WORDS FOR LIFE

Also by Susie Dent

NON-FICTION
How to Talk Like a Local
Susie Dent's Weird Words
Dent's Modern Tribes
Word Perfect
An Emotional Dictionary
Interesting Stories About Curious Words

FICTION
Guilty by Definition

FOR CHILDREN
Roots of Happiness
The Roots We Share

WORDS FOR LIFE

To Boost Every Day of the Year

SUSIE DENT

JOHN MURRAY

First published in Great Britain in 2025 by John Murray (Publishers)

1

Copyright © Susie Dent 2025

The right of Susie Dent to be identified as the Author of the Work has been asserted by her in accordance with the Copyright, Designs and Patents Act 1988.

All rights reserved. No part of this publication may be reproduced, stored in a retrieval system, or transmitted, in any form or by any means without the prior written permission of the publisher, nor be otherwise circulated in any form of binding or cover other than that in which it is published and without a similar condition being imposed on the subsequent purchaser.

A CIP catalogue record for this title is available from the British Library

Hardback ISBN 978-1-399-82065-3
Exclusive hardback ISBN 978-1-399-83155-0
eBook ISBN 978-1-399-82067-7

Typeset in Plantin Light by Hewer Text UK Ltd, Edinburgh
Printed and bound in Great Britain by Clays Ltd, Elcograf S.p.A.

John Murray policy is to use papers that are natural, renewable and recyclable products and made from wood grown in sustainable forests. The logging and manufacturing processes are expected to conform to the environmental regulations of the country of origin.

Carmelite House
50 Victoria Embankment
London EC4Y 0DZ

www.johnmurraypress.co.uk

John Murray Press, part of Hodder & Stoughton Limited
An Hachette UK company

The authorised representative in the EEA is Hachette Ireland, 8 Castlecourt Centre, Dublin 15, D15 XTP3, Ireland (email: info@hbgi.ie)

To my mother, who gave me life *and* words

CONTENTS

Introduction	ix
January	1
February	25
March	49
April	77
May	103
June	131
July	159
August	185
September	213
October	241
November	269
December	295
Acknowledgements	321
Index	323

INTRODUCTION

'If you do not know the words, you can hardly know the thing.' In *Thinking as a Science*, the economist and philosopher Henry Hazlitt explored the connection between a rich vocabulary and the amazing potential of our thoughts. Once we can name something precisely, we can both cope with it better and understand it more fully. Finding the right word is the key to everything.

My love affair with vocabulary has never been a brief fling: what the Victorians called 'firkytoodling', a bit of messing around. It began when I was little, marvelling at everything from street signs to ingredient lists, from *Mandy* annuals to German phrasebooks. Alongside my own random jottings, I gathered my favourites in little notebooks that came with a tiny padlock and key so that I could lock their magic away, daydreaming about their stories.

Those notebooks were full of eavesdroppings. Not the gossipy kind that inspired the word 'eavesdrop', literally nosy neighbours standing outside beneath the 'eavesdrip' of a house to listen covertly to the conversations happening inside. These were the linguistic kind: picking up the nonsensical phrases I could make neither head nor tail of but which still made me smile ('Oh lor!' my mum would occasionally exclaim, leaving me none the wiser); the beauties I couldn't get enough of, like 'icicle' or 'halcyon'; and the words I gleaned from other languages which promised different, distant magics.

It was through learning German at school that my interest grew into a passion. To this day I remember the wonder of discovering the *Libelle*, German's gorgeous term for a dragonfly, a word with such a soft sibilance it seemed to hover in the air exactly like the insect. Only later did I discover that this name was the creation of the father of modern taxonomy Carl Linnaeus, who based it on the Latin for a carpenter's level because he noticed that the dragonfly can stay remarkably level as it hovers. It's one example of the stories I discovered much later, and which have only added to the adventure. Looking back, I can see I have always been a lexicographer of sorts.

Learning another language can bring you up against the fascinating gaps in our own. Why don't we have a word for lingering at the dinner table to chat after a meal is finished, as the Italians do with *sobremesa*? And most of us would happily borrow the Icelandic *sólarfrí*: an unexpectedly sunny day that demands to be taken as an instant holiday.

Happily, while we may be an island nation, our language is far from an island tongue. From the very beginning its speakers have begged, borrowed, and plundered words from every nation and culture they have encountered. Collecting words and phrases from other languages is as thrilling as it is illuminating, and I'm delighted to share some of my favourite untranslatables in the following pages. These range from the sublime – like the Japanese *komorebi*, which captures the dancing pattern of sunlight on a woodland floor, or German's *Zugunruhe*, the migratory restlessness felt by birds as they prepare for their annual flight – to the faintly ridiculous but oh-so-necessary – such as *pelinti* from the Buli language of Ghana, which describes the frantic 'hashashahaaa' sound we make when pushing piping hot food around our mouths.

Our greatest writers knew all about the seasonal urge. Keats loved the spring, Shelley the summer, Frost and Rosetti the winter, and Wordsworth the autumn. Shakespeare found inspiration in each of them. As a lexicographer, I've come to see that language is no different. I find it fascinating how our vocabulary shifts with the time of year, sometimes subtly – the return to our regional roots at Christmastime, perhaps – and sometimes with a bang: what is the word for that unmistakable smell of autumn? In *Words for Life* I'd like to take you on a journey through *my* year, offering you a linguistic vitamin shot for every day from 1 January to 31 December. I want to show you how we each have a wordrobe for every season, a cyclical lexicon for our thoughts, feelings, and experiences.

I've lost count of the times I've been asked, 'Don't you know everything in the dictionary by now?' Fair enough: after all, I've been occupying the umpire's chair and delivering my origin of the day on *Countdown*'s Dictionary Corner for over thirty years. And yet, despite my daily delvings into the lexicon, the answer is always an emphatic 'no'. I still learn something new and surprising every day, from the etymology of a word I once stepped past without a second thought (I was amazed to discover that 'OMG' was coined by an Admiral of the Fleet in 1917), to an example of Gen-Z slang that is suddenly everywhere ('no cap').

Much of our most necessary vocabulary has perplexingly slipped out of view. One of my particular obsessions are the lost positives. It makes me wistful that you can be gormless but not gormful, feckless but not feckful, and ruthless but never ruthful. Yet it's not too late. There is no such thing as an extinct word; it is simply asleep, and we can resuscitate it with one simple kiss of life: usage. By picking up such positives again, we can harness their power and make the world around us a better, more upbeat place in the process.

There is, of course, sadness and confusion in the dictionary too. But there is comfort in knowing that you're not the first to experience something. Even in Old English a word existed for those moments in the middle of the night when worries loom disproportionately large. *Uhtcearu* is literally 'the sorrow before dawn', a dark panicky worry that only begins to dissipate when the sun reappears. For anyone who has ever felt mixed emotions as a holiday approaches – all that packing and airport hassle – the Norwegians have already nailed it with *gruglede*, 'happy dread'. And you will certainly not be the only person to have misread such words as 'cooperation' or 'codeveloper' because they are no longer hyphenated. Welcome to the 'misle', a name based on the easy misreading of 'misled' as the past tense of a mysterious verb.

With other entries, it's more the story that will surprise. I have long relished the fact that Bluetooth technology was named after the tenth-century Scandinavian King Harald Gormsson, nicknamed 'Bluetooth' on account of his prominent dead tooth. Since Gormsson united various Danish tribes with some of their Norwegian neighbours, his name felt a fitting symbol for a technology that is all about connectivity. Not only that: the pioneers of this wirelessness went further still, for the Bluetooth logo combines the ancient runes (Hagall) (ᚼ) and (Bjarkan) (ᛒ) to produce the initials HB, for Harald Bluetooth. My other discoveries include the fact that a lifelong friend was once known as a 'copemate', and that a tongue-twister in sign language is a 'finger-fumbler'.

Writing this book has also given me the opportunity to ask the big questions. Why did we ever stop calling a penguin an 'arsefoot'? How did people get up on time before alarm clocks? Where exactly are the Doldrums? Why was Tolkien so keen on happy endings? And who knew that there is a specific unit of measurement for the smells given off by humans in particular situations? Well, enquire within, the answers may surprise you. They certainly surprised and delighted me.

As for those seasons, *Words for Life* will take you from the dread of returning to work at the start of January to the joy of raising a glass to friends at the year's end. In between it will help you articulate the longing for spring (and the romantic feelings sparked by its arrival) to the joy of summer rain, as well as multiple words for testicles, the strange history of 'arse' and the uncomfortable feeling of new underwear. And when winter comes, I hope this book might dispel the blues with such dictionary treasures as treacle wells and starling murmurations.

INTRODUCTION

My hope is that, as we travel across the year, you will feel the same sense of wonder and magic that I have found in language since I was a child. I have come to believe that there is nothing that cannot be articulated through language: whether it's our own or that of other people. Our vocabulary lives alongside us, following our lead and occasionally pulling us along in its wake.

Coleridge once described prose as words in the best order and poetry as the best words in the best order. This is, I'd like to think, something rather different. I have spent my life looking for the best words – and here they are – but I'm leaving the order and how you use them up to you. I only hope my *Words for Life* are ones you too will want to keep for life.

Susie Dent
Oxford, July 2025

JANUARY

1 January

QUALTAGH

A new year, a new pencil case, a new you: January brings with it a lot of pressures to start afresh. This imperative seems particularly ugsome on 1 January, a day traditionally blighted by crapulence (the worst kind of hangover) or *Katzenjammer* (the German articulation of the throbbing sound of cats yowling in your head). So how exactly *do* you future-proof this shiny new year? In many cultures, the first person you meet on this first day is key. In Scotland and northern England, the first visitor to your home after midnight on New Year's Eve is known as the 'first-footer'. It is considered unlucky for them to be blond (a possible hangover from hundreds of years of savage Viking raids), a doctor, or a priest, but a tall, dark, handsome, male visitor promises to bring good luck throughout the year ahead.

Just as important, however, is that the first-footer should not arrive empty-handed. Coal or silver coins are traditional, whisky preferable, and foods such as buns or biscuits highly desirable. All are designed to bring good cheer but, crucially, they also symbolize prosperity, health, and warmth for the year ahead. In Greece first-footing is known as *podariko* and involves the ceremonious smashing of a pomegranate on the threshold.

On the Isle of Man, the first-footer goes by the name of the *qualtagh*, 'one who is met'. They too are welcomed warmly and may also recite a blessing for the household to ensure good fortune for all its members through the year:

> *Shoh slaynt as shee as eash dy vea,*
> *As maynrys son dy bragh.*

> Here's health and peace and age of life,
> And happiness for ever.

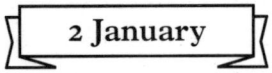

2 January

RESIPISCENCE

Sinners of the 1500s would have been well acquainted with 'resipiscence'. This involved a recognition of one's past misdeeds in the sincere hope of atonement and better things to come. In the centuries that followed, 'resipiscence' broadened its scope, so that achieving it meant coming to one's senses and returning to a better frame of mind. Its inspiration, the Latin *resipiscere*, described both the recovery of reason and the return to sanity. Something most of us – sinners or not – would hope to achieve in the early days of January.

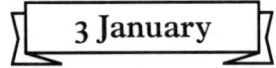

3 January

KNOCKER-UPPER

Confucius said somewhat smugly, 'Choose a job you love, and you will never have to work a day in your life.' But what to do if you don't have that luxury? This tends to be the time when many of us take a hard look at our jobs and consider whether they are making us quite as fulfilled as we'd hoped. It may then be useful (or usefully distracting) to ponder some of the occupations from yesteryear that troubled the minds of our ancestors in such periods of reflection.

One such was the 'knocker-upper', the human predecessor to the alarm clock who would carry a long pole and knock at the door or windows of a house to rouse its occupants. Keen to wake up only their paying customers, the knocker-uppers also used pea-shooters for an even more targeted service. Charles Dickens may not have been a fan: in *Great Expectations*, Mr Wopsle is described as being in such a foul mood, thanks to being knocked up, that he would have 'excommunicated the whole expedition'. If this seems unthinkable to us now, particularly given the lack of a snooze button, spare a thought for the 'gong farmer', a medieval job title for the cleaner of privies and cesspits. Maybe modern working life isn't so bad after all.

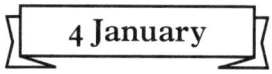

CHISSUP

This is the time of year when a small sniffle has the irritating tendency to turn into a full-blown cold. This key moment is something that dialects, particularly those from traditionally colder and wetter regions of Britain, are particularly good at naming. The six-volume collection of regional vocabulary known as *The English Dialect Dictionary*, compiled by Joseph Wright, a philologist from Oxford, offers the Yorkshire term 'chissup', defined simply as 'to sneeze'. The delightful word may well have been a local variant on 'snickup', which describes a veritable fit of sneezing.

Other local words for what we should properly be calling a 'fneeze' (the original spelling until someone mistook the 'f' for a long medieval 's') include the curious 'pehoy', from Scots, 'sneedge' from Worcestershire, 'tisha' from Lancashire, and 'snirl' from Northumbria, each providing a touch of linguistic consolation for a stuffy nose and sore head.

It was in this week in 1894 that the second-oldest film to be copyrighted in the US was shot, featuring one of the inventor Thomas Edison's assistants sneezing after taking a pinch of snuff. The five-second film is known simply as *Fred Ott's Sneeze*.

Bless you.

5 January

COPEMATE

This is the night when the boughs of holly traditionally brought in to deck the halls are burned and all Christmas decorations must be taken down, or bad luck will be risked for the coming year. On *Oíche Nollaig na mBan*, the Eve of Women's Christmas, the windows of rural Ireland are lit with twelve candles in anticipation of the twelfth and final day of Christmas, the marker of Epiphany and the time when women could gather in each other's homes for a few stolen hours of gaiety, their reward after weeks of wrapping, cooking, and entertaining. Pubs might also be visited, since many women of the household would have raised turkeys or geese for sale at the Christmas market. The proceeds were then put aside as a slush fund for *Nollaig na mBan*, when it was the men's turn to look after the home.

English provides many synonyms for male companions, from 'butty' to 'chum', 'buddy' to 'mucker'. Those for female friends are harder to find, and tend to focus on the activity it is assumed all women engage in when they come together: gossip. 'Gossip' itself is a word that began life in innocence, when a 'god-sib' was a godmother who attended upon her friend at childbirth. The expectation that such help would also entail the exchange of some well-chosen local news led to an altogether different interpretation of 'god-sib', which was soon joined by dozens of epithets describing women of trifling character who delight in idle talk. Better to stick to a far more positive term for a friend who supports you through thick and thin: 'copemate', a sixteenth-century term that bucks the gossipy trend and celebrates women who come together on days such as this.

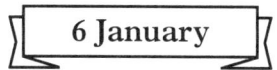

THERMOPOT

If today's mood is sponsored entirely by coffee, you are not alone. Coffee shops have squeezed their way into every chink of our landscape and many of us now wake up to drink coffee rather than the other way round. The language of the barista-hood remains, as it should, predominantly Italian, from the 'espresso' (not 'expresso', however quickly we drink or demand it, and from the Italian for 'pressed out'), to the 'macchiato' ('stained' coffee, thanks to its dash of milk). The 'cappuccino', famously, was inspired by the Capuchins, friars of the order of St Francis. The name was chosen in the 1940s because the appearance of the frothy drink was thought to resemble their coffee-coloured robes.

Are you a 'procaffeinator', one who puts everything on hold until they've had sufficient amounts of coffee? If so, the word 'thermopot' might also come in handy. A term from the eighteenth century for an imbiber of hot liquors, it can be nicely extended to embrace a prolific drinker of any hot drink that takes your fancy.

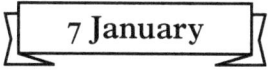

ILUNGA

Tshiluba, also known as Cilubà, is a Bantu language spoken by approximately six million people in the Democratic Republic of the Congo. Within the culture of its speakers is a highly nuanced understanding of forgiveness and the appropriate response to those who offend or harm. This approach is beautifully reflected in its use of the word *ilunga*, which describes someone with a forgiving nature, with one important caveat: this individual is willing to forgive a first and even a second offence, but will not tolerate a third. To transgress in the same way three times implies a pattern of behaviour that is both unchangeable and inexcusable: for the *ilunga*, three strikes means most definitely out.

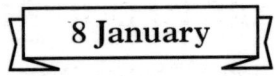

DØRSTOKKMILA

There are days when motivation is so lacking that even getting to the front door feels like a struggle, let alone feeling together enough to walk through it and engage with the outside world. Norwegians have a word for precisely this emotion: *dørstokkmila*, 'the mile to the threshold'. In other words, this is the daunting first step to an activity that will no doubt be worth it, but that just at this moment feels *almost* insurmountable.

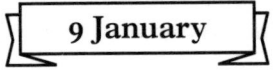

TELETUBBYZURÜCKWINKER

Never let it be said that the English dictionary can't deliver a good insult. Even the briefest of riffles through its pages will demonstrate the richness of the lexicon for put-downs, and the paucity of the same when it comes to compliments. Nevertheless, sometimes a choice barb from another culture and language is too good to pass up, especially if it conjures up a powerful mental image. One of many from German that have been eagerly harnessed by English speakers is *Backpfeifengesicht*, a face that asks to be slapped, but this sits alongside lesser-known insults such as *Bananenbieger* – one who does so little to contribute that they are merely a 'banana-bender' – and *Teletubbyzurückwinker*, one who 'waves back at Teletubbies' on TV, and who consequently may not be overly bright.

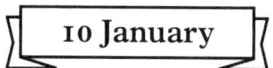

10 January

DOLLARS TO DOUGHNUTS

On this day in 1776, Thomas Paine published *Common Sense*, a fifty-page pamphlet in which the author called for a war of independence against Britain. Over 500,000 copies were sold within a few months. Paine had the authority to galvanize public opinion and to shape an ideology that set his country on the path to revolution.

Most of us are familiar with 'betting our bottom dollar' on something if we feel it is assured to happen, but there are several suitably North American variations available to ring the changes. 'Dollars to doughnuts' is one, as is 'dollars to cobwebs'. Each relies on the dollar as a symbol of American promise and opportunity, with a twist of capitalism and consumerism thrown in. The name of the currency, ironically, is not home-grown, but comes from a German word meaning 'from the valley'. In the sixteenth century, German coins were minted from silver that had been mined at Sankt Joachimsthal, in the kingdom of Bohemia. 'Joachimsthal' itself translates as 'Joachim's valley', referring to the local patron saint. These coins became known as 'Joachimthalers' and then 'thalers', corrupted to 'dalers' and eventually 'dollars'.

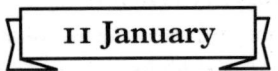

GLUGGAVEÐUR

'Ammil', from Devon, rather exquisitely describes the thin film of ice that lacquers leaves, twigs, and grass blades when a freeze follows a partial thaw, and which in sunlight can cause a whole landscape to glitter. The word is thought to derive from the Old English *amel*, meaning 'enamel'. It finds a companion in an equally evocative word, this time from Icelandic, when a bright blue sky and ammil landscape sparkle invitingly through the glass of your window. Invitingly, that is, until the moment you find yourself outside, whereupon you want to run back inside immediately. *Gluggaveður* is 'window-weather': the kind that looks appealing from inside, only to prove highly undesirable once you're in it.

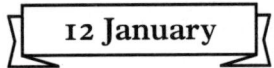

GROWLERY

There was a time when rooms in homes were reserved exclusively for certain occasions – a 'drawing room' was the space to which women would 'withdraw' after dinner, while gentlemen enjoyed a glass of port and a smoke. The 'sitting room' was where you would sit and relax, and the 'parlour' was the place in which to converse (from the French *parler*, 'to talk'; if it was a private conversation, then a 'speak-a-word room' was also on offer). Best of all, the 'sanctum sanctorum', the 'holy of holies', was a person's private retreat, where they could be free from any intrusion.

Some rooms were dedicated to serving particular emotions. A lady's 'boudoir', for example, was intended as a space to which she could retire for some privacy and, if she fancied, a moment of petulance, for the literal translation of the French 'boudoir' is a 'place for sulking'. If anger had the upper hand, then the only recourse was the 'growlery'. This possibility was largely down to Charles Dickens and the sitting room of his character Mr Jarndyce in the novel *Bleak House*. 'Sit down, my dear . . . This, you must know, is the Growlery. When I am out of humour, I come and growl here.'

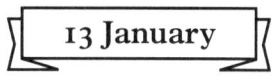

13 January

BINGO!

> Now I do this kind of thing
> On the wing, on the wing!
> Bing!

James Joyce was no stranger to word invention, but he could scarcely have guessed that his use of 'bing' in his epic novel *Ulysses*, giving the *Oxford English Dictionary* its first record of the exclamation, might go on to inspire the name of a game that was to become a nation's favourite. Of all the many theories as to the origin of 'bingo', its use as a shout of joy or surprise is the most plausible. Following the Betting and Gaming Act, which came into effect in January 1960, bingo became not just a new pastime but the source of a whole new language.

Bingo terms range from the self-explanatory to the brilliantly gnarly, from 'sweet sixteen', and 'lucky seven' to 'two fat ladies' (88), 'doctor's orders' (9), 'bed and breakfast' (26), and 'Kelly's eye' (1). This last example is particularly puzzling: some believe it heralds from the 'one-eyed' letterbox helmet famously worn by Australian outlaw Ned Kelly. Others refer to a cartoon in the adventure comic *Valiant*, in which the character Kelly possessed a magic amulet in the shape of an eye. As for 'doctor's orders', a pill known simply as 'number nine' was a laxative given out by army doctors. The traditional price of bed-and-breakfast accommodation in the UK, meanwhile, was 2 shillings and 6 pence, which was always shortened to 'two and six'.

Surely one of the best has to be 'Sherwood Forest' for 33. Why? The home of Robin Hood has 'all the trees'.

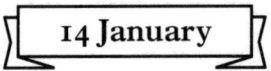

14 January

ARSE-ROPES

This day marks the Feast of the Ass, a medieval Christian festival that celebrates the flight into Egypt and which was borrowed from France, where the *Fête de l'âne* celebrates the many donkey-related stories in the Bible. This 'ass' is of course never to be confused with the anatomical kind, which in US English (and increasingly in British English, where 'arse' is just about holding on) is spelled identically. It is a word which, although far less triggering than many of our modern taboos, might still make modern ears a little twitchy.

Our introduction to this particular four-letter word is courtesy of the *Cleopatra Glossaries*, a manuscript written in the tenth century and so called because, in the seventeenth century, it was stored in a bookcase in the library of Sir Robert Bruce Cotton, below a bust of Cleopatra. The word was far from offensive; 'arse-push' was simply a heavy fall onto one's rump, and 'arsehole' was considered coarse only after the eighteenth century. But surely one of the best uses of the word is courtesy of Wycliffe's Bible in the fourteenth century, in which the Latin text was translated into English. In an early version you will find *Þe arsroppis of hem goyng out stoonkyn*, 'his arse-ropes came out stinking'. This unshrinking word for the 'intestines' is as direct as they come, but there was certainly no sniggering intended, for its appearance came at a time when 'bollocks' was nothing but a straightforward term for a man's testicles. Nevertheless, as sensitivities to bodily parts and functions crept in, the decline in the acceptability of 'arse' was guaranteed – so much so that the brightly rumped bird previously known as a 'white-arse' was rechristened a 'wheatear', despite the sudden inaccuracy of the name.

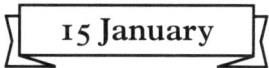

CLINCHPOOP

In 2022, Oxford Dictionaries chose 'goblin mode' as their word of the year. In the aftermath of Covid lockdowns and their impact on behavioural norms, 'goblin mode' describes an unapologetically self-indulgent, let-it-all-hang-out way of life with an extra whiff of disregard for societal expectations and norms. 'Goblin mode' essentially says, 'I no longer care about what anyone thinks about how I look or what I say.' There were once, of course, entirely serviceable words for this variety of goblin that are now marked as obsolete in the dictionary, including 'fustilugs' and 'slug-a-bed'. When it comes to the lack of good manners, we should surely re-embrace the 'clinchpoop', a word first recorded in 1555 in a manual called *The Institucion of a Gentleman*: 'Roysters [wild revellers] doo cal suche one by the name of a Loute, a Clynchepope, or one that knoweth no facyons [fashions].' The 'poop' here, you might be relieved to know, is the aftermost part of a ship, and the reference seems to be to someone who performs the menial task of 'clinching' or nailing together the planks of a ship, and who is thus unlikely to be over-fussed about looking the part.

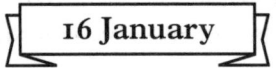

16 January

ECLAIR

Sometimes the only answer is chocolate. The confection of a cream-filled choux finger topped with a chocolate glaze known as an 'eclair' surely heads the solution list for many. Invented in Lyons in the nineteenth century, the cake soon arrived in Britain, where its name was readily adopted. Few at the time may have recognized its etymology, however: *éclair* is French for 'flash of lightning', thanks presumably to the speed with which it goes down. The *Chambers Dictionary* definition of the word is notoriously good: 'a cake, long in shape but short in duration'.

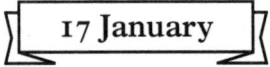

17 January

RENDEZVOUS

Today's 'rendezvous' carry a distinct cachet of romance and thrill-seeking, but it wasn't always that way, even if the word did come to us directly from France, a nation that stereotypically enjoys a hefty dose of both. The precise meaning of 'rendezvous' is 'present yourself', an order issued to soldiers to assemble at a particular hour and place. When the word was borrowed into English in the sixteenth century, it too was used for an army's gathering place before being applied more broadly to the assembly of any group of people. Eventually, 'rendezvous' lost its military moorings and embraced a different kind of arrangement altogether.

Other words in daily use have similar beginnings in the army. 'Alarm' comes from the Italian instruction *all'arme!*, 'to arms!': an audible signal to take up arms and prepare for attack (those who feel physically assaulted by their alarm clocks might sympathize).

'Alert', on the other hand, instructed soldiers to go *all'erta*, or 'to the watchtower', to be on the lookout for the enemy.

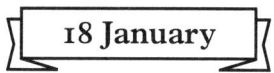

BRUIN

On Winnie-the-Pooh Day, which marks the birthday of A.A. Milne, it is always worth admiring the bear-shaped vocabulary that runs through the English language. One of the least obvious is the expression 'lick into shape', which for all its military feel belongs to the pages of Shakespeare and his contemporaries, who grew up with the belief that bear cubs are born as formless, furry blobs before they are licked into bear shape by their mothers.

Bears populate our geography, astronomy, and mythology. The Arctic takes its name from the Greek *arktikos* ('northern'), which in turn is derived from *arktos*, 'bear'. This refers to the constellation Ursa Major, or Great Bear, which is prominent in the northern sky.

'Bear' itself might be the oldest euphemism we have, with its roots in the reconstructed ancient language of Proto-Indo-European, where the word's ancestor seems to have denoted any wild animal and may be based on a word for 'brown'. For centuries the superstition persisted that to refer to a bear directly would immediately summon it, and so descriptive terms were used to avoid invoking the animal's presence. This phenomenon is often known as 'noa-naming', from the Polynesian *noa*, meaning 'safe'.

In the medieval tales of *Reynard the Fox* the word 'bruin' was used to personify a bear. It too takes its name from the colour brown. Winnie-the-Pooh may be the cuddliest incarnation we have of an animal that has inspired fear and reverence for centuries.

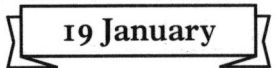

19 January

CLINKABELL

In Kent it's 'aquabob', around Hull and Grimsby they prefer the term 'ice-candle', and elsewhere in Britain you might find a 'cockbell', 'shockle', or 'ice-dagger'. These are all gorgeous terms for an icicle, but there is something particularly magical about the West Country word 'clinkabell', which carries a suitably tinkly, Peter-Panesque feel of wonder.

'Icicle' itself is a tautology, for the second part of the word, 'ickle', means a frozen drop of water, which makes the first part, 'ice', entirely redundant. Perhaps we should follow Yorkshire and simply say 'ickle', but it may be too late to change now. All the more reason to speak of clinkabells when we marvel at the structures tapering down from our eaves.

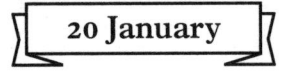

20 January

FORWALLOWED

January, perhaps more than any other month, can leave one exhausted and used up. If worries loom large, sleep doesn't always come easily, leaving us 'forwallowed' – a fifteenth-century description for feeling bone-weary after tossing and turning all night.

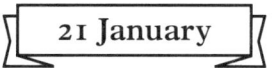

21 January

APAPACHAR

What do the avocado, chilli, tomato, and chocolate all have in common? Apart from possibly rendering you 'poppysmic' (James Joyce's invention for the sound of smacking lips), they are all from Nahuatl, the language of the Aztecs. In Latin America, you will find plenty of other borrowings that have yet to float into English shores. One of these is *apapachar*, meaning 'to hug with the soul', based in turn on the Nahuatl *patzoa*, which literally means 'to knead with love'. Like the Welsh *cwtch*, *apapacho* (the noun) involves far more than a simple hug: it is one designed to wrap someone up with love when they need it most. All of which is highly appropriate for International Hug Day.

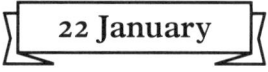

22 January

QWERTYUIOP

The meaning of 'qwertyuiop' surely makes up for its unpronounceability, for it is defined in the *Urban Dictionary* as 'the state of inequivalent boredom, unlike any boredom you have ever known, which makes you type out the letters from left to right on a keyboard'.

That alone would justify its existence, but the word (if we can call it that) also plays a role in the story of the world's very first email. It begins early in 1971, when Ray Tomlinson made history by sending the world's first email. Working on the ARPANET system, a predecessor to the Internet, the computer scientist sent a quick message to himself, thinking little about the contents. 'The test messages were entirely forgettable,' he wrote later. 'Most likely the first message was QWERTYUIOP or something similar.' It may lack romance, but Tomlinson's message would go on to change the way we communicate, shop, bank, and date. Not that he knew it at the time. In fact, he famously remarked to a friend, 'Don't tell anyone! This isn't what we're supposed to be working on.'

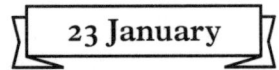

23 January

FRUMBERDLING

For some, January is better known as Manuary, the precursor (in sentiment, at least) to Movember, when many men let their moustaches flourish to raise money for charity. By this time in the month, it is time for chins to be carpeted.

The power and symbolism attached to beards has varied over the centuries. When the Roman Empire crumbled, the history of the ancient world was shaped profoundly by many powerful Germanic tribes, among them the Lombards, who had fought their way across Europe before settling in the Italian Peninsula. Their name came into English from the Italian *lombardo*, itself based on a Germanic compound word meaning 'long beard'.

Into the Middle Ages, beards held a religious and cultural significance that extended far beyond fashion. For a time, they were considered compulsory for any ruler: in the ninth century, King Alfred the Great insisted a fine of twenty shillings be levied on anyone who cut off a man's beard. By the eleventh century, the monk and historian Orderic Vitalis maintained that by growing beards men were essentially admitting that 'they revel in filthy lusts like stinking goats'.

Such an apparent obsession with 'pogonology', the wearing or study of beards, was bound to leave its mark on the English language. To 'beard' someone formidable is to boldly confront them, while in 1587 the English sailor and explorer Francis

Drake described his expedition to Cadiz as 'the singeing of the King of Spain's beard'. The adjective 'rebarbative', meaning 'repellent' or 'disagreeable', may rest on the idea of an itchy beard that chafes the skin.

Far less transparently, some etymologists believe that the word 'bizarre' is an adaptation of the Basque *bizar*, 'beard', an allusion to fully bearded Spanish soldiers arriving in the Pyrenees and provoking considerable surprise in the locals. This may not be far from the truth given that *hombre de bigote*, 'moustached man', is used in Spanish for a 'man of spirit'. And the island of Barbados is said to take its name from the Portuguese *barbado*, 'bearded', perhaps an allusion to the bearded fig trees that grow on the island and are now a national symbol.

Beards have long been the marker of maturity as well as virility, as is proved by a term from Old English for a young man with as yet little experience of life. *Frymbirdling*, or *frumberdling*, is a moniker that translates literally as 'little first beard'.

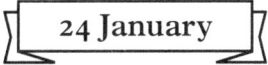

UGSOME

Bishop Hugh Latimer was one of the most popular English Reformers of his time, thanks to his attacks on the lethargy and licentiousness of the clergy and, in the end, to his martyrdom in Oxford alongside Nicholas Ridley and Thomas Cranmer. His final words at the stake to console his companions have long been remembered: 'We shall this day light such a candle, by God's grace, in England as I trust shall never be put out.' Latimer was a highly passionate preacher whose sermons are regarded today as classics of their time: vivid, racy, and profound. He delivered seven sermons before King Edward VI, in which he eloquently denounced contemporary current abuses. In one of them he spoke vehemently of hell as having 'such an evyl favoured face, such an ugsome countenaunce, such an horrible vysage'.

Latimer's choice of the word 'ugsome' was punchy, but it was far from the first. For that we need to look to the Vikings, whom we can thank for many of the earthiest words in English, including 'ransack', 'heathen', 'saga', 'thrall', 'dregs', 'rotten', 'haggle', and 'stagger' – all derived from the Old Norse that crossed the seas with the invaders. As Latimer's sermon showed, much of our Viking inheritance is not for the faint-hearted. To 'ug' was to regard something with dread and revulsion – the word 'ugly' once evoked far stronger emotions than it does today. Something or somebody 'ugsome', including the face of hell, is consequently utterly repugnant.

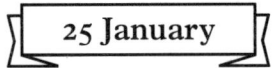

25 January

FINGER-FUMBLER

'Find ninety-nine peppered French fries'; 'good blood, bad blood'; 'clean up the nice school paper': sentences that, though surreal, don't tend to present a challenge to most when read out loud. Try 'red lorry, yellow lorry', however, or 'a proper copper coffee pot', and you might struggle. The latter are of course tongue-twisters, designed to trip up even the most careful enunciators. The former can be just as tricky, though, this time to users of sign language. Each has featured on one or more TikTok videos as examples of 'finger-fumblers' – phrases that are particularly tricky to articulate at speed in sign. An even more challenging finger-fumbler involves asking a sign language user to finger-spell two different words, such as 'cat' and 'dog', on different hands at the same time.

26 January

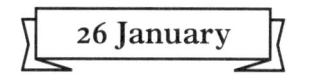

NA'EEMAN

The Japanese have an unusually direct word for looking less attractive after a trip to the hairdresser: *age-otori*. Most of us will notice a new haircut on a friend, even if we do lack a word for the sudden amnesia as to what their hair looked like before. But few of us would think to issue a blessing on top of a compliment, let alone comment on how clean or freshly showered someone looks. This is not the case for Arabic speakers, who like to congratulate others on their fresh look. *Na'eeman* is a salutation used in three specific instances: towards a person who emerges from a shower or bath, sports a new haircut, or displays a fresh beard trim.

It is far from trivial, for at the heart of the word is *nacem*, meaning 'bliss' or 'paradise'. *Na'eeman* reflects the hope that the recipient has both had a pleasant experience and is now blessed by their renewed freshness.

27 January

FAUCHLE

Few words convey the impossibility of concentrating, or of achieving much at all, better than 'fauchle'. Fauchling involves working listlessly because your heart and mind just aren't in the game. The *Dictionaries of the Scots Language* offer some additional definitions that in no way improve matters, for 'fauchle' can also mean to go about things 'in a helpless, bungling fashion', to 'walk with difficulty from lack of strength', and, when used as a noun, 'a small weak person unable to do his own turn and yet trying to do it'. It's a rather pathetic image, but one most of us would recognize. The roots of 'fauchle' may lie in farming, where a 'fauch', in the old infield and outfield system of agriculture, was a part of the outfield ground which was left fallow for four or five years at a time. Perhaps the metaphor was extended to the human version of lying around unproductively with no sign of activity whatsoever. The good news is that fauchling is only temporary.

28 January

PARTING SHOT

On this day in 1896, Walter Arnold of Kent became the first British motorist to be fined for speeding. History doesn't relate his response at the time, but it's safe to say that any smart retort as he exited the scene would have been only marginally slower than the speed he was caught driving at, namely 8 mph in a 2 mph area.

Most of us, including Walter perhaps, would like the idea of delivering a sparkling comeback as we exit such a situation, accompanied by a toss of the hair and a regal flounce. The original 'parting shot', however, was not so much dead witty as lethal in a very real sense, for it began as a 'Parthian shot'. The ancient kingdom of Parthia lay south-east of the Caspian Sea, in modern-day Iran. Parthian horsemen were renowned for their strategy in battle of riding away from the enemy to give the impression of fleeing, before twisting round and discharging their missiles backwards. This skilled manoeuvre was highly effective in taking the opposition by surprise. By the nineteenth century, as the Parthians' history faded, 'parting shot' had become the logical, if far less dramatic, successor to the original.

29 January

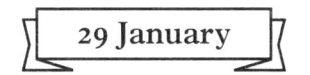

FLIBBERTIGIBBET

Few words are as pleasing to say as 'flibbertigibbet', a not-too-unkind epithet for a flighty person who tends to talk a lot. This is one of many spellings of the medieval word *flepergebet*, which was equally used for a gossip thanks to its sound of meaningless chatter. Things weren't always quite so friendly, however. To the medieval imagination, Flibbertigibbet was the name of a malevolent spirit who kept company with Hoberdidance, Frateretto, and Tocobatto, the four devils of the traditional Morris dance. William Shakespeare retained this devilish twist in *King Lear* by using the name for one of five fiends that Edgar claims are possessing him. The demonic associations thankfully faded, and the word soon settled on frivolity, albeit with the volume turned up on meaningless babble.

30 January

PASSENGER

Mention the word 'passenger' to a medieval pilgrim and they may have looked at you askance. The same would probably be true if they happened across the word 'messenger', 'harbinger', or 'nightingale'. While most of these words would have rung a bell, they would have seemed just a little bit off, for none of them at that point contained a middle 'n'. In the case of 'passenger', the original version was a direct borrowing from French and travellers were consequently known as 'passagers'. A messenger was a 'messager', and a harbinger was a 'harbiger', a mangling of the French *herbergere*, which described a soldier who went ahead to find lodgings for his troop. 'Nightingale' came not from French but rather from a mangling of the Old English *nihtegala*, a night-singer.

The reason for the change? It is what linguists know as the 'intrusive "n"', an emotive title that belies the fact that English speakers, centuries ago, actively chose to put it in to help them pronounce these words better. If you're in any doubt, it might help to remember how many of us whispered about spooky 'skelingtons' when we were young.

31 January

AWKLY

Pizza for breakfast, clothes on inside out, trying out some emordnilaps: National Backwards Day is intended to be a fun exercise in doing things in reverse – including, if you dare, writing, in which 'emordnilap' is a reversal of 'palindrome'. For all the opportunity for laughs, however, choosing the 'wrong way round' has not always proved amusing. In fact, centuries ago it would have inspired both disdain and fear. Left-handedness in particular has long been unfairly associated with bad luck and foolishness, viewed as a reversal of the 'normal' order and inspiring such words as 'cack-handed', 'molly-dooked', and, most famously, 'sinister', from the Latin for 'left', in contrast to the positive associations of such adjectives as 'dextrous' (*dexter*, 'right').

The first meaning of 'awkward', similarly, meant 'from the left hand' or, more generally, 'in the wrong direction'. In the Old Northumbrian of the Lindisfarne Gospels it meant positively 'perverse'. Its root is a word inherited from the Vikings, whose *afug* became 'awk' and produced such useful adverbs as 'awkly', which can mean anything from 'unluckily' or 'clumsily' to, appropriately enough, 'totally back to front'.

FEBRUARY

1 February

MUDLARKING

The Anglo-Saxons knew this month as *Solmonath*, 'Mud Month'. The days after a full moon often see spring tides: the most extreme tides of the month with the highest rises and lowest falls thanks to the combined gravitational pull of the sun and moon. The low tide, when the maximum amount of shoreline becomes accessible, is valuable to those fond of such pursuits as rock-pooling and mudlarking.

In Victorian London, those walking by the shore might notice hunched figures silently seeking out valuables in the tidal mud. These 'mudlarks', as they were known, were frequently children, whose ragged clothes were soon coated in the foul-smelling muck of the shore and the sewers in which they searched for iron and copper lost from vessels moored on the Thames. The journalist and chronicler of the Victorian underclass Henry Mayhew wrote, 'These poor creatures are certainly about the most deplorable in their appearance of any I have met with in the course of my inquiries.'

Charles Dickens was well aware of the horrors of the river, and that people sought their livelihood not just from items caught in the mud but by plundering from the river itself. His novel *Our Mutual Friend* explores the dark trade of those looting valuables from bodies floating in the water.

Today's mudlarks are thankfully more intent on finding historical artefacts or fossils than the wherewithal to live. But to this day the lexicon for mud is rich enough to reflect its importance, not least in the joy it brings those who turn to it for pleasure. From 'squelching' across the 'slubber' to 'plodging' through the 'clart', the modern mudlark has much to choose from.

2 February

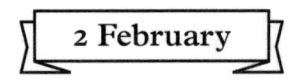

BLAH

It's the shortest month of the year, its birthstone is the peaceful amethyst, and halfway through it celebrates the patron saint of lovers. So why does February seem so determined to bring on the blahs?

The history of 'blah' might help to banish a little of the 'dreichness' that dampens the spirits. The *Oxford English Dictionary*'s first record of these four letters comes from 1918 and the memoir of the US journalist Howard Vincent O'Brien. He was using 'blah' in its original sense of meaningless talk or nonsense: '[He] pulled old blah about "service".' Clearly one blah wasn't enough, and three years later we start to see a double version. Today, the word usually comes in threes, a filler for when a speaker can't muster the energy to relay the precise content of absolute bunkum. It is this sense of emptiness that inspired the use of 'the blahs' for a fit of the blues.

But the blah that represents meaningless chatter is an echo of a sound that ancient Greeks believed all foreigners issued when they opened their mouths. To their ears, foreigners made noises that were no more meaningful than 'bah bah bah'. Worse, they believed such non-natives to be heathens, untrustworthy and menacing, and it is from their indecipherable chatter that 'barbarian' was born. 'Rhubarb' is a close relative, rooted in the Greek *rhēon barbaron*, the second part of which is the same idea of being 'foreign'. It was so called because this was considered an exotic plant, originating as it did in China and Tibet.

3 February

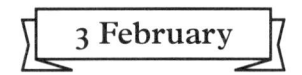

BRASS MONKEYS

These winter months can take their toll on anyone who is 'nesh', or particularly susceptible to the cold. There is a chilly breath of comfort in the fact that, when it comes to cold weather, English at least has a broad vocabulary. Its lexicon includes 'nippy', 'parky', 'utchy', and 'taters' ('potatoes', from the Cockney rhyming slang 'taters in the mould/cold'). But surely one of the best is 'brass monkeys', and attached to it is one of the most famous stories of English etymology.

It is said that cannonballs, during the Napoleonic wars, were stored aboard ships in pyramids, on a brass frame or plate called a 'monkey'. In extremely cold weather, the cannonballs would contract and promptly fall off the brass rack, thereby inspiring the expression 'cold enough to freeze the balls off a brass monkey'.

It's an ingenious explanation, and records of 'monkey' do certainly exist as a term for a cannon itself, but there is no evidence of its being used for the rack holding the ammunition. Moreover, scientists dispute the rate of contraction required to properly shift any cannonballs. Most tellingly of all, one of the earliest forms of the expression involved freezing the tail off a brass monkey rather than any balls (in hot weather, its nose was said to melt). So where does the truth lie? The answer may rest with once-popular figurines of three wise monkeys that, through the respective positions of their hands, represented the maxim 'See no evil, hear no evil, speak no evil'. Today they have been quite literally made iconic through their use in emoji form. Perhaps the idea is that these solid objects could be made to move only in extreme circumstances.

4 February

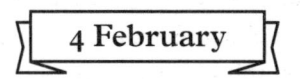

YO-HE-HO

Following the logic of the famous song in *Snow White and the Seven Dwarfs*, released on this day in 1938, do you whistle while you work, or, should the work in question require physical exertion, do you grunt? If the answer to the latter is yes, then you might appreciate not the 'heigh-ho', but the 'yo-he-ho' linguistic theory, which proposes that human speech originated in the sounds produced during the performance of strenuous physical tasks. It sits alongside the 'bow-wow' theory, a term applied to the theory that human speech originated in the imitation of animal sounds – a person might imitate a wolf's howl to warn that a wolf was nearby, for example – and joins the 'pooh-pooh' theory, which posits that all language is the result of natural sounds such as sighs, groans, and cries.

Each of these speculations about the evolution of language, formulated by linguists and philosophers during the eighteenth and nineteenth centuries, rests on the principle that such basic sounds eventually evolved into more complex words with grammatical structures. The true origin of human speech remains a mystery, but anyone tuning into the grunts accompanying a big serve in a tennis match, or to the melodic sing-song we share with our babies, can understand the rich and complicated lexicon of instinctive sounds.

5 February

SPUDDLING

British dialect serves us well when it comes to pottering about rather uselessly. There is 'footling', 'futzing', 'niffle-naffling', 'pingling', 'piddling', and 'quiddling', as well as the more curious 'picking a salad' from the sixteenth century, and the glorious 'fanfreluching' from the seventeenth. But the word 'spuddling' has something extra to add to the mix.

'Spuddling' is a word for the days when you rush around attending to various tasks yet still manage to achieve almost nothing. In other words, to spuddle is to spend a lot of time getting absolutely nowhere. The word is first recorded in the seventeenth century, when it meant to 'puddle' or 'dabble' about in water and, by extension, to work feebly or ineffectively on the land. It was picked up in various dialects across Britain, where its meaning was associated with the word 'spud' (*see* 30 May). This idea of superficially raking over the ground reinforced the idea of being busy without really getting to the bottom of the job at hand.

6 February

KUCHISABISHII

Comfort-eating can be a frequent companion to the winter months, but while English relies on this one, soulless term for a complicated set of emotions, other languages tend to do it much better. German, for example, famously has the term *Kummerspeck*, which specifically describes the overeating that comes after a bad break-up and which neatly translates as 'grief bacon'. In Georgia, diners at a traditionally lavish feast might experience *shemomechama*, which is the act of continuing to eat even when you are completely full.

In Japan, there is a highly specific word for making the umpteenth trip to the fridge to stare at its contents in the hope of finding something new. It describes the feeling of eating not because you're hungry or the food tastes good, but simply for the sake of it. This includes the habit of eating when bored, when it's more about the need for distraction. This is *kuchisabishii* which, when translated, simply and rather beautifully, means 'lonely mouth'.

7 February

NEDOPEREPIL

As Dry January merges into a typically wet February, it is often said that you can take any noun, add an '-ed', and immediately produce an adjective meaning 'drunk'. 'He got utterly lampshaded last night'; 'my neighbours are always totally deckchaired'; 'I've never seen her so chimneyed'. Fun as the game is, none of us really needs to resort to such measures, as English already provides us with hundreds of descriptions for various levels of inebriation.

'Drunk as a skunk', from the 1920s, is one, and was almost certainly chosen purely for its rhyme, but to be 'drunk (or worse) as a newt' is surely even more curious. One theory is that the expression refers to an old (now thankfully obsolete) use of live newts to test the strength of whisky. Others point to the use of 'newt' for new Navy recruits in the time of Nelson, who quickly discovered the delights of rum. Whatever the truth, it's worth knowing that the Romans would compare drunkards to thrushes, thanks to the regular sight of the birds teetering unsteadily around vineyards once they'd feasted upon fermenting grapes. The verb for such dizzy behaviour was *exturdire* (from *turdus*, 'thrush'), and later *étourdi* in French, meaning 'stunned'. When English finally took it over, they may have associated the power of alcohol with impetuosity and, later, strength and vigour, and subsequently coined the adjective 'sturdy'.

Should you need a stronger vocabulary boost for these days, you might borrow from Russian, in which *nedoperepil* is 'to have drunk more than you should have, but less than you could have'. Its literal translation? 'Under-over-drunk'.

8 February

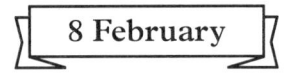

DAALAMIST

One of the beauties of winter mornings is the low-lying mist that shrouds the depths of a valley or lingers over water, gathering overnight before the sun burns it away. In old Scots, this is known as 'daalamist', from the Scandinavian *dal*, 'valley', the source of the English 'dale'. In Britain a mist that hovers on a frosty morning is a 'brume', from the Latin *brumalis*, 'belonging to the winter'.

Other cultures have different but equally evocative ideas. In Icelandic, a low-lying mist that extends stealthily over the ground is a *dalalæða*. Often it will bump into hills and mountains and create spectacular cascades of fog resembling waterfalls. The literal translation of *dalalæða* is 'valley cat': a nod to the way the vapour crawls stealthily across the landscape.

9 February

ORCHIDACEOUS

'England', declared the *Nation and Athenaeum* newspaper in 1921, 'is the great country of kitsch.' A bit harsh, you might think, given that car-mirror dice and nodding-cat figurines were still decades away, but 'kitsch' is a borrowing from German we can't seem to do without, and its origin may surprise, proving appropriate for this Mud Month. Its roots lie in the German verb *kitschen*, which can mean either scraping something together in haste or spreading mud over a surface. The spreading may be key here, for another German import, 'schmaltz', used of excessive sentimentality, originally described chicken or goose fat that was unctuously smeared over food.

It is the equivalent perhaps of the English 'mawkish', whose etymology is possibly even more unappetizing, coming from the medieval word 'mawk', meaning 'maggot'.

If you prefer something altogether more unusual to describe your garden gnome or plastic flamingos, you might opt for 'orchidaceous', which, though nicely flowery, carries a strong hint of over-embellishment and floridness.

10 February

SESQUIPEDALIAN

Most words have a rather abstract connection to the things they describe. The word 'yellow' is not actually yellow. The word 'square' is not a square. Nor do we expect them to be. Such is the arbitrary nature of language. But some words do embody the properties they denote. 'Unhyphenated', 'mellifluous', 'readable': these essentially describe themselves. They are called 'autological', in which 'auto' is the Greek for 'self', because these words possess the very characteristic they describe. 'Pentasyllabic' is an adjective that means 'five-syllabled', and happens to have five syllables. 'Sesquipedalian' is another candidate, a playful description of particularly long or cumbersome words and based on the Latin for 'a foot and a half long'.

The opposite of 'autological' is 'heterological', used of words that categorically don't fit their own definition. Some, like 'four-lettered', 'long', or 'monosyllabic', are obvious; they are joined by others such as 'Spanish', which is clearly not Spanish, and 'plural', which is singular. For those who wish to dig deeper, one popular head-scratcher, named the Grelling–Nelson Paradox after two German philosophers, is whether the word 'heterological' itself is 'heterological' or 'autological' – if we decide on the first, then it must also be 'autological'.

11 February

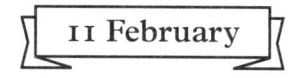

YAKAMOZ

English has no single word for the glittering flashes of light that bounce off the sea as the waves roll beneath the night sky. For this we can look to Turkish, in which *yakamoz* is the magical reflection of moonlight upon the surface of the sea. Or indeed to the Swedish *mångata*, used to describe the light cast upon a body of water, especially during a full moon. Those lucky enough to witness it might glimpse a walkway across the water extending to the moon, literally a 'moon-street'.

12 February

A BIRD IN THE HAND

A Latin proverb from the thirteenth century instructs *plus valet in manibus avis unica quam dupla silvis*: 'one bird in the hands is worth more than two in the woods'. Two centuries later, the same metaphorical warning had firmly settled in English, spawning several variants such as one found in John Heywood's 1546 glossary of 'all the Prouerbes in the Englishe tongue': 'Better one byrde in hande than ten in the wood.'

The advice is the same in each: you should keep what you have and not risk losing it by going after more. In falconry, the expression could be quite literal: a falcon in the hand was valuable enough in itself and worth far more than the possibility of capturing another while risking losing both.

It's an axiom which Charles Darwin, born on this day in 1809, may have ruefully considered one summer's day when he was out collecting beetle specimens. At Cambridge as a student, he had become locked in an intense rivalry with Charles 'Beetles'

Babington, who was to become a prominent entomologist and botanist, with each man striving to be the first to find a new species. Darwin would avidly scoop up any interesting example he unearthed, but one day his enthusiasm led him too far. He recollected in his autobiography:

> on tearing off some old bark, I saw two rare beetles and seized one in each hand; then I saw a third and new kind, which I could not bear to lose, so that I popped the one which I held in my right hand into my mouth. Alas it ejected some intensely acrid fluid, which burnt my tongue so that I was forced to spit the beetle out, which was lost, as well as the third one.

This is, as Darwin discovered to his cost, a defence mechanism of several species, including the bombardier beetle, whose name is explained in a zoological manual from 1803: 'When it is touched we are surprised with a noise resembling the discharge of a musket in miniature, during which a blue smoke may be perceived to proceed from its extremity.'

Darwin had unwittingly provided yet another version of the proverb that has endured for over 800 years.

13 February

JARGON

The Middle Ages saw a significant increase in vocabulary to cover the variety of noises made by birds, from 'chatter' to 'cheep', 'peep' to 'chirp', and 'warble' to 'twitter'. While there was little distinction made as to which bird made what sound, the transfer to human conversation was probably inevitable. Strikingly, such conversation was not viewed in the most positive light. Even the innocuous 'chatter', used for a series of short, quick, and high-pitched bird notes, was simultaneously taken on to describe a distinctly trivial kind of exchange. Once such words landed in the human world, the bird connections drifted away.

'Gobbledygook' was coined in the 1940s by the grandson of cattle baron and politician Samuel Maverick (himself the inspiration for the word 'maverick', someone who goes their own way, thanks to his refusal to brand his cattle) to reflect the confused babble of geese. And 'jargon' gives us another example of a word that was once firmly tethered to the chattering of birds. Its extension to human communication that is barely intelligible to the uninitiated rests on the idea that birds understand each other perfectly – it's the rest of us who are unable to grasp their twittering.

Fittingly enough, on the eve of the most romantic day of the year, a bird was said to choose its mate at precisely this time and to deliver its most beautiful song, which became known as a 'valentine'.

14 February

BASOREXIA

'Hug' is a simple word, which seems to have been a gift from the Vikings – not widely known for their loving embrace – and their word *hugga*, 'to comfort' (a sibling perhaps of the Danish *hygge*, the Scandi cosiness that warms our toes every winter). But 'hug' has a prickly past, for its early uses referred to a bear squeezing a man or dog to death, a somewhat grisly ancestor of the bear hugs we crave today.

'Embrace', at least, is without edge, a nod to the *bras*, or arms, of the French that are still wrapped around their word for kissing, *embrasser* (it is always worth remembering that Samuel Johnson defined a kiss as 'a salute given by joining lips'). For the Germans, a hug is simply an *Umarmung*, or 'arms-around'.

Other English words carry the caress of the past more lightly, though their stories underscore the significance of touch. An 'accolade', a sibling of 'collar', was originally a royal hug, bestowed when honouring a knight in the years before a cold sword became the thing.

As for the recent coinage of 'basorexia', while its medical tone might seem at odds with love and romance, it nonetheless involves a lot of kissing. The term, derived from *basium* (a kiss) and *orexis* (appetite), describes an intense and often obsessive desire to kiss someone. It is a complex emotion that can manifest itself in various ways, including lingering daydreams about kissing and the constant seeking of opportunities that allow for it. It is thought that the release of dopamine that accompanies a kiss can prove particularly addictive.

15 February

FLITTERWOCHEN

The traditional associations of a honeymoon are love, happiness, and serenity. And so it was in the sixteenth century, when writers such as Robert Greene wrote of the days after marriage being spent 'with dauncing and Honney moone'. Sadly a wry note of cynicism soon crept in, and the sense shifted from a time that is as sweet and mellifluous as honey to something akin to the moon's waxing and waning over the course of the lunar cycle – it is full at the start of the marriage, but its light wanes after a time. A note of caution certainly survives in the spirit of the 'honeymoon period': one that may be smooth and easy now, but is destined to fade.

The equivalent term in German is *Flitterwochen* which, given that the usual meaning of *Flitter* is 'sequins' or 'trumpery finery', carries a similar sense of jaded expectations. On a more hopeful note, remembering that this is the day after Valentine's Day, an older sense of the verb *flittern* was 'to laugh or giggle': a far more welcome spin on moonshine.

16 February

SOUBHIYE

It may be dark outside but there is something intensely restorative about getting up before anyone else and savouring a moment of quiet contemplation (and coffee). In Lebanese Arabic, this is known as *soubhiye*, which translates literally as 'morning' but which encompasses a particular moment of private joy.

In Sweden, *gökotta* is an early awakening for the purpose of tuning into the day's first birdsong. Its literal meaning is 'early-morning cuckoo'.

17 February

OLF

Which scientific unit is based on the average office worker, who is generally sedentary and keeps sufficiently warm, with a hygienic routine of around 0.7 baths per day and a skin area of 1.8 square metres? The answer is an 'olf', which is the official unit involved in the measurement of smell. It was introduced by the Danish professor P. Ole Fanger, who based it on the Latin *olfactus*, meaning 'smell', with no doubt a pleasing riff on his name. It is used to measure the strength of pollution sources as well as the smells given off by humans in various situations. A sitting person measures approximately 1 olf, a smoker 25 olf, and an athlete marginally more at 30. Wet dogs, curiously, have not yet been publicly olf-measured.

18 February

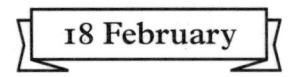

DOOG

Looking for your reswort this morning? Perhaps you need to eevach a doog kool at emoosh.

If these two sentences leave you baffled, they have done their job, for their entire raison d'être is to bemuse and bamboozle. This is back-slang, a coded language that many of us dipped into at school and which has been used by various groups over the last two centuries to evade the ears of outsiders.

One of the earliest of these communities were nineteenth-century butchers, who would regularly use back-slang – or 'pig Latin', as it was appropriately known – to chat about customers or their financial dealings. It was a complicated business, in which words were not just spelled backwards but sometimes gained extra syllables. Thus a 'hel-bat' was a table, and a 'fil-heath' a thief. Costermongers also found it useful, and Cockney rhyming slang similarly operated as a code that provided both entertaining banter as well as privacy.

One of the most recognizable legacies of such slang is the word 'yob', which is simply 'boy' written backwards and is first recorded in a dictionary of slang from 1859. The reversal of the normal state of affairs went on to lend itself well to the idea of a delinquent youth.

As for those first sentences, that would be asking you whether you had lost your trousers (reswort) and need to have a good (doog) look (kool) at home.

19 February

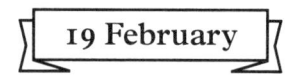

SIGN OF THE MEOW

What do clinging monkeys, little ducks, snails, little worms, strudels, and rollmops have in common? The answer is that they have all been, or still are, nicknames for the @ symbol. They are just a handful of the many terms for the same typographical symbol found across the world's languages: from German, Greek, Italian and Welsh, Hungarian, Hebrew, and Czech respectively. Other choices include 'moon's ear' (*aiqulaq*) in Kazakhstan, *snabela* in Sweden ('a' with an elephant's trunk), and, for the Finns, a sleeping cat (*miukumauku*, literally, 'sign of the meow').

The symbol was originally used by medieval monks as an abbreviation of the Latin *ad*, meaning 'towards', combined with the older form of the letter 'd'. But its modern form began a century or so later, when Florentine merchants used it to denote an amphora, a terracotta vessel that had become a unit of measure for wine and other liquids. It fell largely below the radar until, half a millennium later, it became the cornerstone of connectivity between humans.

20 February

QUEUE

When it comes to words that are curiosities in themselves, we must surely start with 'queue', the British national pastime, the pronunciation of which needs only its first letter while the others just queue up behind. The word is based on French, where it means the tail of an animal, which is what a line of people resembles. Incidentally, there is only one common word in English that has five vowels in a row: 'queueing'.

The etiquette authority Debrett's offers several important instructions on how to queue properly, noting that 'a good queue is essentially a democratic affair; situations where VIPs are allowed to break the rules and are ushered to the head of the queue are much resented.' Among the rules are minding the gap (not too much space, and certainly not too little), deterring queue-bargers by politely pointing them to the back of the line, and willingly participating in queue conversations, which allow for a uniquely liberating anonymity if you are talking to someone while their back is turned.

The British, ever phlegmatic and forbearing, are renowned for their excellent queue skills, leaving us profoundly discombobulated when travelling abroad and the whole idea goes out of the window. Sometimes we should be grateful for the things we love to moan about.

21 February

TITIVIL

Judging by the number of highly coloured words we have for a gossip, from 'prattle-basket' to 'blob-tale', 'church bell' to 'clatterfart', English speakers like nothing better than 'spilling the T'. Today we celebrate such thrilling chatter, but it wasn't always that way. Among the numerous terms for 'tea' in Francis Grose's salty 1785 opus, *A Classical Dictionary of the Vulgar Tongue*, you will find 'prattle broth', 'chatter broth', 'scandal broth', and 'cat lap'. The pamphleteer and political writer William Cobbett (who, incidentally, also coined 'red herring') insisted in 1822 that

> the gossip of the tea-table is no bad preparatory school for the brothel ... the girl that has been brought up merely to boil the tea-kettle, and to assist in the gossip inseparable

from the practice, is a mere consumer of food, a pest to her employer, and a curse to her husband, if any man be so unfortunate as to fix his affections upon her.

There were clearly dark suspicions about what was said at the female-only tea-table.

Among the large lexicon for gossipy types is 'titivil'. It was originally a name, also found as Tutivillus, drawn from mystery and morality plays, where it was given to a devil or demon who collected any words skipped over or mangled in Mass, as well as the idle chit-chat exchanged between churchgoers. The titivil would take such evidence to hell to be used against the perpetrators on Judgement Day.

22 February

DESENRASCANÇO

This day is both Founder's Day for Scouts and Thinking Day for Guides (the shared birthday of founders Robert and Olave Baden-Powell). The famous scout saying 'dyb dyb dyb' is an acronym of their motto: Do Your Best. Luckily for all non-Scouts out there, the Portuguese also have a word for such a can-do attitude.

The literal meaning of *desenrascanço* is 'disentanglement'. It describes an improvised solution born out of the ability to think on your feet, and the often unacknowledged skill of managing a problem you have never encountered before and certainly didn't predict. The closest expression in English is perhaps to 'pull a MacGyver', a tribute to the ever-competent 1980s TV spy Angus MacGyver, who used the laws of science and a Swiss army knife to wrangle himself out of any danger or difficulty.

23 February

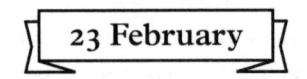

HORNYWINK

As spring approaches, the lapwing is one of many birds out in force. Both its vernacular and scientific names reflect the distinctive flash and hums of its iridescent wings as it flies overhead or zigzags rapidly down to earth. In Latin, it is the *Vanellus vanellus*, the diminutive of *vannus*, a 'winnowing fan', while 'lapwing' was a riff on 'leapwing', meaning 'flickering leap', on account of the bird's floppy, flapping wing movements.

The lapwing is also known for its voice, which gave it another folk-name in English. Its shrill, high-pitched alarm call sounds a little like 'peewit'. It is far from alone in the bird kingdom in being named after its call. The crow, in Old English, was the *crawe*; while the kittiwake, chough, chiffchaff, and cuckoo are similarly named for their sounds. As for the peewit, its roll call of names doesn't stop there: other regional or historical pet names include 'flapjack', 'flopwing', 'hornywink', and 'peesweep'. All of which are poetically interchangeable for when we are lucky enough to observe one of the most beautiful birds on the wing.

24 February

DIGITUS IMPUDICUS

Showing someone the middle finger has been a gesture of obscenity since ancient times. The Romans knew it as the *digitus impudicus*, or 'indecent finger', for it was widely interpreted as a suggestion of an erect penis (by that reckoning, another obscene hand gesture, the V-sign, might suggest a double penis).

The historian Tacitus wrote of a battle in which German tribesmen collectively gave advancing Roman soldiers the middle finger, the predecessors perhaps to the Ukrainian defenders of Snake Island, whose expletive-laden verbal response to Putin's forces on this day in 2022 – 'Russian warship, go fuck yourself' – quickly became an emblem of patriotic courage.

The repertoire of hand gestures can be extensive, shared across different nations as a powerful alternative language. In Elizabethan England, thumb-biting was a distinctly confrontational gesture, involving the placing of the tip of the thumb behind the front teeth and flicking it forward. In some cultures, the spreading of five fingers with the palm facing forward suggests that the recipient has 'five fathers', in other words they are a 'bastard'. The age-old gesture for a 'wanker', meanwhile, is unmistakable to anyone who spends time on a British road.

25 February

NIGHT-WRITING

Nicolas-Marie-Charles Barbier de la Serre knew all about the difficulty that soldiers faced when needing to communicate at night-time without betraying themselves to the enemy. A former fighter in the French artillery, he became interested in linguistic shorthands, and set out to develop a form of writing that could be read silently and in the dark. His system, which relied on a series of raised dots that transcribed phonetic information, dispensed with rules of spelling and punctuation: speed was of the essence, and, as Barbier himself stated, 'useful things can never be too simple'.

The sound equivalents of the dots used by the touch-readable code inspired the name 'sonography'. Barbier himself called it *écriture nocturne*, or 'night-writing'. Its usefulness extended, he knew, far beyond the boundaries of war. In 1821, he took his system to the director of the Royal Institute for Blind Youth, where twelve-year-old pupil Louis Braille was a boarder. The boy was immediately convinced by its raised dots, which were far easier to read than the relief writing used at the time. Braille may have redesigned it to improve accessibility for blind readers, but there is no doubt that a code designed for soldiers communicating in the dark remains at the heart of the system of Braille.

26 February

SCHLIMAZEL

When it comes to bad luck, there are two types in life: those who bring it, and those who invite it – all the time. English happens to have a long-lost word for the former: a 'jettatore'. Straight from the Italian for one who casts the evil eye, a jettatore causes accidents to befall other people, as apparently did one particular duke in the nineteenth century whom, according to one contemporary account, 'all in Naples considered a "jettatore". If he praised any, they fell ill.' The duke's victims might have called themselves total 'schlimazels', if only they had known the word, for these are people to whom unlucky things invariably happen through, it seems, no fault of their own. The typically evocative word comes from Yiddish, in which its closest meaning is 'crooked fortune'.

27 February

HEAD-GEM

Why refer to the sea when you could speak of the 'whale's way'? Or to a ship rather than a 'wave-horse', or the mind as opposed to the 'thought-chamber'? Such exquisite concoctions are known as 'kennings': word hybrids that bring poetry to even the most everyday phenomena. 'Kenning' is a name borrowed from medieval Icelandic studies of poetry: *kenna við* meant 'to name after'. Among the most beautiful examples is surely *merecandel*: Old English for 'sea-candle', a kenning for the sun as it rises or sets over the sea. But one of the most charming is surely the Old English *hēafod-gim* to mean an eye.

Kennings were highly popular in Old Norse and in Old English, where you will find them in works such as *Beowulf* and 'The Seafarer'. They remain common in German today, where a *Drahtesel*, 'wire-donkey', can mean a bicycle; a *Fledermaus*, 'flying mouse', is a bat; a *Stubentiger*, or 'chamber-tiger', is a playful synonym for a cat, and a *Nacktschnecke*, 'naked snail', is a slug. They are sadly largely lacking in modern English, although Seamus Heaney's translation of *Beowulf* illustrates their full power with such wonders as 'bone-house' for the body, 'water-ropes' for icicles, and 'word-hoard' for our vocabulary.

28 February

FROWST

Few of us would expect anything good from the adjective 'frowsty', which sits uncomfortably close to both 'fuggy' and 'fusty' in the dictionary and carries many of the same undertones. A frowsty room is one that smells and feels stuffy. It seems surprising then that simply lopping the 'y' off the word could turn 'frowsty' into something really rather welcoming, but that is exactly what happened in the nineteenth century, when 'frowst' came to mean taking pleasure in a warm atmosphere. You might frowst over a fire, for example, or, if you were a boarder in a public school, you might be given permission to frowst in bed of a Sunday morning or on a special saint's day. The fact that such a lie-in was sanctioned contrasts frowsting with 'hurkle-durkling', old Scots for staying in bed long after you should be up and running.

29 February

MOTHER-IN-LAW'S DREAM

This is a rare day in the calendar that falls once every four years: famously the one day when women are encouraged to seize the initiative and propose. The important question has to be: how do you know that someone really is 'the one'? The presentiment of love upon first meeting – the sense that the person in front of you will go on to be special in your life – has no single expression in English. Thankfully, Japanese does have one, in *koi no yokan*. A phrase that has become highly popular thanks to manga comics aimed specifically at teen girls, it describes the instant conviction upon meeting someone that they will eventually take over your heart.

Of course, in situations such as these, it also pays to ignore your mother's advice. In Swedish, a *svärmorsdröm*, or 'mother-in-law's dream', is someone a hypothetical mother might consider extremely eligible as a potential son- or daughter-in-law on account of being well-mannered and successful – and potentially very boring.

MARCH

1 March

BRETHYN CARTREF

Today is St David's Day, celebrated with an outpouring of fervour, or *hwyl*, and kindness. The Welsh language has a distinct preoccupation with the importance of home. It harbours, after all, such beauty as *hiraeth*, a deep longing, especially for one's home and one's place within it; there is a wistfulness and nostalgia to it that extends far beyond homesickness.

The deep agricultural roots of Wales are revealed in the old distinctions between seasonal dwellings. A summer home is the *hafod*, to which a household and its livestock could move to make use of higher summer pasture. *Hendref*, meaning 'old home', sits on lowland pasture and is where a household would spend the winter months.

Cartref is another member of the homeful lexicon, which is made up of *câr* ('kin') and *tref* ('homestead'). This is both the physical building and the emotional and familiar aspects within it. Its range is broad, covering such things as *gwaith cartref*, 'homework', and *bara cartref*, 'home-baked bread'. Best of all is surely the *brethyn cartref*, used to describe a Welsh blanket, with the literal meaning of 'homely cloth' – it's an evocative idiom for the comfort and familiarity of childhood. It features in a Welsh ballad:

> *Brethyn gwlan y defaid man,*
> *Dyna fel y gwisgai'r oes o'r blan*
> *Felly elai gynt i garu –*
> *Yn ei frethyn cartre.*

> The fine sheep's wool cloth,
> That is how it was worn the era before
> So the sooner to love –
> In his homely cloth.

2 March

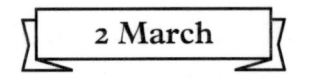

WABBIT

'Wabbit' has nothing to do with Elmer Fudd and his endless pursuit of Bugs Bunny, 'that wascally wabbit', even if their first adventure, *Elmer's Candid Camera*, was released today in 1940. Instead, in nineteenth-century Scots, to be 'wabbit' was to feel decidedly feeble and listless. If you are feeling a bit 'meh' on top, then you might also borrow 'frobly-mobly' from the same lexicon, which describes an elusive sense of unease with no directly explicable cause. Put it together with 'wabbit', and you essentially have the historical equivalent of the shrugging emoji.

3 March

WELSH RAREBIT

Were you to boast of enjoying Welsh rarebit and a spot of Albany beef for luncheon, you would be unknowingly pulling together a thread of linguistic connections, with three items that are not all they are sometimes held to be. 'Welsh rarebit', for starters, was not the original that was later bastardized to 'Welsh rabbit'; it was the other way round. The rather unappetizing original name of the dish was one of many insults lobbed towards the Welsh, insinuating that Welsh citizens couldn't afford to buy real rabbit and had to resort to cheese on toast instead. 'Rarebit' was a successful later attempt by chefs to suggest something altogether fancier. 'Albany beef', similarly, contains no beef at all. Rather this is sturgeon, a fish that was so plentiful in the Hudson River Valley during the eighteenth and nineteenth centuries that the town of Albany was known as 'Sturgeontown'. As for 'luncheon' being the progenitor of 'lunch', the latter is actually recorded first, in 1591, in the sense of a thick hunk of food such as bread or bacon. 'Lunch' as the name for a midday meal began to emerge in the 1820s, when it was frowned upon as a mere vulgarism and fashionable affectation.

4 March

FECKFUL

The end of winter is finally in sight and it's time to start thinking about the joys of spring: at least that might be our aim as we begin to look forward to a season that is erumpent with new life and fresh intentions. We can certainly all hope to become more 'feckful', the unknown antonym to 'feckless' in which 'feck' is simply short for 'effect'. To be feckful is to be powerful, vigorous, and effective. This is one of our language's many lost positives, dropped in favour of their negative offspring and consigned to the recesses of the historical dictionary. Our pessimism bias has led us to drop such wonders as 'ruthful' (full of compassion), 'kempt' (well-combed), 'couth' (highly polite), and 'full of gorm' (attentiveness). Recent research has shown that embracing positive vocabulary helps us live longer, feel happier, and visit the doctor less. So as springtime approaches, here's to the gruntled and the consolate, the ept and the ruly: they deserve to blossom once more.

5 March

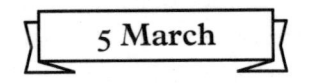

PELINTI

English needs a word for the sharp intake of breath and subsequent 'hashashahhh' sound we make when we put overly hot food or beverages into our mouth. The gulp can be even louder if the mouthful in question is ice cold and we have dental sensitivity. While English can't yet oblige, the Buli language, spoken in the upper east region of Ghana, certainly can. *Pelinti* describes the frantic pushing of piping-hot food around your mouth in a vain attempt to avoid burning your tongue.

6 March

RIGMAROLE

Say the word 'ribble-rabble' out loud and you might catch the sound of a motley crew of disorderly characters muttering away. Beneath it in the *Oxford English Dictionary* is a word with an equally discomfiting feel: 'ribble-row', which is accompanied by an example from a seventeenth-century burlesque poem: 'This Witch a ribble-row rehearses,/ Of scurvy names in scurvy verses.' A ribble-row is a charade of little substance – a rigmarole, in other words.

'Rigmarole', meaning a rambling disconnected account, an unending yarn, or a tiresomely lengthy process, has its own curious story, taking us back to the thirteenth century, when Scottish noblemen signed a declaration of loyalty to King Edward I. Each of them fixed their seal to the deed, and when all the attachments were joined together the document was rolled up to be presented to the king. It became known as the

Ragman Roll, based on the name of a medieval game containing verses that described various characters, among them Ragemon le bon, or 'Ragemon the good'. The unrolled document, made up of more than thirty-five pieces of parchment with 2,000 signatures, was over forty feet long, and it was this, together with the complexity of drawing it up in a short period of time, that inspired the 'rigmaroles' we complain of to this day.

7 March

FUDGEL

The Dutch verb *epibreren* describes a pretence many of us are familiar with, namely making a relatively trivial task look important as a means of avoiding proper work. The term was apparently resurrected by Simon Carmiggelt, a Dutch newspaper columnist who explained that it had been revealed to him in 1953 by a civil servant from whom he had requested some papers. The civil servant said that the papers still required some *epibreren*. Not knowing what he meant, Carmiggelt pushed him to explain, and the civil servant eventually confessed that he had invented the term in order to fend off unwelcome enquiries.

Nathan Bailey's *Universal Etymological Dictionary* can provide an English word that proves our ancestors were just as susceptible to distraction when they really should be working. The verb 'fudgel' he defines as 'to make a Shew of doing somewhat to no purpose; to trifle'. In other words, fudgelling involves pretending to be incredibly industrious while achieving nothing at all.

8 March

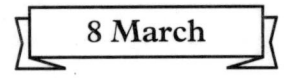

TONSTRIX

Any historical dictionary will tell you that, for centuries, women were more talked about than talking, the object of the male gaze or the recipient of their favours. Consequently, the names of roles within society were male by default, with a suffix added if the female version was needed. A governor became a governess, and a seamster a seamstress. English was far from alone in this: whenever a Roman wanted to indicate the female version of a male role, they would add the suffix -*trix*; a female barber, for example, was a *tonstrix*. Many such titles, once imported into English, survived for a while, and the 'aviatrix', 'editrix', 'creatrix', 'doctrix', and 'monitrix' all walked the professional stage at various times in the past. Other titles related more to a woman's character and were characteristically judgemental: a 'consolatrix' was a woman who soothed a man's brow, while a 'persecutrix' was nothing less than a harridan. Today, only one remains in common use, recorded in English as early as the sixteenth century, when 'dominatrix' described a woman who was particularly tough or overbearing. Today's suggestion of sexual dominance arose much later, in the 1960s. On International Women's Day, it is also worth noting that there is just one word in English where the female category provides the default and a suffix is required for the male counterpart, namely: 'widow' and 'widower'.

9 March

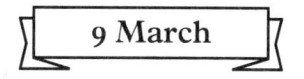

UHTCEARU

The darkest hour (unfortunately) is always before the dawn. The Germans have a specific word for the uniform colour that we tend to perceive in total darkness, when light signals are absent. This is *Eigengrau*, 'instrinsic grey', and many of us will encounter it in the sleepless hours just before sunrise, when worries can loom unmanageably, shrinking back into proportion only when day breaks. There is some solace in knowing that we are not alone, for this dark spiral of anxiety was known in Old English as *uhtcearu*: the 'sorrow before dawn'. Hang on in there.

10 March

IT AIN'T OVER TILL THE FAT LADY SINGS

'Oh, yeah, it was vintage Carpenter. He was one of the world's funniest guys.' So said a visitor to the press box at a Southwest Conference men's basketball tournament on this day in 1976 after overhearing an organizer comment on a game that looked to be all over bar the shouting. Ralph Carpenter's exact words were 'The opera ain't over until the fat lady sings'.

It was, in fact, far from the first outing for an expression that has survived in various forms to this day. Nor was it originally restricted to opera, for regional US English had several similar proverbs that follow the same pattern, including 'Church ain't out till the fat lady sings'. Nonetheless, it was in the final rousing performance of an opera singer that the expression found its home. The 'fat lady' in question is usually held to be the Valkyrie Brünnhilde, traditionally played by a buxom woman in armour and a horned helmet. Brünnhilde's farewell scene is peak opera, lasting almost twenty hard-singing minutes and leading directly to the finale of *Götterdämmerung*, the last of Wagner's Ring Cycle. As it is about the end of the world (or at least the world of the Norse gods), in a very significant way it really is 'all over when the fat lady sings'.

11 March

BAGSY

Most of us of a certain age will know about claiming something for ourselves by 'bagsying' it. We might have shouted, 'Bagsy lick the bowl!', for example, while making a cake with our siblings, or have 'bagsied' the comfiest bed on holiday. It seems a curious choice on the face of it, but it is simply a contraction of 'bags I' – you 'bag' the last lick of the spoon by declaring your interest in it, based on the principle that *possession is nine points of the law* – bags something and it is yours. Today's children might instead 'call shotgun', particularly when claiming the passenger seat of a car. The reference here is far more precarious: armed guards were frequently required when travelling across the American prairies to protect against bandits, and would sit in readiness next to a stagecoach driver. The dictionary's first record comes from a 1940 issue of the Californian *Pony Express Courier*.

12 March

FOOL'S BALLOCKS

'Beldairy, bleeding willow, bull's bags, bullsegg, cuckoo, cuckoo-flower, dandy goshen, dead man's fingers, fool's ballocks, fool's stones.' This extract from Winifred Brenchley's

Weeds of Farm Land, published in 1920, gives a sense of the vernacular terms for plants that were more typically known by their scientific Latin names, in this case *Orchis morio*. The Doctrine of Signatures, a theory in folk medicine, rested on the belief that herbs or animals have physical or behavioural traits that mirror the ailment or body part that they can successfully treat. Walnuts, for example, were considered curatives for head ailments because, according to the seventeenth-century botanist William Coles, they 'have the perfect Signatures of the Head'. The plants heartsease and eyebright were thought to heal diseases of the heart and eye, while lungwort eased breathing troubles, and liverwort ailments of the liver. Kidney beans, of course, were thought useful for maintaining kidney health.

Not all plant names were determined exclusively by their role in medicine. Some are simply descriptive, but can seem surprisingly blunt to modern ears. 'Dead man's fingers' was applied to many plants with noticeably finger-like flowers, while the orchid 'fool's ballocks' is so called on account of its testicular shape ('orchid' itself is a borrowing from Greek for the same part of the anatomy, thanks to the appearance of the frequently paired tubers of the species). That said, orchids were particularly prized for their purported use as an aphrodisiac, so their place in the Doctrine of Signatures was surely guaranteed.

13 March

BRANCH WOBBLER

Storms in Britain are supervised by the Met Office, and not just meteorologically. In 2015, it launched the project 'Name Our Storms', issuing a new list of names each September to be used for future storms of sufficient strength to require an amber or red warning to the public. The list is compiled jointly with Met Éireann and KNMI, the Dutch national weather-forecasting service, and together they are known as the 'western storm-naming group'. Further afield, it is the World Meteorological Organization that has naming power, maintaining six alphabetical lists to be used on a six-year cycle and alternating between masculine and feminine epithets.

The Met Office relies heavily on suggestions from the public for future consideration. Unsurprisingly, given the result of a democratic vote on the name of a government's multimillion polar research ship (arise *Boaty McBoatface*), the Met Office has had to dismiss a good few of them. The *Sun* newspaper recently revealed some of the 'wacky suggestions' that were submitted, and summarily rejected, in the space of one year. It includes 'Voldemort', 'Sweet Caroline', 'Megatron', 'In a Teacup', and 'Branch Wobbler'.

14 March

EIGHT MINUTES

The 1920s were a time of linguistic exuberance, a chance to shake off the dark days of war and embrace a good time. The Roaring Twenties, as they became known, saw a wealth of expressions for excellence. Some, such as 'the gnat's elbows', 'the kipper's knickers', 'the oyster's earrings', and the 'tadpole's teddies', have been lost to time, but the 'bee's knees' and 'the cat's whiskers' (as well as its occasional pyjamas) have happily survived. All of these would have been well known to the flappers: highly fashionable young women who loved nothing more than flouting convention and enjoying themselves to the max. They may have taken their name from the use of 'flap' in US dialect for a newly fledged bird, even if inevitably 'flapper' was soon taken to mean a 'woman of loose character'. But, like all groups with a shared passion, the flappers had their own jargon too. Within it, a tough or cynical individual was known as an 'eight minutes' because they were 'hard-boiled'. A *particularly* hard-boiled character became, naturally, a 'ten minutes'.

15 March

BACKFRIEND

'The saddest thing about betrayal is that it never comes from your enemies': anonymous words that Julius Caesar might have reflected upon on this day, the Ides of March, when he spotted his former friend Brutus among the conspirators sent to topple him. The events of his assassination amply fulfilled the etymology of 'betrayal', whose origins lie in the Latin *tradere*, 'to hand over'.

In 1765, the lexicographer Samuel Johnson included in his *Dictionary of the English Language* the word 'backfriend', which he defined as 'a friend backwards; an enemy in secret'. Its successor in pretence is today's 'frienemy', a seeming friend that is recorded since 1891. As they say, snakes don't hiss any more, they call you 'mate' instead.

Of course, between the friends and the foes there will always be the sycophants in the middle. In the seventeenth century they would have been known as the 'catchfarts': servants who followed the boss a bit too closely for comfort. The key, as always, is to differentiate between those who have your back and those who want to stab you in it. Perhaps Tennessee Williams had it right when he said, 'We have to distrust each other. It is our only defense against betrayal.'

16 March

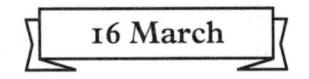

ALUMINUM

When it comes to language, there is one subject that is guaranteed to cause a ruction. Mention is usually made of such abominations as 'color', 'Can I get a cappuccino?', an athlete 'medalling', and artificially extended terms such as 'transportation'. The subject of course is US English, and its inexorable infestation of the 'proper' kind.

Most lexicographers will take pains to show how each of these examples was already prevalent in British English before it crossed the Atlantic – in the case of 'medalling', the dictionary's first mention is in a letter written in 1860 by the English novelist William Makepeace Thackeray when he spoke of a friend 'medalled by the King'. Spellings such as 'color' and 'realize' are to be found in Shakespeare's First Folio and outscore the 'British' version by some margin.

Howsoever these land, one of the biggest surprises for those who abhor the steady creep of US English revolves around the name of the metal we know as 'aluminium', and its apparently random respelling by American tongues to 'aluminum'. The truth is that 'aluminum' coexisted alongside 'aluminium' throughout the nineteenth century, depending on whether the speaker wished to follow the model of 'platinum' or 'magnesium'. Sir Humphry Davy, inventor of the famous Davy lamp, wrote in 1812, 'As yet Aluminum has not been obtained in a perfectly free state.' Eventually, as the desire for independence in language as much as territory grew, 'aluminum' settled in North America, while British English exclusively embraced the other.

Oscar Wilde may have said, 'We have really everything in common with America nowadays except, of course, language,' but that language is a good deal more united than we think.

17 March

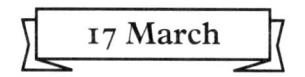

AMAINIRIS

The ancient language of Irish can feel unfamiliar to new ears, even though it is a linguistic cousin to Welsh, Scots, and Manx. Its beauty is undeniable, as are its sounds, and St Patrick's Day is as good a time as any to appreciate it. Beyond the words that have been readily absorbed into English, such as *craic* and *sláinte*, quite apart from those that have lost their Irish moorings completely, such as 'trousers', 'galore', 'whiskey', and 'drumlin', lies a rich and useful language that can frequently fill a gap in our own.

English has, for example, lost many of its old markers of time. The sixteenth-century 'overmorrow', meaning 'the day after tomorrow', has inexplicably drifted into obscurity. In Latin, the *perendinus* was the day after tomorrow, giving English the verb 'perendinate', to put something on hold until then. But Irish can do one better, for *amainiris* means precisely *two* days after tomorrow.

18 March

SHOTCLOG

March is not always a pleasant month. In the words of Garrison Keillor, this is 'the month God created to show people who don't drink what a hangover is like.' For those who do know exactly how a sore head feels, poor weather and the need for consolation means their money can run out long before the end of the month. Thankfully the historical dictionary provides a few words to describe those who refuse to let empty pockets stop them having a good time. Take the 'snecklifter':

someone who lifts the 'sneck' or latch of the tavern door and peers in to see if they know anyone who might stand them a drink. A 'lanspresado', originally a non-commissioned officer of the lowest grade, is alternatively defined in a slang glossary from 1699 as 'he that comes into Company with but Two pence in his pocket'. In other words, this is the person who professes to be continually broke and who relies on the generosity (or forgetfulness) of their friends. Better to be them, however, than the 'shot-clog': seventeenth-century slang for an unwelcome member of a group tolerated solely because they're buying the next round.

19 March

GLIMMER-GOWK

A nineteenth-century glossary of words from Lincolnshire lists the exquisite 'glimmer-gowk' as a local term for an owl, whose wings reflect the soft light of the moon as it sweeps across the night sky.

In its beauty the name easily outclasses the adjective 'strigiform', which can be used of anything pertaining to owls. Its root is the ancient Greek *strix*, which may descend from a long-lost language of the eastern Mediterranean. *Strix* moved into Latin as *striga*, which in turn took on a variety of dark meanings considered in keeping with this swooping king of the night, from an evil spirit to a vampire or witch.

The owl's association with intelligence may stem from its depiction in Greek mythology, where the creature was the messenger of Athena, the goddess of wisdom. The Ainu, the indigenous people of northern Japan, believe that the owl is a harbinger of good luck. It is said that if a person hears the sound of falling rain when walking beneath a tree in which an owl is perched, surely they will become rich.

20 March

TWAT

'Twat' is a curious offering in the swearing smorgasbord in that we have never quite decided how 'bad' it is. Deemed inoffensive enough to feature in 12-certificate films, it is still considered 'strong language' for TV and therefore unacceptable for family viewing.

From the outset, 'twat' could be used as a purely anatomical description. One of its earliest mentions is in a seventeenth-century collection of epigrams, which offers the curious 'Give not male names then to such things as thine,/But think thou hast two Twats oh wife of mine.' A century later, Nathan Bailey included in his *Universal Etymological English Dictionary* the term 'twat-scowerer: a Surgeon or Doctor'. Things weren't always quite so straightforward, however. Robert Browning added his own – and as it turned out, erroneous – interpretation in his 1841 poem *Pippa Passes*, where he uses it to mean part of a nun's habit: 'Then, owls and bats, cowls and twats,/Monks and nuns, in a cloister's moods,/Adjourn to the oak-stump pantry!' Browning seems to have misunderstood a poem from two hundred years earlier: 'They talk't of his having a Cardinalls hat,/They'd send him as soon an Old Nun's Twat' (something that no one was ever likely to see).

The origins of 'twat' are elusive. One theory, as yet unproved, is that it derives from the Old English *thwitan*, meaning 'to cut off' – the idea being that a woman's genitals are simply the amputated versions of those of a man. The leading slang lexicographer Jonathon Green has found a more plausible relationship with the dialect terms 'twitchel', meaning a narrow passage, and 'twatch', a gap in a hedge.

The *Oxford English Dictionary* adds another possibility, that the word may originate from syllables used in a refrain in songs.

One particularly bawdy tune from 1602 has the chorus 'Twittye twitty twatty foole', which resulted in a seventeenth-century synonym for the vagina: 'twit-twat'. (The idea is not as far-fetched as it sounds, given that the word 'dildo' also began as a pair of nonsense syllables in sixteenth-century songs, in the style of 'hey diddle diddle'.)

Whatever its story, 'twat' is a multitasker in the swearing world. And sometimes no other word will do – as the poet John Cooper Clarke will confirm:

> What kind of creature bore you,
> Was it some kind of bat?
> They can't find a good word for you,
> but I can . . . TWAT.

21 March

KOMOREBI

Nature has a rightfully prominent place in the lexicon of Japan. This is a culture, after all, which encourages *shinrin-yoku*, or 'forest-bathing': a total immersion in the peace of a forest to promote calm and well-being. The annual ritual of *hanami*, literally a 'flower viewing', draws an entire nation to marvel at the transient beauty of cherry blossom. Both traditions involve the quiet observation of nature's processes as a way of restoring a sense of harmony, and they are joined by possibly the most specific and special expression of all, *komorebi*, which describes the beauty of nature's play with light and shadow.

The three-kanji word – its Chinese characters roughly translate as 'trees', 'leaking through', and 'sun' – describes the shards of light that dance on the floor of a forest as the sun breaks through the trees. It is what the poet Gerard Manley Hopkins knew as 'shivelight'. Like most untranslatable words, *komorebi* captures more than its literal meaning, for it is viewed metaphorically as small dots of brightness that can punctuate the darkest times, which is perhaps truer to life than the trope of light at the end of the tunnel, with its insistence on a perfect ending. Life is far more often like *komorebi*: dark and light in varying measures throughout. As the writer Renu Vijayanand explains:

> The other thing about *komorebi* is that it doesn't just describe the way ordinary sunlight is pretty. It's a special kind of beauty that's only made possible by the dark foliage of trees. The beauty of *komorebi* isn't just in the sunlight. It's in the shadows, too.

22 March

SPIZZERINCTUM

Now, there's a word! It isn't in the dictionary, but any veteran Scouter will tell you that boys are full of it. Spiz – zer – inc – tum ! for speed, life, zip . . .

The Annual Report for the Boy Scouts of America, from 1960, was clearly on to something, even when 'spizzerinctum' was taking its time to find a way into the dictionary. Despite a lack of formal recognition, however, it served as a useful exuberant byword for vim, vigour, and all-round enthusiasm. The word's roots seem to be the dialect 'spizarinctum', meaning cash, itself a riff on 'specie', which was a term for money in the form of coins. The extension to the idea of pep and zing may have connected cash in one's pocket with a renewed enthusiasm for life.

23 March

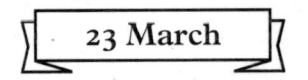

OCHLOCRACY

The dictionary offers various terms for styles of government, as well as the individuals who create them. Over on the dark side, 'kakistocracy' is the very worst kind of government. An 'aristocracy', originally, was ruled by the best (Greek *aristos*) of citizens. And no one wants a 'boobocracy': a government of boobs (i.e. fools).

We also have 'democracy', of course, but take that too far and you might end up with an 'ochlocracy', which comes from the Greek *ochlo*s, a 'crowd', making an ochlocracy more akin to mob rule (social media, anyone?).

A 'logocracy', on the other hand, is surely one of the best, for this is a community or system of government in which the only ruling powers are words.

24 March

DOING A HARRY

The chills of winter may be ebbing but there is still time to catch a Vincent, thanks to a Miley Cyrus, sending you potentially into a right two-and-eight. Better to have a Rosie Lee at the gates of Rome until you feel less moby.

Most of us would recognize a few of the formulae here, part of a long-standing tribal banter that risks becoming fossilized as its usage drops. Cockney rhyming slang, for all its humour, can tell us a lot about secret languages and their functions across the centuries.

Some of the first formal glossaries of language involved the secret vocabulary or 'cant' of the criminal underworld.

Documenting it wasn't easy: one magistrate, intent on exposing these 'counterfeit cranks' who sought to hoodwink or 'honeyfuggle' honest citizens, threatened to whip those who came in front of the bench unless they revealed their code. It was never freely given, but we do have occasional glimpses of this criminal sub-language, such as 'the Wit be burnt': a signal exchanged in the dead of night between highwaymen to indicate that the person one of them might be eyeing up as their next victim has already been robbed by another.

Cockney rhyming slang began in a similar fashion in the opening decades of the nineteenth century. The secret language of costermongers – market traders selling, among other things, 'costards' or cooking apples – was both joyful banter and a necessary private lingo designed to evade outsiders, whether the police or the occasional customer. They wanted a language that neither the authorities nor the 'Billy Bunters' (punters) could understand as they bartered in the markets around London's Whitechapel and Petticoat Lane. It makes sense that classic rhyming slang often references the products that these traders sold, such as 'apples and pears' for 'stairs', 'porky pies' for 'lies', 'loaf (of bread)' for 'head', and 'blowing a raspberry (tart)' for 'fart'.

But this wasn't just the language of the market. As a bold, irreverent, and sometimes complex code it was perfect for the 'flash language' of the Victorian underworld, where it thrived among criminals. To this day, it is said to be popular within prisons, where it clearly marks out those in the know from those who aren't.

Rhyming slang received an unexpected boost during the Second World War, when troops from the East End of London chose to baffle and bamboozle the regiments fighting alongside them in the trenches. Perhaps it was also the sound of home they longed for, inspiring them to dip into the banter they had left behind to comfort and fortify them as they ripped into the 'Rabbit Run' (Hun).

In recent decades Australians have heartily embraced the idea, producing their own homespun versions of rhyming slang with flourishes such as a 'Cobra shower' for 'flower' and, of course, 'Reg Grundies' for 'undies'. To 'do a Harry', meanwhile, is to do a runner, on the formula 'do a Harry Holt/bolt'. The phrase is from the name of former Australian prime minister Harold Holt, who disappeared, presumed drowned, while swimming at Portsea, Victoria, in 1967.

As for its future, even if the glory days have passed, rhyming slang is far from brown bread. A little moby, maybe (Moby Dick/sick). As for the rest of that first paragraph, this was of course referring to catching a Vincent van Gogh/cough, thanks to a Miley Cyrus/virus, sending you into a right two-and-eight/state, forcing you to have a Rosie Lee/tea at the gates of Rome/home.

25 March

DEIPNOSOPHIST

The culture of the ancient Greeks was underpinned by storytelling and a deep spirit of inquiry. The impulse for self-education and the desire to question received opinion were strong, and the boundaries between education and pleasure were thinly drawn, if at all. The earliest myths show mankind actively scrutinizing the demands of the Olympian gods, and Greek comedies were expressly designed to subject politicians and public figures to ridicule if it was felt to be deserved.

Much of this, of course, was reflected in the vocabulary of the time. The Greek *skholē*, the foundation for English 'school', described both leisure and philosophy, as well as a venue for debate. For the ancient Greeks, leisure time was spent as much on intellectual pursuits as physical recreation. The word *sumposion*, which was to become the English 'symposium', meant a 'drinking companion', since symposia perfectly blended entertainment and learning, involving choreographed discussions held after a banquet, together with music and games.

This world also provided us with the 'deipnosophist', a master of the art of dining and discussion: in other words a 'table philosopher'. In modern terms, a deipnosophist is a seasoned dinner party guest, but its meaning can surely be extended to those who enjoy a proper and extended conversation over food rather than a meal on a tray eaten silently in front of the TV.

26 March

OMG

The dictionary holds many surprises when it comes to the age of words we assume to be entirely modern. Teenagers might be horrified to learn, for example, that 'OMG' was first uttered in 1917, notably by Admiral of the Fleet John 'Jacky' Arbuthnot Fisher in a letter to Winston Churchill: 'I hear that a new order of Knighthood is on the tapis – O.M.G. (Oh! My God!) – Shower it on the Admiralty!!'

Fisher may well have been making a punning riff on the initials of the Order of St Michael and St George, which had been without a chancellor for several years until one was appointed on 4 October of the same year. Nonetheless, his exclamation continues to provide us with the earliest record of an abbreviation that has dominated communications over the last two decades.

'LOL' is similarly first recorded a good three decades before its popularity exploded in the 1990s. In this instance, however, the meaning has changed quite dramatically, since the cops of San Francisco knew it only as an acronym for 'Little Old Lady'.

'Text-speak' nonetheless predates both of these by some margin. The British Library holds a love poem written in the nineteenth century that might otherwise have graced the blinking screen of an old Nokia:

> He says he loves U 2 X S,
> U R virtuous and Y's,
> In X L N C U X L
> All others in his i's.

27 March

MONDEGREEN

Ask anyone for their greatest hits of misheard song lyrics, and conversation will come alive. We all have our own versions, usually several, of what are sometimes known as 'mondegreens', a name that began with a misinterpretation of the lyrics from the seventeenth-century Scottish ballad 'The Bonnie Earl of Moray'. 'They hae slain the Earl o' Moray/And laid him on the green' suddenly became 'They hae slain the Earl o' Moray/And Lady Mondegreen'.

Among the most commonly quoted mondegreens are 'money for nothing and your chips for free' by Dire Straits (arguably better than the original, which involves 'chicks for free'), and Starship's 'we built this city on sausage rolls'. The comedian Peter Kay has spoken for us all with his interpretation of the line 'just let me state for the record', from Sister Sledge's 'We Are Family', as 'just let me staple the vicar'. Boy George surely *meant* to sing about a 'comma chameleon', and as for Bob Dylan, more than a few listeners have grown up believing he is reassuring us all that 'the ants are my friends, they're blowin' in the wind'.

28 March

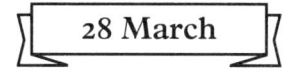

FERNWEH

Language offers many words for the emotional pull of home, but fewer for the longing to be far away from it. 'Dromomania', a coinage describing the urge to flee, is used in medical circles for a compulsion to escape, which is also known as 'vagabond neurosis' or 'travelling fugue'. German, however, does it far more poetically with *Fernweh*, 'far-sickness', or the aching for distant places. It is similar to, but not at all identical with, *Wanderlust*, a word that already sits comfortably in English to describe a joyful desire for travel. *Fernweh* is a more complex, melancholy emotion, for it can be a yearning for places you have never seen. Its story is said to have begun with the fantastically named landscape gardener and great traveller Prince Hermann Ludwig Heinrich von Pückler-Muskau, author of a bestselling book that detailed his exotic adventures across Europe and North Africa. In 1835, Pückler-Muskau wrote that he never suffered from homesickness, but was instead greatly afflicted by its opposite condition, *Fernweh*.

29 March

AUBADE

Today's dawn chorus is more likely to come from drills, dustbin lorries, or nesting birds – the embodiment of what were once known as 'joblijocks': disturbers of domestic peace. Rewind a few centuries, and the sounds might have been far more pleasing. A dictionary from 1678 marvels in the French word 'aubade', defining it as 'Songs, or Instrumentall music, sung, or playd under any ones Chamber window in the morning'. Such sentimental music would probably emanate from a suitor or lover as the sun rises, and might consist of a 'reverdie', another French borrowing for a song that rejoices in the arrival of spring. The genre of the reverdie was highly popular in Chaucer's time, when such songs or poems were sung by minstrels and troubadours, and often featured spring personified as a beautiful woman. The literal meaning of reverdie, rather beautifully, is a 'regreening'.

30 March

SPREZZATURA

'What: this old thing?' For many of us this is the knee-jerk response to any compliment we receive on an item of our clothing, suggesting that we just threw said garment on without a second thought having bought it for under a tenner a decade ago, and yet somehow managed a look of enviable elegance and style. The truth might well be very different, even if we would never admit it – this is probably a rather expensive item that we tried on after any number of rejected alternatives. This, for the Italians, is *sprezzatura*, a studied kind of nonchalance that implies not a single bead of sweat has been exerted in achieving something that is really quite impressive. Most recently, it has also come to embrace a kind of aesthetic rebellion, such as a watch worn over a shirt cuff. But the sense of it is very much the same: of a carefully constructed insouciance.

31 March

UITWAAIEN

March comes in like a lion and leaves like a lamb, the old proverb goes. It's certainly notable for its blustering winds. The Dutch, coming as they do from an extremely flat and windy country, can offer us the word *uitwaaien*, literally an 'outblowing', for the predilection for the desire to walk in particularly windy weather. The name comes from the concept of replacing bad air with the good kind, and comes with the added invigorating bonus of clearing the stuffiest of heads.

APRIL

1 April

MOUNTWEAZEL

When is an entry in a dictionary a fake one? When it's a 'mountweazel', a term that describes a fictitious entry planted by a reference book or map publisher in order to ensure their text is not plagiarized. The 1975 edition of *The New Columbia Encyclopedia* included a biography of one Lillian Virginia Mountweazel, an American photographer from Ohio who became famous for her unusual subject choices such as French cemeteries and rural mailboxes. The entry explains that Ms Mountweazel died in her early thirties from an explosion while on assignment for *Combustibles* magazine.

The fake addition is one of many spurious insertions in reference works, planted as copyright traps. Fictitious streets, known as 'trap streets', regularly find their way into city maps, such as the small cul-de-sac Lye Close which featured in an A–Z street map of Bristol. In 2005, the *New Oxford American Dictionary* added the word 'esquivalience' to its pages. Its entry was clearly a similar in-joke at the expense of would-be plagiarizers, for the definition reads, 'the wilful avoidance of one's official responsibilities'.

2 April

GLAZOMER

The first day of April is also, rather ironically, known as International Problem-Solving Day, which makes the positioning of National DIY Day on 2 April all the more appropriate. As a nation of enthusiastic bodgers we might appreciate a word to describe the skill of wrangling with a devilishly complicated flat-pack and turning it into a work of art. For the Germans, this is *Fingerspitzengefühl*, 'fingertips feeling', which describes an intuitive flair and situational awareness that leads to making the right choices. Russian, meanwhile, has a word for the ability to measure without any instruments: *glazomer* is a compound word meaning 'eye measurement'. On days like today, a good *glazomer* will serve you very well.

3 April

ABSOLUTELY CUCKOO

The classic joky gesture of making 'bunny ears' behind someone's head in a photograph has an unexpectedly dark history.

Traditional sayings fail to agree which day of April the cuckoo should arrive but the month itself is not disputed:

> The cuckoo comes in April,
> Stays the month of May,
> Sings a song at Midsummer,
> And then a goes away.

The bird *Cuculus canorus* is known for the call of the male during mating time. It is a migratory bird, and its arrival is traditionally welcomed as the harbinger of spring. In both Latin and English, the cuckoo's name is echoic, imitating the male's call. The bird has a curious linguistic relation in the 'cuckold', the husband of an unfaithful wife, thanks to its habit of laying its egg in another bird's nest.

The Old English word for a 'cuckoo' is *gowk*, still found in northern England and simultaneously used for a dimwit or simpleton: an April gowk is an April fool. This may be in reference to the cuckoo's monotonous call, or to the fact that the cuckoo dupes other birds into hatching their own eggs. Those aren't bunny ears you're making, they are cuckold's horns.

4 April

EXSUFFLATE

Spring-cleaning need not apply only to our cupboards. This is surely also the season to 'exsufflate' our bodily cobwebs and quicken our steps to match the energy of the season. This seventeenth-century word for 'blowing away' anything unwanted has been used for everything from demons to flies from a horse's nose. Thankfully most potential uses are a little more pedestrian.

The antonym of 'exsufflate' is of course 'insufflate': to blow air or gas into a cavity of the body. This might be the more poetic version of 'blowing smoke up someone's arse', a synonym for hoodwinking that some say arose from the use of tobacco enemas in the seventeenth and eighteenth centuries. These were sometimes used as a means of quite literal resuscitation of a drowning victim, for it was said to have a particularly galvanizing effect. An alternative explanation looks to the First World War, when British troops in the trenches would lift a papier-mâché dummy over the parapet to attract snipers and determine their position. According to this story, the fake Tommy would have a cigarette in its mouth, and a soldier crouching below him would blow smoke out of it through a tube inserted below.

Attractive as these theories are, there is little evidence for either. More likely is a coarser version of 'blowing smoke' to mean deception. After all, the word 'camouflage' began with an old sense of the French word *camouflet*: the act of blowing smoke into someone's eyes.

5 April

SMITHFIELD BARGAIN

'I'd marry again if I found a man who had fifteen million dollars, would sign over half to me, and guarantee that he'd be dead within a year.' The actor Bette Davis, one of the greatest in Hollywood history, was born on this day in 1908. A mistress of sardonic put-downs, she was equally happy to take swipes at herself. She endured three divorces as well as widowhood and concluded later in life that 'none of my husbands was ever man enough to be Mr Bette Davis'.

The historical lexicon for marriage displayed a similar level of cynicism. To be married (or to enter the 'parson's mouse-trap') was to be 'leg-shackled' or even 'noozed' (as good as hanged). 'Marriage music' was far from desirable; rather it described the squalling and crying of children. A 'Westminster wedding' was a match 'between a whore and a rogue'; to have been to an 'Irish wedding' was to have a black eye; and a 'Smithfield bargain' was a match contracted solely on the basis of one partner's interest – usually the man, with the implication that his choice of wife could be bought and sold as easily as cattle in a meat market.

If, however, 'the grey mare is the better horse' and the boot was on the other foot, then a 'hen house' was one where the wife ruled the roost, with her 'hen-pecked' husband said to live in Queen Street, or at the sign of the Queen's Head.

6 April

CREPITUS

Anyone who winces when they hear another person loudly crack their knuckles may at least like to know the name for the sound that joints can make when pulled: 'crepitus'. This term, from the Latin *crepare*, meaning to 'crack' or 'creak', can also describe the crackling of pneumonic lungs as well as the sounds of grasshoppers and rattlesnakes. It belongs to a large lexicon of medical terms for everyday physical events. Should you find that one of your limbs has fallen asleep after prolonged pressure, you are suffering from 'obdormition', while the involuntary twitch in your eyelid is 'fasciculation', named from the Latin *fasciculus*, 'little bundle', because it is caused by the contraction of a small number of muscle fibres. The technical term for sneezing is 'sternutation', while a growling stomach is 'borborygmus'. Finally, there is a real term for the brain freeze you experience when eating ice cream: say hello (carefully) to 'sphenopalatine ganglioneuralgia'.

7 April

TOSSPOT

In the arsenal of insults, 'tosspot' occupies a bit of a sweet spot. Less offensive than 'tosser' but stronger than 'numpty', it is considered passable enough to be used in the Harry Potter film franchise. While many would assume it to be the quieter sibling of the full-frontal 'tosser', it has a very different origin. One seventeenth-century account of a voyage by early settlers across the Atlantic to New England gives us an (unpleasant) flavour of its use with mention of a radical cure: 'The eggs of an owl put into the liquor that a tosspot useth to be drunk with, will make him loathe drunkenness.' A 'tosspot' was literally one who tossed back one pot of beer and immediately asked for another. The line between drunkenness and idiocy being notoriously thin, the word soon took on the mantle of a much broader insult. A word journey it might be good to bear in mind on this, National Beer Day.

8 April

CORDATE

The peepul tree, also known as the bodhi tree or *Ficus religiosa*, is a type of fig tree native to India, China, and South-East Asia, where it is considered sacred by Hindus and Buddhists. In Bihar, India, stands a bodhi tree that is believed to be the descendant of one that is particularly revered, for beneath it the spiritual teacher Siddhartha Gautama is said to have attained enlightenment. The same teacher became known as the Buddha, whose birthday is celebrated on this date in Japan. The name 'bodhi tree' means 'tree of awakening'.

The bodhi tree is known for its heart-shaped leaves, said to represent peace and happiness, a key feature in the tree's iconography. One such leaf features on the medal for India's highest civilian award, the Bharat Ratna. The adjective for 'heart-shaped' is *cordate*, based upon the Latin *cor*, 'heart', which sits at the head of an important family in English, including 'cordial', 'accord', and 'concord'.

9 April

KALSARIKÄNNI

Having dominated the mood of this century's first two decades, 'FOMO' is facing an unexpected threat. The fear of missing out is being nudged aside by its polar opposite: 'JOMO', aka the joy of missing out, especially when not attending an event to which one has been pressingly invited but which is then cancelled by the other party.

On Finnish Language Day, it is worth noting that the Finns have a very specific adjunct to JOMO. Finnish, a member of the Finno-Ugric family, has penetrated everyday English vocabulary very little, with the exception of 'sauna'. We may need to make room for at least one more, however, as for those of us who embrace not going out, the Finns can offer *kalsarikänni*, the highly specific pleasure that comes with staying at home and getting drunk in your underwear.

10 April

OFF ONE'S OWN BAT

On this day in 2004, Brian Lara scored 400 not out against England in Antigua, securing the record for the highest number of runs achieved by an individual, off their own bat, in Test cricket history. Or was it off his own 'back'?

Many expressions in English exist in two versions, and it can be hard to distinguish the original from the imposter. Is it a 'vicious circle' of a 'vicious cycle'? And do we have another 'thing', or 'think', coming?

To answer the first question, for the umpire's decision as to whether Lara scored from his back or bat we need to look to our earliest record of the phrase, which dates from 1742 and a book by the cricket historian Henry Thomas Waghorn. In it we read, 'The Betts on the Slendon Man's Head that he got 40 Notches off his own Bat were lost' (the Slendon Man is likely to have been Richard Newland, one of the sport's earliest left-handed batters who played for Slindon and Sussex). In the decades that followed, 'off one's own bat' continued to refer to scores in cricket that resulted from one player's hits, but by the middle of the nineteenth century it was being used more broadly for achievements from a single individual's exertions. 'Off one's own back' emerged as a mishearing in the twentieth century, influenced perhaps by the phrase 'off the back of'.

As for 'vicious cycle/circle', the first version of the phrase involved a circle, and had a firm place in the field of logic. It is first recorded from 1792, with a 'vicious cycle' joining the ranks some fifty years later. Meanwhile, 'another think coming' seems to be the standard version, dating back to 1896. But it only just knocked 'another thing coming' off the top spot, preceding it – at least as current records stand – by just a single year.

11 April

RECRUDESCENCE

Spring may be bursting forth all over and giving us a sense of energy renewed, but sometimes the things that break out afresh are not always welcome. Illness, or a highly undesirable leader, or a schism in a relationship you thought was mended: all have the capacity to come back with a vengeance even after a period of reprieve. In the seventeenth century, such an unwelcome return was known as a 'recrudescence': a recurrence of an unwanted set of circumstances after a period of remission. At its heart is the Latin *re-*, 'again', and *crudescere*, 'to become raw', as of a wound that reopens and brings even more pain than the first time around. Since its appearance in the early eighteenth century, recrudescence has been applied to undesirables as varied as syphilis and smallpox, sham politicians, and extreme ideologies. Its very sound makes it one to avoid.

12 April

FOLEY ARTIST

On this day in 1891, Jack Donovan Foley was born. Over the course of his life he worked variously as a cartoonist, an accountant, a stuntman, a baseball player, a writer, and a film director, but it was his final role that was to ensure his lasting fame, as well as the immortalization of his name in language.

After the success in 1927 of *The Jazz Singer*, the first feature-length motion film featuring sound in the form of synchronized recorded music, other major studios rapidly adopted the idea. Foley quickly saw the potential of this early technology, and began to concentrate on the means of producing an array of different sound effects. Initially, these involved such arduous tasks as marching on the spot in order to imitate the stride and motion of characters on the screen. When an actor put on a jacket, so Foley would too, in order to precisely replicate the rustle of the fabric. Glasses would be clinked, shotguns fired, doors slammed – all in synchronicity with the action of the film.

Foley created detailed soundscapes for stars as big as Sandra Dee, Rock Hudson, and Laurence Olivier. He painstakingly learned the traits and gait of each of them, noting that James Cagney had 'clipped' footsteps, while those of Marlon Brando were 'soft'. Recreating these personal characteristics became known as 'Foley art', and his crew, performers in their own right, were the 'Foley artists'. On today's film credits 'Foley artist' remains an official job title for those following in the suitably loud footsteps of this pioneer of sound.

13 April

KEEN AS MUSTARD

Mustard has been relished as a spicy addition to food for thousands of years. At various points in its history people would crunch mustard seeds to clean their teeth during meals, use it as a food preservative, and apply it in medicine to various illnesses from hysteria to snakebites.

Up until the eighteenth century, mustard was brought to the table unprepared, as seeds that guests needed to crush and add to a liquid such as vinegar. But in London in 1742, in the appropriately named Garlick Hill (so called from a thoroughfare where garlic was sold, having been transported from the now-lost dock Garlickhythe), a factory for the manufacture of mustard was established by Messrs Keen and Sons. Their name was to become the most famous in mustard-making, until they were bought by Colman's in the early twentieth century.

It is tempting to attribute the state of being 'as keen as mustard' to the same family name, but the expression was already entrenched in the language long before, having been first recorded in 1672. It makes the association between the heat of mustard and the zest and energy of people's behaviour, a link also seen in the phrase 'cut the mustard'. Both expressions were no doubt helped along by the stereotypical image of ale-drinking yeomen tucking into sides of roast beef, to which mustard was thought to be an essential companion. By the early twentieth century, the idea of vigour and enthusiasm was so strong that 'mustard' was used on its own to describe something excellent or, to extend the metaphor, 'hot stuff'.

14 April

QUANTUM LEAP

It would be easy to see how a 'quantum leap' might belong in the same category as a 'meteoric rise'. Both after all describe a major advance in the course of a particular event or career. All is not as it seems, however, for meteors fall, not rise. And a quantum leap, strictly speaking, does not describe a large change at all, but a tiny one.

The word 'quantum' began with the Latin *quantus*, meaning 'how big?' or 'how much?', and originally had the very simple definition of 'a quantity or amount'. The term was introduced into science by the physicist Max Planck in the early twentieth century, and describes the minimum amount of energy that can exist in any given situation – in other words, a very small amount. A 'quantum jump' is the abrupt change of an electron or atom from one energy state to another. Our modern interpretation came about because, although this is a tiny jump in terms of size, it is an instantaneous and dramatic one, and so it was harnessed to mean a sudden or explosive increase, or a major advance. Today happens to be World Quantum Day, chosen because 4.14 are the first digits of Planck's constant, a fundamental constant in quantum physics that explains the behaviour of subatomic particles.

15 April

PEREPODVYPODVERT

What do you call the presentation of a simple idea that does more to obfuscate than explain? It may be the result of BAFFLEGAB (*see* 8 September): pretentious verbiage that is cheek-puffingly inflated and near incomprehensible. But sometimes, despite our best efforts, we make a meal out of something that is really quite straightforward. In such cases we should take a deep breath and try to utter the Russian word *perepodvypodvert*, a fanciful coinage that means doing something in an unnecessarily complicated way. It effectively describes itself, for this mouthful of a word largely consists of a pile of prefixes before it gets to the point. It is, as the inventor of the game League of the Lexicon, Joshua Blackburn, describes it, 'overtranscompliconvoluted'.

16 April

MISOPHONIA

Today is World Voice Day, encouraging us all to nurture and appreciate the phenomenon of the human voice. The root of our word 'voice', the Latin *vox*, has produced a vast family of words in English. It has given us 'vocal', 'vocabulary', 'vociferous', 'equivocate', 'evoke', 'vouch', and 'vowel'.

The appreciation of any voice or sound is of course utterly subjective, as anyone who has witnessed the abbreviation 'ASMR' do a lot of heavy lifting on social media in recent years will agree. Short for 'autonomous sensory meridian response', this is a feeling of well-being and sensory delight in response to certain stimuli, particularly auditory ones. They might include the sound of a soft whisper, of bubble wrap steadily popping, or even a crisp being crunched close to a microphone. All of these and more have proved highly popular on platforms such as TikTok but anathema to anyone with 'misophonia', a condition in which certain noises prove extremely distressing. Far better to stick with more mellifluous – (a word that literally means 'flowing honey') – vocals.

17 April

PHLOEM

'Nanny Ogg knew how to start spelling "banana", but didn't know how you stopped.' Terry Pratchett's observation about one aspect of a banana isn't the only thing that bothers people. Even diehard lovers of the fruit, who may raise a glass to it on National Banana Day, struggle with the strings that run down its interior, which go by the equally unattractive name of 'phloem bundles'. Most of us give them a miss when it comes to the eating of a banana, but at least we now have a name for them.

If you're looking for further fruity facts, in Malay *pisan zapra* is said to mean the time needed to eat a banana, measured at approximately two minutes.

18 April

SNOLLYGOSTER

The word 'snollygoster' may describe a shrewd but unprincipled politician, but its beginnings lie far from the political sphere. In the US state of Maryland, a 'snallygaster' was a mythical monster said to prey on animals and children. Its name would be invoked by exasperated parents in order to scare their children into good behaviour. It is this that seems to be the inspiration behind 'snollygoster', a measure perhaps of the odium often felt towards those in office. An edition of an Ohio newspaper from 1895 put it rather billowingly: 'A Georgia editor kindly explains that "a snollygoster is a fellow who wants office, regardless of party, platform or principles, and who, whenever he wins, gets there by the sheer force of monumental talknophical assumnacy".'

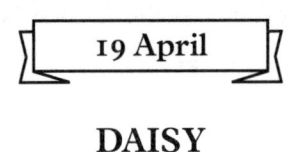

19 April

DAISY

The birth flower for April is the daisy. In Norse mythology, it is a symbol of love and ferility: a nod perhaps to the fact that it is a composite flower, made up of two flowers blended together.

In floriography, the language of flowers, the daisy is also associated with the keeping of secrets: giving someone a daisy in Victorian times was a symbol of the important information they were keeping safe. In medieval love poetry, meanwhile, the flower is the symbol of innocence, in particular that of young women. It features in 'Marguerite' poetry, so called after the French name for the daisy, which itself is based on the Latin for 'pearl'. In Shakespeare's *Hamlet*, Ophelia distributes flowers to members of the court, each with a personalized hidden meaning. The daisy she gives to no one, for there is no innocence to be found at the Danish court.

The story of the daisy carries a beautiful metaphor that reflects this simple flower's behaviour. In Old English, the flower was known as the *dæges éage*, or 'day's eye': a nod to the flower's closing its petals at dusk, concealing its central sunny disk, and opening them again in the morning.

20 April

DREIKANTER

Most of us overlook the pebbles that fill up our flower beds or drives, or that we kick along a path as we walk. The technical definition of their name relies on measurement: a fragment of rock with a particle size of between 4 and 64 mm (0.16–2.52 in) according to the Udden-Wentworth scale of sedimentology.

Many pebbles are smooth and rounded pieces of a fine-grained rock type known as quartzite, which happens to be one of the birthstones of April. While many may look bland and uninspiring, their journey has been immense, originating as sand in ancient seas nearly half a billion years ago. These sand layers were slowly transformed into buckled quartzite rock layers in mountain chains; as they eroded, the pebbles were often shunted by flooding over huge distances. Pink quartzite was transported over miles of terrain in the stomachs of dinosaurs, who swallowed rocks to grind up the food they ate. Such stones are known as 'bezoars'.

These rich histories have inspired a lexicon of names not just for the types of rocks and pebbles we see today, but for their characteristics too. One such name is a 'dreikanter', a pebble that has been shaped and faceted by sand, often with three faces. The German *Dreikanter* means a 'three-edged thing'. The winds of millennia have effectively rendered them 'ventifacts', stones that have been configured by windblown sand.

'Pebbling', meanwhile, is a term for the collecting and sharing of little things – from coins and flowers to memes and photos – with someone you care for as a means of forming a bond. Its name was rather wonderfully inspired by the behaviour of gentoo penguins in Antarctica, who declare their interest in mating by sharing pebbles or rocks to help build nests. In both the gentoo and human worlds, pebbling is a small but significant bridge to a deeper relationship.

21 April

PLUVIAL

April is, of course, notorious for its showers, and the vocabulary for rain rarely disappoints. One of its best offerings is surely the 'thunderplump': the kind of heavy rain shower that catches you completely unawares and soaks you to the skin in seconds.

In the seventeenth and eighteenth centuries, senior clerics as well as monarchs would wear long cloaks as ceremonial vestments, intended to protect them against the rain during processions. These cloaks were consequently known as 'pluvials', from the Latin term for rain.

To go with your pluvial, you might want to take a 'bumbershoot', the Victorian nickname for the umbrella regarded in America as an archetypal British expression but which actually originated on that side of the Atlantic. It is comprised of 'bumber', a riff on the first half of 'umbrella', and 'shoot', a nod to its resemblance to a parachute.

22 April

VEDRITI

Sometimes the real joy for true 'pluviophiles' – rain-lovers – lies as much in finding a spot to shelter from it as in standing beneath it. The Slovenian word *vedriti* means exactly this, to take refuge from a rainstorm, but it also carries the more metaphorical sense of seeking sanctuary from a tough moment in life and waiting for it to pass. There is reassurance in the fact that the same Slovenian verb can also be used to describe stormy weather that is clearing up.

Other languages are equally expressive when it comes to rain. Swedish speakers, for example, distinguish between *hundväder* ('dog weather', the equivalent of our raining cats and dogs) and *vargaväder* ('wolf weather', the kind that is so unpleasant only wolves can bear it). And in Dutch, there is *onweer* or, as we once said in English, *unweder*, which literally means 'unweather' and which describes a severe and violent tempest.

23 April

BATED BREATH

What exactly is the 'beck' in 'beck and call'? Or the 'fro' in 'to and fro', and the 'cob' in 'cobweb'? All of these familiar expressions contain at least one element that is not used anywhere else. They are linguistic fossils, surviving in one form only. Most examples tend to slip past us unnoticed: the 'fell' in 'one fell swoop' that once meant 'savage', for example, as when a bird of prey swoops from the sky. Today's 'bobs' (shillings and, by extension, miscellaneous items collecting in one's pocket) only come with 'bits', just as 'spick and span' only come as a pair thanks to their alliterative appeal. When do we ever use the word 'riddance' without 'good' in front, or (fittingly) 'yore' in anything other than 'days of yore'?

The 'beck' in 'beck and call' is a much earlier form of 'beckon' and was used in the sixteenth century to mean the slightest desire or command, and therefore absolute control. As for 'fro', this was once a common abbreviation of 'from', so that 'to and fro' means alternating movement in opposite directions.

Verbs, as well as nouns, can sometimes be odd survivors. The 'bate' in 'bated breath', so often misspelled as 'baited', is a fossilized shortening of 'abated', with the sense of 'suspended' or 'restrained'. The US actor and comedian W.C. Fields made full use of the opportunity for wordplay with 'The clever cat eats cheese and breathes down rat holes with baited breath.'

24 April

APRICATE

The pleasure of 'apricating' in spring sunshine is a universal pleasure. Almost as rare as its close cousin 'apricity', the warmth of the sun on a winter's day, the word manages just four records within the *Oxford English Dictionary* before, like a linguistic mayfly, it perplexingly disappeared. Thankfully, 'apricating' is not restricted to the colder months; rather it means to bask in sunshine and relish its warmth on your back. The restorative power of nature can bring us back to earth like nothing else.

Icelandic offers us another possibility on days like this: a *sólarfrí* is a 'sun holiday', when workers are granted unexpected time off to enjoy a particularly sunny day.

25 April

ARSEFOOT

Today is the day we celebrate the wonderful creature that takes its name from the Welsh *pen gwyn*, 'white head'. Sailors and fishermen first gave that title to the now extinct great auk of the seas around Newfoundland in the sixteenth century: another flightless waterfowl with black and white plumage adapted to life in freezing waters, before bestowing it upon the penguin.

Surely the best title for the seabird, however, is 'arsefoot', a nickname given to it by eighteenth-century sailors. It perfectly describes a waddling bird whose diminutive legs are set far back on its body. Just don't ask whether penguins have knees.

26 April

SOCKDOLAGER

The US of the 1830s was a political and economic powerhouse. Linguistically, the decade was equally expansive, characterized by a frivolity that ignored the shadow of an ideology that was to ensure the powerful would extend their nation – as well as capitalism and slavery – beyond their own continent. The time saw a fashion for wordplay, obscure abbreviations, fanciful coinages, and puns. Most fell by the wayside, drowned out perhaps by the Civil War and the decades of tension that preceded it. It is a shame that among such lost words was 'explaterate', a robust verb that essentially and onomatopoeically means 'shoot off at the mouth'. Some inventions of the period did survive, albeit at the margins, including 'absquatulate', to leave somewhere in a hurry, and 'hornswoggle', a florid term meaning to hoax someone.

The highly useful 'sockdolager' was another, originally describing the knockout blow in a fight but soon broadening to anything that was exceptional, particularly a very large fish. Fishermen, after all, have long been noted for their hyperbole when it comes to the one that got away. But the term has also gone down in history as one of the last words that Abraham Lincoln heard before he was assassinated in April 1865. The president was at the theatre watching a performance of Tom Taylor's *Our American Cousin* and, as the audience laughed loudly at the line 'Well, I guess I know enough to turn you inside out, old gal – you sockdologizing old man-trap', John Wilkes Booth fired the fatal shot.

27 April

STRUTHIOUS

The naming of animals in ancient times was often the result of guesswork. Those who had never witnessed an exotic species at first hand had to rely on the accounts and descriptions of travellers who had. Consequently, many names are more an approximation of which other living creature the animal or bird resembled. The giraffe, for example, was once a 'camelopard', a nod perhaps to the strange creature's long neck. The first part of the word 'ostrich' is from the Latin *avis*, 'bird', but the second part harks from the Greek name for an unlikely example: *strouthos*, meaning 'sparrow'. The fuller term in ancient Greek was *megas strouthos*, 'large sparrow', while yet another Greek name, *strouthokamēlos*, found its way into seventeenth-century English as 'struthiocamel', 'sparrow camel'.

Legend once held that hunted ostriches would bury their heads in the sand in the belief this would hide them from view. Any humans who metaphorically do the same, muttering, 'Problem? What problem?', we can safely call 'struthious', a handy adjective meaning 'ostrich-like'.

28 April

BRAIN ROT

First we had 'doomscrolling', then we had 'brain rot': a coupling that gives us a useful example of cause and effect. But while 'doomscrolling' was a new word, coined during the Covid pandemic for our mindless phone-shuffling from one bad news story to the next, 'brain rot' has form. Used to mean the deterioration of a person's mental or intellectual state, it was introduced by the US writer and philosopher Henry Thoreau in 1845, when he lamented the inability of contemporary minds to grasp complex ideas and the tendency instead to 'level downward to our dullest perception'. Today, the expression has landed on a major preoccupation for many of us: the overconsumption of low-quality, low-value content and its negative impact on our happiness.

Ironically, the main popularizers of 'brain rot' are the very communities who are most responsible for it, or at least for the digital content that causes it. The turning of our minds to mush has been a major theme on TikTok, one of the homes of vacant scrolling. But perhaps the revival of the term is a cheeky self-dig among younger generations who seem all too familiar with the harmful impact of the very media they've helped create.

29 April

DONALD DUCKING

One of the less predictable outcomes of the global pandemic were the endless rounds of office Celebrity Squares on computer screens for months on end, as online meetings became the only way we could communicate visually at a time when we were quite literally out of touch. Such meetings quickly extended to virtual social gatherings, in which families would assemble around their respective tech and drink wine or even eat dinner together-apart. Zoom etiquette quickly became an essential education, and involved a good degree of what seventeenth-century writers knew (though writing from an entirely screenless perspective) as 'nod-craftiness': that is, the art of nodding along to conversations as though you understand absolutely everything that is being said, when you actually tuned out some time ago.

Wardrobe became another dilemma: what to wear for your online business meeting when logging on from your office (if you're lucky) or beneath your children's bunk bed? Many resorted to smart shirts and jackets on top, the only visible portion, and shorts or pyjama bottoms down below. In Hungarian, *Donaldkacsázás* involves taking it a step further, by wearing a T-shirt and nothing else. They are 'Donald Ducking'.

30 April

PORONKUSEMA

Beyond the quibbles over metric vs imperial, most of us measure out our lives in traditional distances. Many are rooted in the footsteps of the past: for the Romans, *mille passus*, a thousand paces marched by disciplined troops, became a fixed and useful measurement of distance, later shortened to a 'mile'. The yard as a unit of length descends from Old English *gerd*, 'twig, stick', which was used as a measuring rod for three feet.

Such stories pale into insignificance when compared with some of the measurements calculated by other cultures, most notably the Finns. *Poronkusema*, for example, once denoted a distance of approximately 7.5 kilometres, the distance a reindeer can travel before needing to urinate. *Peninkulma*, on the other hand, refers to the distance at which a barking dog can be heard in still air. One of the most curious, surely, is *sian pierema*: the distance a pig can fart (roughly one to two feet, if you're interested). And when it comes to the tiniest of measurements, *muggeseggele* is a word from the German Swabian dialect for a proverbially small distance or quantity. It literally means 'a housefly's scrotum'.

MAY

1 May

ERUMPENT

An underused adjective from the seventeenth century describes buds and blossom that are bursting forth with vigour. Happily, 'erumpent' can also be used of energetic humans.

Each year on May Morning, the city of Oxford comes alive to celebrate the victory of summer over winter, birth over death. Dating back over half a millennium, the ritual inspires thousands of people (many of whom have stayed up all night) to gather at dawn beneath the tower of Magdalen College. Many in the crowd will be dressed in green, an unknowing nod to Flora, the Roman goddess of flowers. Like Christmas, the celebration of May Day was cancelled by Oliver Cromwell only to be reinstated by the returning king, Charles II, in 1660. There are many lively May Day traditions, from Bringing in the May and the erection of maypoles (it's all about fertility after all), to Beltane bonfires that mark the beginning of the month. Even the dew of May was believed to have particularly beneficial properties. The most potent May dew was the one that was collected on this very morning: folk belief had it that any woman lucky enough to wash her face in it would be restored to perfect beauty.

None of this is to be confused with the international distress signal 'Mayday', which comes from a mangling of the French call for help 'm'aidez'. May Day (two separate words) is all about fun and games.

2 May

EX CAPPA

On this day in 1568, Mary, Queen of Scots, escaped from Lochleven Castle, where she had been imprisoned after failing to quash a rebellion by Scottish nobles in protest at her marriage to the Earl of Bothwell. With the help of someone she had befriended at the castle, she was able to flee and cross by boat to the mainland.

The word 'escape' is one of many in English that wear their hearts on their sleeves. When it emerged in English in the fourteenth century, it rested on the metaphor of a criminal fleeing a scene and shrugging off their heavy coat as they did so, leaving their pursuer grasping nothing but cloth. 'Escape' comes from the Latin *ex cappa*, 'out of one's cape'.

There are many more such examples of words that bear their history so explicitly. Look at the word 'secretary' and you'll see it involves the word 'secret', for the original duty of medieval secretaries was to keep their boss's secrets. A secretary in the Middle Ages was someone privy to confidences, regardless of their employment. By the fifteenth century, the title became annexed to the officer who conducted the correspondence of a king, and who necessarily guarded the monarch's secrets closely. The private secretary to a prime minister, as well as a secretary of state or foreign secretary, are direct descendants of these early letter-writers, whose output may have been secreted in a 'secretaire', a desk with a folding table and lockable drawers.

Any modern freelancer, meanwhile, might like to know that their early namesakes were knight-adventurers unattached to any lord or manor, who were free to use their lances for payment.

Often the very words that wear their hearts on their sleeves slink by unnoticed, simply because we have changed the pronunciation. We no longer think of breaking our night-time fast when we have breakfast, of illustrators adding 'lustre' with their paintbrush, nor of becoming 'at one' with a friend we have offended when we 'atone'. Similarly, when we are alone, we are 'all one'; there is something rather poignant in the fact that the 'l' migrated to join the 'one' and created the word 'lonely'.

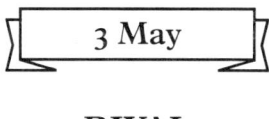

3 May

RIVAL

It is a curious fact that the words 'river' and 'rival' descend from the same Latin root – a rival was originally someone who competed for precious water from the same stream, or who tussled over the rights to a particular riverbank. The story of the Rivals of May, who competed for resources, love, and power, forms an important part of Celtic and Irish myth.

For citizens of the ancient world, the constellation of Gemini, which is visible in the skies between September and May, represented Castor and Pollux, the twins who inspired its brightest stars. But for the Celts, the constellation told a very different tale, of two men in love with one woman. Creiddylad lived at the court of King Arthur. Considered to be the most beautiful woman in the British Isles, she was loved by two of Arthur's warriors: Gwythyr and Gwyn. These rival suitors became embroiled in conflict when Creiddylad was betrothed to Gwythyr, driving Gwyn, the king of the Otherworld, to obsessive jealousy and the decision to abduct Creiddylad from his competitor-in-love. A bloody battle ensued, forcing King Arthur to intervene and decree that the two rivals must fight in single combat every May Day until Judgement Day, when the winner would have Creiddylad's hand. This eternal battle is said to be played out in the sky for all to see.

4 May

MISLE

Written in a stream of consciousness, *Finnegans Wake*, published on this day in 1939, is considered to be one of the gnarliest books in English. It is said that one day, while James Joyce was dictating the story to Samuel Beckett, there was a knock at the door. Beckett didn't realize that Joyce's 'Come in' wasn't part of the dictation, and added it in. Later on, Joyce noticed the unexpected addition but decided to keep the mistake in. No one quite knows whether the tale is true, but Beckett liked to recount the incident to illustrate that mistakes, invented or otherwise, can always teach us something.

At the end of the day, what is an error, anyway? Some pronunciation debates, for example, run and run. Even 'pronunciation' is now, ironically, often rendered 'pronounciation'. The sounds of words are as subject to evolution as our vocabulary and in many cases the dictionary will either (depending on your point of view) sit on the fence or stay loyal to its democratic principles by listing more than one pronunciation. 'Scone', famously, can be pronounced to rhyme with both 'cone' or 'gone' depending on your geography. In many cases, the dictionary offers two pronunciations because English users, a democracy, cannot quite make up their mind. So seems to be the case with 'biopic', which can be either 'biOpic' to rhyme with 'myopic', or as a word of two halves, 'bio-pic'.

There is a third category when it comes to such pronunciation conundrums, namely the words we learned growing up but which we have really only ever seen written down. 'Oxymoron', for example, might inspire you to create something rather more sophisticated than 'oxy-moron' and invent a gliding flourish for it instead, with 'ox-imm-o-ruhn'. Conversely, you might think that 'epitome' has to be 'epi-tome', and 'hyperbole' must be 'hyper-bole'.

None of this is entirely our fault – the vagaries of English spelling can render many words so ambiguous that we are bound to imagine them differently. This can occur particularly with words with more than one syllable which we 'rebracket' or divide up the wrong way so that we lose sight of where one word ends and another begins. This has become a particular problem since hyphens are on the wane. Just consider 'deice', 'corespondent', 'sundried', 'unshed', 'coworker', and, rather unfortunately, 'mishit'.

Such terms are known as 'misles', a name based on an easy misreading of the hyphenless 'misled', which led one writer to conclude it must be the past tense of a verb 'misle'. It follows that there is also now a verb for the state of being momentarily confused – if you happen to misread 'codeveloper' in any way that involves a fish, then you've been mizzled.

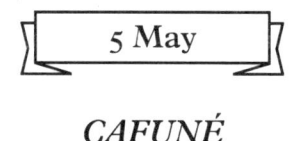

5 May

CAFUNÉ

Spring has sprung and love is in the air – or at the very least 'vernalagnia': the romantic feelings that are bursting forth as enthusiastically as the buds and blossom around us. What better phrase to borrow then than *cafuné*, from Brazil: an untranslatable Portuguese expression for the act of tenderly running one's fingers through a loved one's hair. It need not be exclusive to romance, however, for *cafuné* can be applied just as well to the affectionate stroking of our pets.

In Chinese, the word *pán* is also all about the human touch, this time in relation to objects which, once turned over and over in the hand and rendered smooth and shiny, are thought to take on a mystical connection to their owner. It is used both with reference to jewellery, in which they become a little like worry stones, and to the gentle, repeated stroking of pets in order to accustom them to being handled.

6 May

NECTAR

This is the time of year when we welcome the sight of bees in our gardens. The bumblebee, once also nicknamed 'dumbledore', 'drumbler', and 'humble-bee', takes its moniker from the use of 'bumble' to imitate a buzzing, humming, or droning sound. J.K. Rowling once said she chose the name Dumbledore for the headmaster of Hogwarts because she liked to imagine him humming to himself as he walked around the castle.

In May we are likely to see at least four species: buff-tailed, white-tailed, early, and tree bumblebees. As the weather warms up and flowers start to bloom, the insects are busy foraging for nectar and pollen. In ancient Greek, 'nectar' was the drink of the gods, often savoured alongside 'ambrosia', divine nourishment and the elixir of life. 'Ambrosia' is rooted in the Greek for 'immortal', while 'nectar' enjoys a similar etymology, in which *nek* means 'death', and *tar* means 'overcoming'.

The ancient world was baffled by the origin of bees and came up with a very imaginative theory. In a biblical story, Samson makes a wager by setting his wedding guests a challenge in the form of a riddle, 'Out of the eater came something to eat, And out of the strong came something sweet'. Its inspiration? A discovery Samson had once made of a busy beehive in the carcass of a slain lion. 'Out of the strong came forth sweetness', words from Judges, the seventh book of the Old Testament, are still written on the side of tins of golden syrup – the modern world's attempt to create their own honey-like condiment.

The theory behind such a strange nesting place was known to the Greeks as *bous*, 'ox', and *gonē*, 'progeny', rendered in English as 'bugonia'. For Samson, it was fitting that the king of the insects arose from the king of the beasts. Later, the Roman politician Florentinus reported as fact that rotten animal entrails produced pollinating bees, while from a buried warhorse came the hornet. This reference to burial was also important: burying a cow or ox was thought to encourage a hive. Better still, if the ox was buried so that its horns projected from the ground, bees would surely emerge from their base.

As for the riddle, the wedding guests were unable to solve it and resorted to threatening Samson's wife for the answer, which she was forced to give up. Enraged by his wife's actions, Samson went on to kill thirty Philistine men to fulfil the wager he had lost.

7 May

KEKEKE

The first Sunday in May is World Laughter Day. 'Ha ha' has become a frequent indication of laughter on our screens, used with irony or straightforward humour just as it is 'IRL', in real life. Its predecessor 'LOL' has now been consigned by Gens Z and Alpha to the dustbin that belongs to parents and the elderly. Yet few of us engaging in e-laughter appreciate how other cultures do things differently.

In transliterated Korean, for example, quiet laughter is typically represented as *kekeke* or *hhh*. A vowel is added if laughing out loud is in order, which brings it close to something more familiar: 'haha' or 'hoho'. For Brazilians, laughter sounds a little like 'kakakakakakaka' or 'huehuehue', while *rsrsrs* is an elongation of *rs*, itself an abbreviation for *risos*, 'laughter'. Peninsular Spanish has *jajajaja* or *jjj*. *Www* is the Japanese laugh, while in Thailand, given that the number five is pronounced *ha*, laughter on screen becomes '5555' ad infinitum, according to just how funny something is.

8 May

ZUGUNRUHE

In classical times the flight patterns of birds were said to foretell the future. Superstition surrounded their habits, too: before we came to 'MURMURATION' as a collective noun for starlings, we had a 'mutation', born out of the belief that starlings shed their legs at the age of ten, and grew new ones.

As for where birds go in the winter months, this attracted much curiosity. Samuel Johnson maintained that swallows would sleep all winter in the beds of rivers – 'A number of them conglobulate together, by flying round and round, then all in a heap throw themselves under water' – while other naturalists believed they migrated to the moon. Even as late as 1837, the *Kendal Mercury* reported a man who claimed to have observed several swallows emerging at springtime from the water of Grasmere in the form of 'bell-shaped bubbles, from each of which a Swallow burst forth'.

Myths aside, for many birds the urge to migrate is irresistible. Their behaviour exhibits a build-up of anticipation and tension as a long flight beckons, and it is said that even caged robins and garden warblers will turn repeatedly towards the north when their free family members are making their annual flight. In German, this is known as *Zugunruhe*, literally 'migration restlessness'. It is a word that can be co-opted for the human impulse to move, especially when ordinary life becomes too much.

9 May

MAN-DREAM

An outbreak of boisterous merriment associated with springtime, demonstrated most obviously in the gambolling of lambs, was once known as 'man-dream'. The expression draws on the original, Old English sense of 'dream', which was mirth and jubilation. Such joy came particularly in response to music and song, a delight once known as a 'glee-dream'. Etymologists are not yet clear whether this use of 'dream' is related to the kind we experience in sleep, but the semantic route may have travelled from ecstasy to the often-fanciful images seen at night-time. Certainly the word 'widden-dream', which described a state of mental disturbance, seems to straddle both meanings. But it is delirium exclusively of the joyful kind that informs 'man-dream' and its associations with hilarity; 'man' here is used in the sense of a 'person', irrespective of gender.

'Hilarity' is in fact another word that shares a connection with springtime. In ancient Rome, the Hilaria were religious festivals full of celebration, pomp, and extravagant masquerades, held at the spring equinox to celebrate the renewal of life.

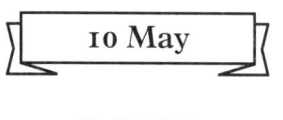

10 May

RANÇO

We all have one – or more: an irrational dislike of someone who in truth is quite innocuous, yet who inexplicably rubs us up the wrong way. In the slang of Brazilian Portuguese, this form of irrational aversion is known as *ranço*. In literal terms it means 'rancidity', as of foul-smelling old fat, with the idea that our resentment and spite fester away within, even while we are unable to put our finger on exactly why.

11 May

UNCANNY VALLEY

This was the day in 1997 that Garry Kasparov, the world chess champion, admitted defeat to Deep Blue, a supercomputer produced by IBM. It was a clear indication to many that artificial intelligence was on the march. In his book about his encounters with Deep Blue, Kasparov acknowledged a deep respect for the computer and a growing anthropomorphism (the attribution of a human response to a non-human object) in his relationship with it.

In psychology, the 'uncanny valley' hypothesis predicts that an entity which closely mimics human behaviour is likely to elicit an eerily emotional reaction. Its name is a translation from the Japanese *bukimi no tani*, the title of a book by the robotics professor Masahiro Mori, who introduced the concept in 1970. Mori describes a curve of emotional responses to the behaviour of a robot as it becomes increasingly more humanoid. As it begins to take on human-like characteristics, the reaction is strong and empathetic and continues in this direction until the robot becomes almost human, at which point the response quickly becomes one of revulsion. This changes again when the gap between machine and human is near indistinguishable, when the emotional response becomes positive again and approaches human-to-human empathy levels. The appearance of this response curve, when plotted on a graph, shows a rise followed by a steep fall and a rise again, hence Mori's choice of 'valley' for his name.

The term clearly has wider applications, far beyond robotics. Recently it has been harnessed for film-watchers' reactions to the CGI-altered appearance of real actors, whose looks the producers considered too old or imperfect for the role. Viewers frequently feel discomfited by the eerie 'uncanny valley' effect of such virtual makeovers, which blur the lines between reality and fantasy to the extent that everything seems unreliable.

12 May

SMEUSE

If you've ever spotted a small hole in a hedge or wall you may not know that you are witnessing a 'smeuse', an opening created by a small animal passing through and used as a doorway. The word may be a blend of the dialect words 'meuse', meaning a hiding place, and 'smoot', a small hole or opening. Alternatively it may be a relative of the Welsh *mwg* (pronounced 'moog'), meaning 'smoke', implying something flimsy or insubstantial and very easily overlooked. As for the users of a smeuse, one Essex term for wriggling through a hedge is 'squiggle'.

13 May

FIZMER

A nineteenth-century glossary of 'provincialisms' includes an entry for 'fizmer', a gem of a word meaning 'to fidget unquietly, and make a great stir about trifles, making little or no progress'. It adds that the 'fizz' element may have been inspired by the noise 'produced by these petty agitations', and thankfully suggests no relationship with 'fizzle', whose original meaning was to 'fart quietly'. That said, the dialect of the Cambridgeshire Fenlands has taken it one step windier, harnessing 'fizmer' to mean the light rustling sound of grass in the breeze.

Regional dialects are indeed rich with the vocabulary of the wind. A 'williwaw', for example, is a sudden downward gust. Most beautiful of all, perhaps, is a 'wimpling': the rippling motion in a bird's wing feathers caused by the flow of the wind.

14 May

SKUNK

On 14 May 1607, after many failed attempts, the adventurous spirit and resolve of the first English colonists took them to Jamestown, a North American peninsula in the James river named after James I. The writer William Wood documented in detail his observations of geography, climate, and nature during his stay in New England between 1629 and 1634. In his *New Englands* [sic] *Prospect* he makes reference to 'beasts of offence' including 'Squunckes, Ferrets, Foxes'.

Many of the terms recorded from these early encounters were borrowed or plundered from native languages, in which animals were often named after their appearance or behaviour. The indigenous Mi'kmaq people used the word *qalipu*, 'caribou' in English, to describe an animal with 'snow-shovelling' hoofs. 'Moose' was taken from the native Abenaki language, in which *moz* literally describes an animal that 'strips bark from a tree'. The same language gave us 'skunk', the English spelling of which was finally settled at the turn of the eighteenth century and which probably translates as 'urinating fox'. It has since become shorthand for everything that stinks, from a non-payer of bills to a cheat, and from pungent drugs to devastatingly defeating an opponent in a game.

15 May

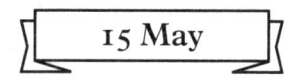

BLURB

The *London Magazine*, in 1732, defined one sense of the term 'puff' as 'a cant word for the applause that writers or booksellers give their own books &c. to promote their sale.' By this time the use of 'puff' for such self-publicizing was already more than a century old: one work from the early 1600s writes of 'the flattering puffes/Of spungy Sycophants'. 'Puff' in this sense survives to this day, but it has been knocked off the top spot by another word for much the same thing: 'blurb'.

It is a rare thing for lexicographers to know the exact moment a word or phrase was born. In most cases they can determine a rough chronology for any new coinage, but a precise attribution to a word's inventor is far less common than you might think. 'Blurb' offers us one of those, for it was a calculated creation by the American comic author and cartoonist Gelett Burgess, who on 15 May 1907 handed out copies of his new book at an American Booksellers' Association banquet. He had called it *Are You a Bromide?*, and billed its contents as 'researches into the psychology of boredom'. Burgess even produced a special wrapper for the book that featured a beautiful young woman, 'Miss Belinda Blurb', caught, so the copy itself notes, 'in the act of blurbing'. Her gushingly shameless speech begins, 'Say! Ain't this book a 90.-H. P., six-cylinder Seller? If WE do say it as shouldn't.' Her assertions become increasingly preposterous: 'It has that Certain Something which makes you want to crawl through thirty miles of dense tropical jungle and bite somebody in the neck.'

As a blend of 'blab' and 'blurt', 'blurb' certainly works. And while Burgess's satirical fun-poking was far from subtle, his coinage has served the language ever since. The author himself even provided the dictionary with a helpful definition: 'Blurb, 1. A flamboyant advertisement; an inspired testimonial. 2. Fulsome praise; a sound like a publisher ... abounding in agile adjectives and adverbs, attesting that this book is the "sensation of the year".'

16 May

HETEROGRAM

What do 'subdermatoglyphic', 'dermatoglyphics', and 'uncopyrightables' have in common? The first two seem easy bedmates, defined respectively as a layer of skin beneath the fingertips, and the scientific study of the ridges, lines, and mounts of fingers, palms, soles, and toes. 'Uncopyrightables' skews the equation somewhat, and so you might rightly guess that this is a purely linguistic puzzle. They are all 'heterograms', a category of vocabulary in which no letter is repeated. It derives from the Greek *hetero-*, meaning 'different', and *-gram*, 'written'.

17 May

SHIBBOLETH

The Old Testament story of the warring Ephraimites and the Gileadites is said to have given us the first password in Western literature. The Book of Judges tells how the Gileadites defeat the Ephraimites, and stand guard by the Jordan as the fleeing Ephraimites attempt to cross. Each person approaching the river is commanded to say the word 'shibboleth'. The Ephraimites, having no 'sh' sound in their language, pronounce the word with a simple 's', unwittingly revealing themselves as the enemy. Their failure results in some 42,000 Ephraimites being killed. In English, 'shibboleth' subsequently came to mean a long-standing catchword or slogan associated with a particular group. It is said that during the Second World War US soldiers would test the ability of suspected Japanese spies to pronounce 'lollapalooza'.

A different category of shibboleth involves group codes, allowing members to discreetly make themselves known while keeping outsiders in the dark. Members of Alcoholics Anonymous might, for example, announce that they are 'a friend of Bill W', a reference to William Wilson, the founder of the group. And while the expression 'friend of Dorothy' has become a joky self-reference within the gay community that is understood by all, it was not always so open. At a time when homosexuality was illegal, a US sailor might well use the term as a nod to the gay icon Judy Garland in the 1939 film *The Wizard of Oz* based on a book by L. Frank Baum that was published on this day in 1900. This code was said to be so effective that when the Naval Investigative Service learned of it they assumed the Dorothy in question was a real woman with connections to gay servicemen.

As for 'shibboleth', it is also used today for an IT community password that doesn't reveal individual identities.

18 May

HIRPLE

There is, famously, no rhyme for 'orange'. Nor, if you believe the Internet, for 'purple' or 'silver'. In truth the dictionary does contain rhymes for each of these, even if we do need to drag them from its dustiest corners. For 'orange', for example, we have 'sporange', a sac-like structure in which a plant's spores are produced. A 'milver' is someone who shares an interest in a particular topic such as words and wordplay. As for 'purple', there is more than one option. A horse's 'curple' is its rump, and Robert Burns clearly saw its potential for an unusual rhyme:

> *I'd be mair vauntie o' my hap,*
> *Douse hingin o're my curple,*
> *Than ony ermine ever lap,*
> *Or proud imperial purple.*

> I would be more proud of my wrap,
> Sedately hanging over my buttocks,
> Than any ermine ever folded,
> Or proud imperial purple.

The Scots word 'hirple' is arguably even more useful, for it means to walk slowly and painfully or with a limp, or, as the *Oxford English Dictionary* bluntly puts it, 'to drag a limb' or 'to move with a gait between walking and crawling'. Predictably, many of the word's uses seem to be allied closely with alcohol. Robert Fergusson's eighteenth-century poem 'Leith Races' describes the result of one drinking spree with 'Great feck gae hirpling hame like fools,/The cripple lead the blind.'

Does this mean *everything* in language has a rhyme? The answer is no, for 'month', 'bulb', 'angel', 'husband', and 'woman' are just a few of the words that don't.

19 May

HOT-SPONG

'Cast ne'er a clout till May be out' goes the old saying (in which a 'clout' is an item of clothing). But should you venture outdoors on a late spring day, over-optimistically leaving that jumper or coat behind, you might find yourself longing for a 'hot-spong'. In East Anglian dialect, this is the rush of welcome heat that hits you when the sun emerges from a bank of clouds. The word 'spong', a variation on 'spang', also carries the meaning of a narrow stretch of land. The allusion here is to a strip of sunshine whose warmth is short-lived and leaves its recipient longing for more.

20 May

ECLOSION

This month brings us the romance of mayflies, dancing hopefully across the air as they look for a mate before their twenty-four hours of life is up. If successful, the male will release the female after mating, who then descends to the water to lay her eggs on its surface. There she will lie motionless, spent, her wings flattened, to be picked off by birds or fish, while the male soon dies on the nearby land.

The beginning of their fleeting cycle, before flight, involves the process of 'eclosion', which describes the emergence of an insect from its pupal case or, in this case, the process of hatching from an egg. Mayflies eclose from their stage as water nymphs and transition to winged adults. They show a remarkable synchronicity in their eclosion, emerging simultaneously in vast numbers to fill the sky with their lacy wings, as those of us who are lucky enough to sit by a stream and watch them in this special month can attest.

21 May

FRENCH MARBLES

For all the advances in learning in the later Middle Ages, superstition still reigned supreme. Illness in particular had strong moral associations; some diseases were viewed as divine intervention for wrongs committed. When a patient had a stroke, for example, they would have been thought in the sixteenth century to have suffered 'a stroke from God's hand'. The most effective treatment for the lymphatic disease scrofula, popularly known as the 'King's evil', was thought to be the touch of a monarch. Such stroking of patients had originated in legends of ancient gods performing miraculous cures by touch.

Syphilis was equally thought to be the result of divine retribution. It was also so strongly associated with moral depravity that it required several euphemistic names, including 'Cupid's measles', 'French marbles', and by Shakespeare, 'Neapolitan bone-ache'. The stigma of the affliction was such that each nation blamed it on another: the Italians called syphilis *morbus Gallicus*, and the Germans the 'Spanish itch'. Still, a medical illustration attributed to the Renaissance painter Albrecht Dürer, who was born on this day in 1471, depicts a man whose skin is covered with the cankers and rash associated with syphilis. Above his head is a globe carrying the signs of the zodiac, showing that the disease was also firmly believed to be the result of astrological influence.

22 May

INCUNABULA

In his *Dictionary of Obscure Sorrows* (2022), the writer John Koenig introduces us to the word 'vellichor', which he defines as 'the strange wistfulness of used bookstores, which are somehow infused with the passage of time [...] a hidden annex littered with thoughts left just as they were on the day they were captured.' It would be hard to put it more eloquently, but Koenig might be reflecting too on the unmistakable smell of secondhand bookshops, one of leathery cracked spines and pages yellowed by age.

In France, there exists a word for the magic of delving into old books, one which an AI translator might plainly define as 'to read' but which is much more than that. The verb *bouquiner* has a touch of ancient magic about it, a tribute to the 'bouquinists' who sell antiquarian books on their green stalls, such as you might see dotted along the river Seine. Its roots are the Middle French *boucquain*, meaning a 'rare old book'.

Some of the rarest printed old books are 'incunabula', a term given to those that were printed before 1501. In the first decades of the sixteenth century, the invention of the printing press revolutionized the way books were made and dramatically increased their number and availability to readers. *Incunabula* comes from the Latin for 'swaddling clothes' as well as the bands that secured a baby in a cradle. These were 'baby' books, produced when the art of printing was still in its infancy.

23 May

DOUP-SCUD

The eighteenth-century Scots word 'doup' designated the bottom of an egg as well as that of a human. A 'doup-skelper', for a time, was another name for a schoolmaster, for its literal meaning was 'bottom-smacker'. A 'doup-scud', meanwhile, was a 'thump on the buttocks from a fall' – in other words, an uncommonly painful landing on one's backside and the more unpleasant sister to what English would comedically call a 'pratfall'. The original meaning of 'prat' was a single buttock, which is how it broadened its application to a fool and, to reference a different part of the body altogether, a right plonker.

24 May

LES GODDAMS

It is probably appropriate that the word 'risqué' is French, since we have been associating the French people with sauciness for four centuries or more. The terms 'French kiss', 'French knickers', and 'French maid' all reinforce the assumption that our Gallic neighbours know far more about decadence and naughtiness than we do ourselves. As Henry Fielding put it in his novel *Tom Jones* (1749): 'I would wish to draw a Curtain over ... certain French novels'. Condoms have been called 'French letters' since the early 1800s. *The Man of Pleasure's Companion* from 1844 advised that 'Gentlemen who live in London will be at no loss in easily obtaining these French Letters.' 'Letter' in this instance was simply a euphemistic way of describing something sent over by the French.

The English, on the other hand, were known for other habits. Notoriously, they were called *les rosbifs* by the French thanks to their appetite, and the pejorative ping-pong between the nations continued with the retaliatory 'frog'. But while the French were considered saucy and sassy, the English were clearly seen as oafish, not least in their excessive swearing. Their propensity for profanity during the Hundred Years War, which is said to have commenced on this day in 1337 with the confiscation of the English-held duchy of Guyenne by French King Philip VI, led to the English receiving the slur *les goddams* from their French enemies.

25 May

HARPENDEN

Today is Towel Day, which celebrates the author Douglas Adams, in whose *Hitchhiker's Guide to the Galaxy* it is decreed that 'A towel . . . is about the most massively useful thing an interstellar hitchhiker can have.' Logophiles everywhere celebrate another work by Adams, *The Meaning of Liff*, which he co-wrote with John Lloyd, creator of *Blackadder* and *QI* among many other comedy successes. This glorious volume attempts to fill gaps in our language by allocating them a suitable-sounding place name. The result is such gems as 'Abilene: Descriptive of the pleasing coolness on the reverse side of the pillow', 'Winkley: A lost object which turns up immediately you've gone and bought a replacement for it', and 'Thrupp: To hold a ruler on one end on a desk and make the other end go bbddbbddbbrrbrrrrddrr.'

Surely one of the most useful entries, however, offers a word for the endless goodbyes required when ending a phone call: 'Harpenden: The coda to a phone conversation, consisting of about eight exchanges, by which people try gracefully to get off the line.'

If only we could return to a once-standard farewell in the early days of telephony: 'That is all', followed by a swift replacement of the receiver.

26 May

OWL-LIGHT

As the hour hovers between night and day and the sun dips below the horizon, a soft glow suffuses the air until objects become barely distinguishable. A French expression for this time of day is *entre chien et loup*, 'between dog and wolf', because the light is such that you might scarcely tell the difference.

The symbolism of twilight has inspired reflections on loss, transcendence, and transition for centuries. In scientific terms, the phenomenon is created by the earth's atmosphere as it scatters the sun's rays; the moon, which has no atmosphere, has no such limbo light: here darkness falls instantly.

Astronomers recognize three stages of twilight. The first, covering the time from the sun's disappearance to its centre falling six degrees below the horizon, is known as 'civil twilight', when street lamps and car headlights come on. The second stage is 'nautical twilight', when the centre of the sun is between six and twelve degrees below the horizon. Its name reflects the fact that it ends when the distant line between sea and sky is no longer visible. This is also the time when bright stars are more noticeable, which sailors once used for navigation. Finally, we have 'astronomical twilight', when far fainter stars and constellations are discernible in the night sky.

Should you wish to add more magic to this time of day, you would do well to consider a seventeenth-century description of it: 'twitterlight', which evokes a sense of trembling between two states as the skies 'darkle' (sixteenth century). Other terms include 'cockshut', since this is the time cockerels go to sleep, 'crepuscule', 'dimmit', 'forenight', 'gloaming', 'owl-light', 'mirkning', and 'the blue hour'. Irish Gaelic also gives us *amhdhorchacht*, whose literal meaning is 'raw, uncooked darkness'.

Each of them might just be eclipsed, at least in language, by 'dimpsy', a term from England's south-west that is born from the adjective 'dim' but has a far more exquisite sound.

27 May

EYETHIRL

On 27 May 1703, Tsar Peter the Great of Russia founded St Petersburg. The new city was to serve as the capital of the Russian Empire for over two centuries. Peter the Great intended it to be a showcase of Russian imperial power and culture, while simultaneously opening a 'window to the West'.

The Russian for 'window' is *okno*, which is a relative of *oko*, meaning 'eye'. This metaphorical thread runs through English too: before we had windows, we had 'eyethirls', in which a 'thirl' was an opening or aperture. The word 'window' was a legacy of the Vikings, and is not without its own poetry, for in Old Norse, *vindauga* meant 'eye of the wind'.

As for thirls, they survive in the word 'nostril', which was originally a 'nose-thirl', or 'nose-hole'. It is an unlikely relative of the word 'thrill', which once meant to 'pierce with a sword' such as to make a hole in the victim. Thankfully, today's thrills only pierce us with excitement.

28 May

BATH DAY

The English names for months of the year reflect an enduring Roman influence. Many celebrate classical deities, prominent leaders, and traditions, while others are built upon numerals taken from Latin. They were chosen over older names such as *primilce*, or 'three milk', for May, and *blótmónaþ*, or 'blood month', for November, a month marked by blood sacrifices designed to appease the gods.

But if these Anglo-Saxon names are now lost to us, we can still find Old English influences in the days of the week, which are founded upon a Germanic revision of the Roman Empire's system of naming. This followed a planetary system which at the time included the sun and the moon. Old English retained the spirit of the Latin *dies Solis* and *dies Lunae* ('moon day') for Sunday and Monday, but then substituted the Germanic gods Tiw for Mars, to give 'Tuesday', Woden for Mercury for 'Wednesday', chose Thor the thunder god over Jupiter for Thursday, while Frig, goddess of love and the inspiration for 'Friday', replaced Venus. The name of the Roman god Saturn remained largely intact to produce 'Saturday'.

Other cultures followed a similarly haphazard system. Swedish, for example, dedicates all but one day of the week to the gods of Norse mythology, although the exception was certainly inspired by the Vikings. The trend-bucker is *lördag*, Saturday, which was once set aside for washing and which comes straight from the Old Norse *laugardagr*, 'bath day'.

29 May

CABAL

Charles II, who was born on this day in 1630, was advised by a council of five ministers, Thomas Clifford, Henry Arlington, George Buckingham, Anthony Ashley, and John Maitland, Earl of Lauderdale. The group was marked by political infighting. The French ambassador to England at the time wrote,

> The council [Cabal] consists of ministers with a mortal hatred of one another, who seek only to be avenged upon each other at the expense of their master's service; this means that there is great uncertainty in the resolutions which are taken ... that one can never be sure of anything.

The name 'cabal' was an acronym, formed from the ministers' surnames, and it is they who popularized the use of the word for a clique or political faction. This wasn't the earliest use of the term, however, for the Kaballah (sometimes Cabal for short), is the ancient Jewish tradition of mystical interpretation of the Bible, based on a rabbinical Hebrew word for 'tradition'. The decisions of Charles' Cabal were, for some commentators, mysterious enough to surpass human understanding.

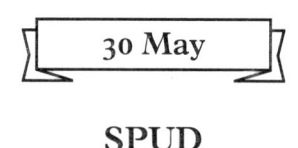

30 May

SPUD

'Let the sky rain potatoes,' urges Falstaff in Shakespeare's play *The Merry Wives of Windsor*. As desires go, this one seems particularly bizarre, but what he is really wishing for is erotic prowess, for he is referring not to the humble spud but to sweet potatoes, which, like tomatoes, were once strongly believed to have aphrodisiacal qualities. The white spuds we celebrate today on International Potato Day arrived in the late sixteenth century. They took their name from the Spanish *patata*, confusingly itself a riff on an old Caribbean word *batata*, 'sweet potato'.

The affectionate term 'spud' emerged around the mid-nineteenth century, when English speakers borrowed it from New Zealanders. Before that, 'spud' was a short digging implement, which is most probably related to a Viking word *spjot*, 'spear', rather than our word 'spade'.

That fact hasn't stopped the invention of an entirely different story to explain the nickname. For centuries, the potato was thought to cause leprosy, to the extent that it was shunned in France as nothing more than pig feed. In early nineteenth-century Britain, an activist group named the Society for the Prevention of an Unwholesome Diet actively protested against the growing of potatoes, more likely out of fear that it would overshadow their wheat crops. S.P.U.D., the society's acronym, therefore led to potatoes being called spuds. Among lexicographers, this is what is known as a 'backronym', a juicy acronym invented retrospectively to account for a word's origin.

31 May

HAMMER AND THONGS

Newspaper corrections have long been a source of a dark laugh or two. The *Morning Star* once had to apologize for an unfortunate error in a regular music section: 'In yesterday's paper in Chris Seare's jazz albums column, we incorrectly referred to Don Rendell as a "terrorist" when it clearly should have been "tenorist". We apologize for any offence.' This is almost as good as when the *Guardian* quoted the Chairman of Wolverhampton Wanderers: 'Our team was the worst in the First Division and I'm sure it will be the worst in the Premier League.' What he actually said, the paper later confessed, was 'Our tea is the worst in the First Division and I'm sure it will be the worst in the Premier League.'

Sometimes, we need to look closer to home for our gaffes. The category of 'eggcorns' – a term coined to describe slips of the tongue or ear which we are often convinced are correct, as in hearing 'eggcorn' for 'acorn' – includes such entertaining manglings as going at something 'hammer and thongs', 'like a bowl in a china shop', or being a total 'pre-Madonna', as if every diva that ever existed was leading up to one unique pop icon.

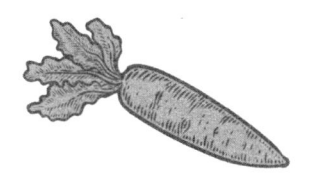

JUNE

1 June

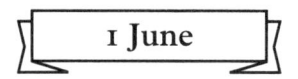

CUSHTY

DEL BOY: No, no, no, no. Everything's cushty. Yeah, no, no, no. You've got nothing to worry about.'
(John Sullivan, *Only Fools and Horses*, 1985)

Slang is the most mobile form of language – those vivid words that nail a staple experience or object in life and are too good not to run with. So it makes sense that many of the core terms we use have been picked up from travellers, people who are generally on the move, whether in a caravan or a three-wheeled Robin Reliant.

June is Gypsy, Roma and Traveller History Month, and English is full of liftings from their rich languages. 'Roma' itself comes from *rom*, a man or in this case a Gypsy, a word that itself is a shortening of 'Egyptian'. The Roma language is a hybrid tongue, based ultimately on Sanskrit but full of borrowings from other languages as its speakers moved west, including Hebrew, Greek, German, and the Romance languages. Many have slipped into our mainstream so successfully that they have become largely untethered from their past. 'Chav', which began life as a Romany word for a child before metamorphosing into a classist insult, is one, as are 'bloke', 'pal', 'gaff', 'nark', 'rozzer', 'zhoosh', and 'wonga'. This slang term for money is derived from the Romany *wonger*, meaning 'coal', a possible allusion to the practice of collecting coal fallen from passing trains which would then be used as currency.

'Cushty', meaning 'good' or 'pleasing', is a favourite Cockney expression that sounds straight out of cushiony, comfortable Peckham, but is in fact another word that travelled all the way from India with the Roma.

2 June

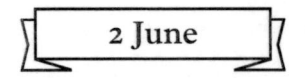

LITTORAL

The Scottish Gaelic word *machair* describes a unique habitat of flat, low-lying strips of land in western Scotland and Ireland that overlie shell sand – the kind that consists almost entirely of powdery seashells deposited over thousands of years and heaped together by tides and currents. It is home to a variety of wading birds as well as poppies, field pansies, and daisies, and rarer species of flowers such as the butterfly orchid, so called because of its wing-shaped petals.

Ecologically, the hinterland between low and high tide is also known as the 'littoral' zone, from the Latin *litus, litoris*, 'shore'. It is used primarily in the military, where a littoral combat ship is a fast and manoeuvrable vessel designed for use in coastal waters. In marine ecology, these shallow waters are characterized by abundant species and organisms such as lichen, seaweed, barnacles, crabs, and molluscs. Their home is defined by the motion of waves, constantly changing with the interaction between land and sea. Like the shores of *machair*, our littoral spaces are a feast for the eyes and ears.

3 June

PLIMSOLL LINE

'Daps', 'sannies', 'pumps', 'mutton dummies', 'kicks', 'sneakers', and 'squeakers': the soft, rubber-soled shoes we wear for PE, sport, and flashy fashion are about the only item in the shoe world that attracts a diversity of names on a national scale. While the universal term today may be 'trainers', for boomers born in the fifties and sixties, the humble gym shoe would often be called a 'plimsoll'.

On London's Victoria Embankment, overlooking the Thames, stands a statue dedicated to a man who died on this day in 1898 and whose memory has faded somewhat in the years since. In his lifetime Samuel Plimsoll was celebrated as a pioneering reformer known to many as the 'sailor's friend', for he campaigned tirelessly for better safety measures at sea. One of the many issues concerning him was the overloading of vessels by unscrupulous merchants, which resulted in what Plimsoll called 'coffin ships', so high was the fatality rate of those who dared sail in them. In 1873, he published a booklet entitled *Our Seamen: An Appeal*, a passionate entreaty for greater safety that was based on the voices of sailors and their families. The pamphlet's contents were described by *Vanity Fair* as 'a book jumbled together in the fashion of an insane farrago, written without method and without art, but powerful and eloquent beyond any work that has appeared for years because it is the simple cry of a simple honest man'.

By 1876, the Merchant Shipping Act had come into force, allowing the authorities stringent inspection rights and introducing the 'Plimsoll line', a fixed loading line which was to be painted on the hull of every British ship to ensure it would never be too low in the water. The 'plimsoll' shoe is so called because of its thick rubber band which resembles the line on a boat's hull.

4 June

OMFIETSWIJN

The word 'wine' is a borrowing from the Latin *vinum*, but it is also a distant relative of the Greek *oinos*. Given our habit of borrowing from Greek for our passions as well as our phobias, 'oenophile' was chosen as the word for a 'wine-lover'. It is clearly also appropriate for the person who coined the Dutch word *omfietswijn* to describe exceptional wine. This is detour wine: the kind that is worth cycling the extra mile for.

5 June

SHIMMY

On this day in 1956, Elvis Presley first performed 'Hound Dog' on television, earning him the nickname 'Elvis the Pelvis'. Presley was less than enamoured with the sobriquet, which he pronounced to be 'childish'. Nonetheless, his performance was declared 'unfit for family viewing' and, following a performance in Wisconsin, the FBI director J. Edgar Hoover received an urgent message from a local Catholic newsletter, warning that 'Presley is a definite danger to the security of the United States . . . [His] actions and motions were such as to rouse the sexual passions of teenaged youth.' When asked whether he regretted these effects of what was called his 'grunt and groin' style, Elvis replied, 'How would rock-'n'-roll music make anyone rebel against their parents?'

Presley would surely want us to focus instead on his considerable dance skills, not all of which were apparently deliberate, at least early on in his career. It is said that his stage fright was such that it made him shake, resulting in a hip- and leg-quivering shimmy that he later capitalized on to the max.

The word 'shimmy' began with a Latin word for 'shirt', *camisia*, which became *chemise* in French. Rather than describing such embellished garments as those worn by the King of Bling, the first 'shimmies' were women's one-piece undergarments, but after the First World War an entirely new sense of the word was added, and 'shimmy' moved to describe a type of popular dance characterized by an energetic and suggestive shaking of the shoulders and arms. According to a US newspaper of 1919, not all responses were favourable. '"Vulgar!" cried the sensitive; "Absurd!" was the verdict of the scornful; "Difficult, but darned attractive!" modern art expressed it.' All of which might be a description of Elvis's dance moves a few decades later. Shimmy, Rattle and Roll.

6 June

MULBERRY HARBOUR

Before 6 June 1944 the term 'D-Day' was already well established within the military to indicate the designated day of a military operation. The 'D' here stands simply for 'Day' and was employed for reasons of secrecy to avoid publicizing an exact date. The term has since become inextricably linked to the day when the Allied troops landed in Normandy to liberate western Europe from Nazi Germany.

Another term associated strongly with that day is 'Mulberry harbour', describing two temporary floating harbours built under great secrecy to allow for the rapid offloading of reinforcement troops, vehicles, and supplies for the Normandy offensive. 'Mulberry' was the code name given to the structures (their constituent parts were 'gooseberries', and their pier heads were 'spuds'). It was chosen from a rotation of available code names, but must have seemed fitting given that mulberry trees grow quickly to great heights, just as the harbours were assembled at speed in under a year.

7 June

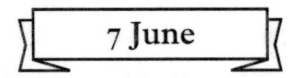

VERSCHLIMMBESSERUNG

'Even German is preferable to death.' Mark Twain had a notoriously thorny relationship with the language of Goethe and Beethoven. His main beef was with its knotty grammar: 'Whenever the literary German dives into a sentence,' he wrote, 'that is the last you are going to see of him till he emerges on the other side of the Atlantic with his verb in his mouth.' He wasn't overly fond of its vocabulary either: 'These things are not words, they are alphabetical processions ... Whenever I come across a good one, I stuff it and put it in my museum.'

Thankfully, many of the best German compounds are actively used rather than simply observed as artefacts of a weird propensity to find the longest word possible. Yet many a German student would recognize Twain's perplexed awe at a language that positively encourages Lego-like word-building (which, if it existed, would go something like *Bauklotzartigewortzusammensetzung*). And yet whenever we look to fill a hole in our language, it has become almost traditional to declare, 'I bet German has a word for it.' To be fair, it often does. The word *Verschlimmbesserung* is a prime example, managing to combine the practical (or, in this case, impractical) and the emotional. Its meaning requires an entire sentence in English, namely 'an attempt to improve a situation that only ends up making things worse'.

8 June

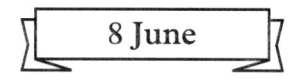

ALL MY EYE AND BETTY MARTIN

There are numerous theories as to the origin of this strange expression, which is an eighteenth-century exclamation akin to 'hogwash!' One of the most plausible is that it is a corruption of a Latin prayer dedicated to St Martin (in which *beate Martine* means 'blessed Martin'), but others point to a mysterious Betty Martin who lived in London in the late eighteenth century. If the latter, she would belong in the ghostly collection that also includes Flipping Ada, Flaming Nora, and Mickey Bliss – he who gave us the rhyming slang Mickey Bliss/piss, and the inspiration for 'taking the Mickey'.

Sometimes, the people populating these expressions actually existed. 'Jack the Lad', famously, was the nickname given to a thief in eighteenth-century London whose daring escapes from prison made him a folk hero. Similarly, the original 'Smart Alec' may have been Aleck Hoag, a notorious pimp, thief, and confidence man in New York in the 1840s, who was dubbed 'smart Aleck' by the NYPD because he was too smart for his own good.

Far darker is the story of 'sweet Fanny Adams', which involves one of the grisliest murder cases of Victorian times. In 1867, a twenty-four-year-old solicitor's clerk named Frederick Baker was arrested for the brutal murder of eight-year-old Fanny Adams, in Alton, Hampshire. Baker abducted Fanny on a hot afternoon near her home and killed her, before cutting up her body into small pieces, some of which were never found. It was thanks to the dark humour of sailors in the Royal Navy, who began to use 'Fanny Adams' for the new and unpopular rations of tinned mutton that were introduced in 1869, that the phrase 'sweet Fanny Adams' came to mean 'not much' or 'nothing at all'.

9 June

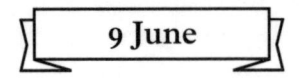

COMMODORE

On this day in 1978 the American group the Commodores released the song 'Three Times a Lady'. It became the band's first number one in the *Billboard* top 100. The song was a smash hit and propelled them to greater fame, but it also had a linguistic consequence that they could not possibly have foreseen, involving a famous piece of rhyming slang and an entry in the slang lexicon for money.

A 'fiver', or five-pound note, became in 1960s Cockney a 'Lady Godiva'. In *Fletcher's Book of Rhyming Slang*, Ronnie Barker drew on his *Porridge* sitcom persona with the immortal sentence, 'Take this Lady Godiva for your froth and bubble [trouble].' A 'Commodore', consequently, was fifteen pounds, because, of course, it was 'three times a lady'.

10 June

NUWOSEO TTEOK MEOKGI

Whatever the problem, cake is almost always the solution. It is consequently often used figuratively in English as a good thing, from expressions such as 'have one's cake and eat it', to 'it's a piece of cake'. The latter example may have been inspired by the use of cakes as prizes, particularly in the 'cakewalk' dancing competitions in the southern states of America. Ancient Greeks also gave cakes as prizes, notably to the person who could last the longest in a drinking contest. While today something that 'takes the biscuit' tops an already bad situation, the idiom's original use was less ironic, for it meant simply to carry off the honours by excelling at something. It is a development of an earlier expression with that same meaning of winning: 'that takes the cake', first recorded at the end of the nineteenth century.

As for 'a piece of cake', arguably an even better choice for declaring something to be a cinch is the Korean *nuwoseo tteok meokgi*, which adds a whole new dimension by likening an easy win to 'eating cakes while lying down'.

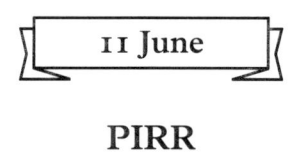

11 June

PIRR

A light breath of wind that ripples the surface of a puddle or stream is known by some delightful terms in English dialect, from a 'cat's paw' to a 'shirr' or 'cockle'. In the Shetlands it is a 'pirr', a word that clearly matured as it went on, for in its earliest appearances in the sixteenth century its usual meaning was a sudden onset of agitation or anger, as well as a flurry of activity. That energy subsided so that 'pirr' became a gentle zephyr rather than anything stronger, but the baton was taken up by 'pirrie', used for a sudden squall or storm. This is entirely unrelated to the 'pirrie' that riffs on 'perry', a cider-like drink made from pear juice, although it's feasible that one might bring on a metaphorical instance of the other.

12 June

DOUBLET

It is said that Camus, Sartre, and Proust all found inspiration in ennui, the uniquely French emotion that is less than depression and more than boredom: it is a world-weary listlessness that drives some people to try unusual antidotes. The poet Gérard de Nerval tried to banish his ennui by taking

Thibault, a lobster he had rescued from a restaurant tank, for walks in Paris's Palais-Royal. When challenged, Nerval was said to have replied calmly, 'I have affection for lobsters. They are tranquil, serious and they know the secrets of the sea.'

Curiously, a close relative of 'ennui' is 'annoy', something altogether more provoking. Both words occupy a category known as doublets, in which words with distinct meanings and histories nonetheless derive from the same parent. Many are surprising: 'clock' and 'cloak' are from the same family, for example, since the ancestor of both is the Latin *clocca*, 'bell': clock towers often contain bells, while a cloak (or cloche, another relative) is 'bell-shaped'. The words 'vanilla' and 'vagina' are also doublets, both deriving from the Latin for a 'sheath' or 'pod', while 'capital', 'chattel', and 'cattle' are strictly speaking triplets, each descending from the Latin *caput*, 'head'. Cattle was considered an important commodity for trading, and trading was often done by cattle headcounts. Today's use of 'goods and chattels' in law bears no trace of a bovine influence but the idea is the same: one's personal possessions.

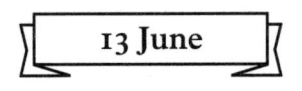

13 June

NOHOW

A liberal sprinkling of 'like' in conversation is one of the biggest peeves of viewers of such programmes as *Love Island*, where the tic regularly inspires multiple memes on social media of contestants using it in every sentence. But the habit has a surprisingly long pedigree and can be traced back over 250 years to the works of Frances 'Fanny' Burney, born on this day in 1752 who went on to become one of the most prominent social commentators of her time. In seven decades of diary-writing, she chronicled personalities and events in a journalistic and natural style of storytelling that was years ahead of its time.

Burney, or Madame d'Arblay as she became after her marriage, is credited with many first uses in the *Oxford English Dictionary*. Some were too tricksy to survive, such as 'preparationing' and 'negativing', while others remain elusive despite their usefulness – the adjective 'nohow', for example, was used by Burney to mean 'out of sorts; just so-so'. Many more of her creations are still firmly cemented in the language – 'dawdling', 'fatigued', 'fidgeted', 'grumpy', 'conversational', and 'puppyish' are all first recorded in her diaries and letters. These might seem rather late given the ease with which we use them now, but another of Fanny Burney's first uses feels the most modern of all – that use of 'like' as a filler. In a novel which Burney published anonymously in 1778, *Evelina, or the History of a Young Lady's Entrance into the World*, we can read, 'Father grew quite uneasy, like, for fear of his Lordship's taking offence.'

14 June

EUTRAPELY

The prefix *eu* is a particularly happy one. You will find it in such words as 'euphemism', meaning 'to speak fair'; 'eulogy', meaning 'to speak well of'; 'euphonious', 'pleasing to the ear'; 'euthanasia', literally, 'an easy death'; 'eucatastrophe', J.R.R. Tolkien's coinage meaning a 'happy ending'; and even in 'eucalyptus', whose name means 'well-covered' because its unopened flowers are protected by a form of cap. And you will also find it in a word that, though now obsolete, is particularly suited to the approach of summer: 'eutrapely', which comes from the Greek for 'pleasant in conversation' and which was listed among Aristotle's seven moral virtues. In essence it conveys the ease with which we slip into happy and comforting exchanges with old friends.

15 June

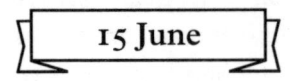

KADIGAN

According to the British National Corpus, a database containing billions of words of current language, the word 'thing' is used a whopping 2,500 times in every one million words. It has become such a multitasker that it can stand in for 'something', 'anything', and 'nothing'. And yet for such an unspecific word, it is one with a powerful history.

In Old English, 'thing' denoted an assembly of the people as well as a formal parliament. A word inherited from Germanic, it may come from an ancient root meaning 'stretch', referring perhaps to a stretch of time appointed for a meeting or assembly. This sense of a place in which important matters were discussed is still found in the name of the oldest surviving parliament in the world, Iceland's *Althing*. It is hidden too in the word 'hustings', which comes from the Old Norse *hústhing*, a 'household assembly held by a leader', and which was applied in Middle English to the highest court of the City of London and subsequently to the platform in Guildhall where the Lord Mayor and aldermen presided. Eventually 'hustings' attached itself to the temporary platform on which parliamentary candidates were nominated, hence the sense 'electoral proceedings'. As for 'thing' itself, this took on the meaning of the subject of a discussion until relaxing yet further to embrace any old thing.

Not content with just one word, English has an entire lexicon for unspecified objects such as 'thingamajig', 'doohickey', 'doodad', 'whatchamacallit', and dozens more. Such placeholder words are known as 'kadigans', a term coined by the American writer, poet, and editor Willard R. Espy, perhaps after someone bearing the Irish or Welsh surname Cadigan who liked to use them. Kadigans can be found in almost every language, and even in this realm of nameless things there is often a hierarchy of specificity – a 'gizmo' or 'dingus', for example, suggests some sort of device, whereas 'oojamaflip' can be used of a person or object whose name you can't put a finger on. 'Thing', however, remains universally applicable – perhaps there is some grandeur in it still.

16 June

FATHOM-HEALTH

In the summer of 1953 a fantastical horror-melodrama arrived in the movie theatres of North America. *The Beast from 20,000 Fathoms* was lauded for its spectacular special effects, which had a dinosaur called the 'Rhedosaurus' rampage through downtown New York while the city's comparatively tiny citizens made a desperate run for cover. The critical reception was mixed, not least because the dinosaur was judged to look highly unrealistic, but the movie nonetheless became a sleeper hit, helped no doubt by its sensational title.

The fathoms in question, of course, were from the depths of the sea, taking their name from an ancient word that is as old as English itself. In 824, the year of our earliest record, it meant something rather different. For the Anglo-Saxons 'fathom' meant arms that were outstretched, as in an embrace. This was later standardized to a distance of six feet (apparently the average span of both arms), both above and below water. In the 1600s, a 'fathom-health' was a toast of honour that was drunk 'fathoms deep'. Over time, the word took a metaphorical turn so that to fathom something meant to grasp it intellectually rather than physically. Something unfathomable therefore could not be grasped – much like the Rhedosaurus.

17 June

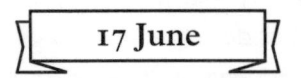

GREEN-METE

Today is National Eat Your Vegetables Day, designed presumably by parents as a way of encouraging recalcitrant children to eat their broccoli even if they can't spell the word. Were we to take the concept back a millennium, we might have been talking of 'Green-Mete Day', for that was once the term of choice for the humble vegetable. It rests on the earliest meaning of *mete*, in Old English, which denoted any kind of food. As diets began to expand, adjectives were added to specify the food in question – 'green-mete' became the collective term for vegetables, while 'sweet-mete' encompassed any sweet confection. As vocabulary proliferated, so the meaning of 'meat' narrowed, and came to rest on the animal flesh we know it as today.

18 June

MEETING YOUR WATERLOO

The seemingly unstoppable rise of Napoleon Bonaparte that so terrified the rest of Europe at the start of the nineteenth century ended on this day in 1815, on the muddy battlefields of Waterloo in Belgium. His British nemesis, the 'Iron' Duke of Wellington, is celebrated to this day whenever we eat beef Wellington or wear wellington boots. Thanks to his victory, the phrase 'meet your Waterloo' became popular in English as a metaphor for a decisive and crushing defeat – a turning point at which a challenge becomes insurmountable. It has since been used in various contexts far beyond military and political scenarios, often to describe personal or professional failures, although we shouldn't forget ABBA's own twist on the idea with their Eurovision-winning 'Waterloo', whose lyrics explored the idea of falling in love as akin to meeting your Waterloo. While Napoleon lost the battle, he may have (linguistically speaking at least) won the war.

19 June

COCKALORUM

Is it not delightful and instructive, to hear the unintelligible jargon of *presto! – pausto! – maunto! – cockalorum! – yaw!*

What better way to remark upon a series of exclamations than by piling up the exclamation marks oneself. This was clearly the strategy of the author of an *Essay on Satirical Entertainment*, written in 1772, who also gives us our earliest record of the word 'cockalorum', a shout that accompanied the final flourish of a conjuring trick or the winning move in the wonderfully named game of 'snip-snap-snorum'. Its origin is unclear, but it may well be a mangling of the liturgical phrase *saecula saeculorum*, 'for all future time', used to end prayers.

The story of 'cockalorum' did not end there, however. Thanks to our long-standing equation in language between a strutting cockerel and pomposity, the word shifted to describe a self-important and highly conceited individual. In the form 'high cockalorum', this would be one such person in public office.

20 June

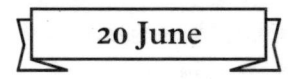

TANDSMØR

'Do you like butter?' Holding a buttercup under someone's chin is one childhood test everyone seems to pass. The truth is that these delicate summer flowers reflect yellow on all chins, due to an illumination from the epidermal layer of their petals as intense as the reflection of glass: a liking for butter is largely irrelevant. For those who really do love its creamy rich taste, however, there is a wonderful Danish word describing the impression left on a thickly spread piece of bread as we bite into it: *tandsmør*, literally 'tooth butter'.

21 June

PHILOCALY

> What is this life if, full of care,
> We have no time to stand and stare.

In his poem 'Leisure', W.H. Davies describes the necessity of pausing to appreciate what is happening on our doorstep. Taking pleasure in the small joys of life is known as 'philocaly', which is based on Greek *kalos*, meaning 'beautiful', and *philo*, meaning 'love'. It follows that a 'philocalist' is a lover of beautiful things, wherever they may find them.

Beauty is of course subjective, and *kalos* is also at the heart of the word 'callipygian', 'having beautiful buttocks'. It was originally used as an epithet for a statue of Aphrodite.

22 June

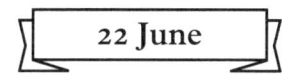

DRECKLY

It says quite a bit about human nature that the very first meaning of 'soon', in Old English, was 'forthwith', 'immediately', and 'without delay'. There was therefore no point in having the comparative 'sooner' or the superlative 'soonest', because whatever was being referred to would already have been done. Inevitably perhaps, given our propensity for procrastination, 'soon' relaxed to the point that its uses range from 'in a short while' to 'on the never-never' – what the Spaniards would call *mañana* and Devonians would describe as 'dreckly' (which is short for 'directly', but generally means anything but).

None of this has stopped us from talking about speed and immediacy as an elusive desirable. In the *Historical Thesaurus of English*, there are over 250 synonyms meaning 'straight away', including 'in a whiff', 'in two ups', 'in the twinkling of a look', and 'upon the nines'. This compares with an equal number of synonyms for 'drunk', suggesting perhaps that doing things 'dreckly' might necessitate a diversion along the way.

23 June

ATTERCOP

As the weather gets warmer, so the spider mating season begins. The thought may induce a shudder, but spiders are vital to the world's ecosystem: without them we would be facing famine, as all of our crops would be consumed by the pests that spiders prey upon.

The Anglo-Saxons took a very different view, one that might appeal to most arachnophobes, for they believed spiders to be universally poisonous, with a bite that required considerable efforts to address. The *Leechbook*, a tenth-century collection of medical cures, recipes, diagnostic guides, and charms which survives in a single manuscript held at the British Library, includes one remedy that might raise a modern eyebrow:

> *Uiþ gongewifran bite nim henne æg, gnid on ealu hreaw & sceapes tord niwe, swa he nyte, sele him drincan godne scenc fulne.*

> Against the bite of a spider, take a hen's egg, mix it raw in ale with a fresh sheep's turd, so that he does not know, give him a good cup full to drink.

Here a spider is rather wonderfully known as a *gongewifran*, or a 'walking weaver'. A more usual word for the arthropod in Old English was the *attercop*, or 'poison-head'. That *cop*, incidentally, also explains the 'cob' in 'cobweb'.

Spiders have, of course, also proved inspirational. A popular story relates how Robert the Bruce, who was established as Robert I on this day in 1314, noticed a spider in a cave a few days before the Battle of Bannockburn. He saw how the web that the spider was diligently weaving faltered again and again, and yet the creature continued undeterred. On the seventh attempt the threads of silk came together perfectly. The moral that Bruce took from the encounter was that a determination to succeed is everything, giving him the resolve to command a decisive victory over the English. Some maintain that it was also this event that led to the proverb 'If at first you don't succeed, try, try, and try again'.

24 June

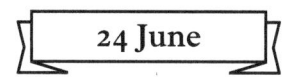

BELLADONNA

The US newspaper magnate William Randolph Hearst presided over a considerable empire. Among his employees was the writer Ambrose Bierce, born on this day in 1841, a fiercely clever, wry, and difficult figure who worked on Hearst's *San Francisco Examiner* for over twenty years. Bierce gave the newspaper considerable intellectual prestige thanks to his razor-sharp, frequently excoriating wit. One story relates how Hearst once began to speak proudly of his extensive collections of buildings, art, books, and tapestries, eventually asking Bierce if he collected anything in particular. Bierce's response was typically withering:

> I collect words. And ideas. Like you, I also store them. But in the reservoir of my mind. I can take them out and display them at a moment's notice. Eminently portable, Mr Hearst. And I don't find it necessary to show them all at the same time.

Many of the words that Bierce collected can be found in his *Devil's Dictionary*, a glossary of everyday words that are given spoof definitions that amply reflect Bierce's acerbic take on life. Many are still quoted today, such as 'Politics, *n.* The conduct of public affairs for private advantage,' or 'Reporter, *n.* A writer who guesses his way to the truth and dispels it with a tempest of words.'

Others are so cynical they can make the reader wince: 'Back, *n.* That part of your friend which it is your privilege to contemplate in your adversity,' or 'Piano, *n.* A parlor utensil for subduing the impenitent visitor. It is operated by depressing the keys of the machine and the spirits of the audience.'

For the most part, however, the collection is so insightful that it elicits knowing laughter on every page. 'Belladonna' is defined as 'In Italian a beautiful lady; in English a deadly poison. A striking example of the essential identity of the two tongues.'

The Devil's Dictionary added significantly to Bierce's notoriety, and it was lauded and despised in equal measure. Perhaps he expected nothing less, judging by the entry for 'applause', which is defined somewhat bitterly as 'The echo of a platitude.'

25 June

SOULMATE

It's an ancient concept. Plato's *Symposium* describes humans as originally having four arms, four legs, and one head made of two faces, but then they were split in half by Zeus, king of the gods, leaving each torn creature to search for its missing counterpart. Each of us, in Plato's imagining, is a 'matching half' of a human whole, and each of us is forever seeking the other half. If a person is lucky enough to find them, something wonderful happens: 'the two are struck from their senses by love, by a sense of belonging to one another, and by desire, and they don't want to be separated from one another, not even for a moment.'

It took a further two millennia for the right word to be coined in English, however. The Romantic poet Samuel Taylor Coleridge, who died on this day in 1834, bequeathed English several words and expressions. Most famously, his *Rime of the Ancient Mariner* gave us the idiom of 'an albatross around one's neck', an image central to the narrative of the poem in which the mariner shoots an albatross and is thereafter obliged to carry the burden of the bird around his neck ever after, as a reminder of his ill deed. Other coinages include 'pleasure dome', 'suspension of disbelief', and, thankfully, 'soulmate'. In a 'Letter to a Young Lady', Coleridge insists, 'You must have a

Soul-mate as well as a House or a Yoke-mate.' Perhaps he was aware of one poetic theory as to the etymology of the word 'soul', which is that it heralds from the same Germanic root as 'sea': Germanic peoples believed that the spirit of the soul came from the oceans and returned to the water after death.

26 June

SEA-LAWYER

Steven Spielberg's *Jaws* was released in the summer of 1975, destined to become a blockbuster with a score by John Williams that continues to induce shudders in those who hear it. The word 'shark' has its own dark underbelly, introduced by the sailors of an expedition undertaken by the slave trader Captain Hawkins, who brought back tales of a creature 'like unto those which we call dogge-fishes' but far more 'ravenous'. In 1569, a crew of fishermen trawling mackerel in the English Channel were astounded by a colossal fish that rushed at their nets, almost capsizing them. They managed to capture it, marvelling at a creature that was seventeen feet long and had razor-edged teeth; its skin was subsequently stuffed and put on display in a tavern in London's Fleet Street. But it still lacked a name. According to *A Collection of Seventy-Nine Black-Letter Ballads and Broadsides, Printed in the Reign of Queen Elizabeth*, one witness said of the 'marveilous straunge Fishe ... Ther is no proper name for it that I knowe, but that sertayne men of Captayne Haukinses doth call it a sharke.'

No one quite knows where Hawkins heard the name, but perhaps, given his iniquitous career, we should have gone with an alternative name bequeathed to the feared fish over a century later, namely 'sea-lawyer', a homage to its cunning and ferocity.

27 June

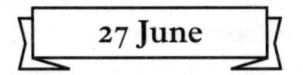

THREE-PIPE PROBLEM

The German Reich's wartime ciphering system known as the Enigma was considered unbreakable. It was the Germans' most sophisticated method of encrypting secret information, transmitted via a machine that resembled a typewriter and that had originally been intended for business purposes, before being co-opted for military use. By the time Germany invaded Poland in 1939, the British had cracked many of the Enigma codes used on the Western Front, but with the subsequent invasion of Russia the Allies desperately needed to intercept the messages regarding German troop movements and planned offensives. On this day in 1941, Alan Turing and his team managed to decode the cipher that underpinned the German army's direction of its military operations on the Eastern Front.

The cryptanalysis of the Enigma clearly required extensive, collective time and brainpower. Greater certainly than what Sherlock Holmes considered to be a 'three-pipe problem': a vexatious issue that demands deep thought for the duration of smoking three pipes of tobacco. In Arthur Conan Doyle's *The Red-Headed League*, the detective helpfully puts a time frame on it: 'It is quite a three-pipe problem, and I beg that you won't speak to me for fifty minutes.'

28 June

BRIDEWELL

'To Bridewell with these roagues,' exhorted the Church of England clergyman Henry Smith in 1591. Bridewell was at this time a prison in the City of London, but its original construction had been intended for sumptuous banquets for the monarchy rather than the punishment of vagabonds and Smith's 'roagues'. It was built in the early sixteenth century on the banks of the Fleet River (now a subterranean river used as a sewer) as a residence for Henry VIII, taking its name from the nearby well of St Bride. It was the setting for Hans Holbein's painting *The Ambassadors* and in its time saw lavish masquerades and the entertainment of such notables as Charles V, who had been invested as Holy Roman Emperor on this day in 1519.

Such luxury was short-lived, for just half a century later the rambling palace was donated by Edward VI to the City of London with the aim of addressing the burning issue of vagrancy. Its use was to be as a house of correction for small-time offenders who were guilty of such crimes as vagabonding, peddling without a licence, prostitution, and petty pilfering. The inmates were immediately put to hard labour; refusal to participate resulted in such punishments as flogging. The model was regarded as successful enough to warrant the establishment of further institutions for the 'correction' of vagrants, which also took on the name of 'bridewells'.

The use of 'clink' to mean a prison shares a similar history – the original Clink was a prison in Southwark that operated well into the eighteenth century. Once again, its name slipped into slang as a byword for jail. Newgate Prison, meanwhile, was arguably even more productive, in language at least. Among the dark additions to the dictionary were a 'Newgate hornpipe', a hanging, and 'Newgate tree', the gallows. A 'Newgate lawyer', meanwhile, was a third-rate lawyer who hung around the prison in the hope of finding work, the predecessor to today's 'ambulance-chaser'.

29 June

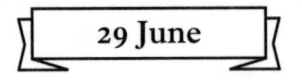

HAPLESS

On a warm, dry evening in the early summer of 1613, crowds packed the auditorium of the Globe playhouse on London's Bankside. They were there to see a performance of *All is True*, co-written by the forty-nine-year-old William Shakespeare and a younger playwright, John Fletcher. The drama's focus was on the divorce of Henry VIII and Catherine of Aragon, and the excitement at this new collaboration was heightened by the play's considerable use of pageantry and special effects, including the firing of several cannons on stage right in front of the expectant audience. As the high drama unfolded, few of them noticed a terrible mishap, in which a piece of wadding, used to press down the gunpowder, caught alight and flew up and ignited the Globe's thatched roof. The resultant fire consumed the theatre's wooden structure, which burned to the ground in less than an hour.

The news was feverishly reported across London, and not all were sorry to hear it. Some puritans, who considered theatres to be dens for heathens, viewed the fire as divine vengeance. Others clearly enjoyed the tale of one hapless member of the audience, who was noted by an eyewitness to have 'had his breeches set on fire, that would perhaps have broyled him, if he had not by the benefit of a provident wit, put it out with a bottle of ale'.

The word 'hap' carried the meaning of 'fortune' or 'chance'. It survives not only in 'hapless' (unfortunate), but also in 'mishap', 'perhaps' (by chance), and 'happen', used of actions that come to pass by fortune or chance. To be 'happy', it followed, was to be favoured by fortune. She had certainly not smiled upon London that day, where what had promised to be a huge success quickly became an unfortunate one. To quote Shakespeare himself: 'If haply won, perhaps a hapless gain.'

30 June

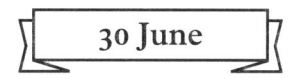

POPUTCHIK

Alfred Hitchcock's *Strangers on a Train* was released on this day in 1951. Based on the novel by Patricia Highsmith, its story involves a tennis star who strikes up a conversation with a total stranger and thereby sets in motion a deadly chain of events.

In Russian, the word *poputchik* once had political connotations, denoting someone who sympathized with such causes as Bolshevism and Naziism. Its modern incarnation is far less tarnished, used of a 'fellow traveller' who happens to share your carriage on a train. The freedom of anonymity invites the sharing of confidences in the knowledge that your new friend *pro tempore* will then disappear into the night, never to be encountered again.

JULY

1 July

PECUNIA NON OLET

Vespasian, who was proclaimed emperor of Rome by his troops on this day in AD 69, is largely known for his fiscal reforms and consolidation of the empire, as well as the commissioning of the construction of the Colosseum. After his takeover, Vespasian and his advisers sought every avenue possible for raising taxes in order to shore up the public finances. Notoriously, these included the *vectigal urinae*: a tax on the contents of public urinals in Rome. More specifically, this was a tariff levied on those who purchased urine for such trades as tanning leather, laundry, cloth-making, and even dentistry, for Romans would use a mixture of urine and goat's milk to whiten their teeth.

Despite the tax's success in bringing in revenue, it did not meet with universal favour. Vespasian's son and eventual successor, Titus, maintained this was a degrading way for the imperial exchequer to make money. According to the Roman historian Cassius Dio, Vespasian handed his son a gold coin and asked, 'See, my son, if this has any smell?'

It is from this account that English took the axiom *pecunia non olet*, 'money does not smell', used to imply that coins hold the same value regardless of their origin.

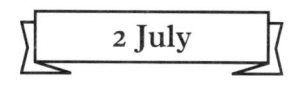

2 July

GRENADO

The fruit of the tree *Punica granatum*, the pomegranate, has served as a symbol of many things, from resurrection to fertility, unity to chastity. In classical mythology, it was particularly associated with the indissolubility of marriage, thanks to the story of Persephone, who was duped by Hades into remaining in the underworld for six months of every year by eating six pomegranate seeds.

The name of the fruit comes from the Old French *pome*, 'apple', and *grenate*, based on the Latin *granatum*, 'many-seeded' (similarly, the perforated sweet-smelling container known as a 'pomander' is from the Latin *pomum de ambre*, 'apple of ambergris'). It went by various names before settling on 'pomegranate', including 'garnet-apple', 'apple Punic', and 'grenado'. If the latter looks familiar, it is because it is related to 'grenade', the small bomb that is similar in shape to the fruit, and shatters into seed-like fragments on impact. Confusingly, a hand grenade has, since the First World War, been informally known as a 'pineapple'.

3 July

SOBREMESA

There is a cultural eloquence in the Spanish word *sobremesa*: the conversation at the table when dinner is finished, and which translates simply as 'upon the table'. This is the time when the focus shifts to conviviality and debate, when time seems elastic, and idleness is anything but empty. English simply has no word for it, perhaps because – sadly – such conversation, once the food has gone, rarely happens.

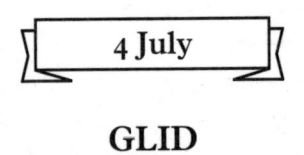

4 July

GLID

The language of our ancestors was full of 'strong' verbs – those which change their vowel on altering their tense, such as 'write' and 'wrote', 'bind' and 'bound', 'bite' and 'bit', 'speak' and 'spoke'. Old English had no fewer than seven classes of strong verb, each with its own signature conjugation. In the centuries that followed, some of these flipped over into 'weak' verbs, namely those that simply add a syllable or letter, such as 'love' and 'loved', or 'text' and 'texted'.

Some verbs still hover between the two classifications. We can, for example, say we 'strove' towards a solution as well as 'strived', while regional English and Scots opt for 'tret' rather than 'treated', and 'jamp' for 'jumped'. US English still favours a strong verb in many cases: it prefers 'snuck' over 'sneaked', for instance, and 'dove' for 'dived'. It is just one reflection, on this Independence Day, of how the language-keepers of North America and Britain sought linguistic separation as well as the political kind. For the Americans, rejecting the King's English was tantamount to rejecting the king (for more on this, *see* MASHEEN, 16 October). And so it is that British English embraced the weaker version of many verbs. Some of its losses are surely to be lamented: how much more poetic is 'glid' instead of 'glided', 'chid' for 'chided', and 'snew' for 'snowed'?

5 July

SIDLER

'Double-dipping', 'regifting', 'mimbo', 'yada yada yada'. The pilot of the US comedy series *Seinfeld* first aired on the US network NBC on this day in 1989, changing the way that sitcoms were written and – despite calling itself 'a show about nothing' – propelling several words and expressions into the English language. They also include 'sidler', a perennially useful epithet for the work colleague who appears out of nowhere to take a share of the credit for something they didn't contribute to, and who can equally disappear in a flash when any criticism is meted out.

6 July

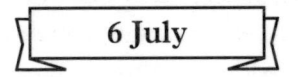

WISTFUL

Instagram is full of posts featuring mournful photographs superimposed with the German words *Fernweh*, the longing to be far away, and *Sehnsucht*, a melancholic yearning. They are each so beautiful that it's easy to overlook that English also does yearning exceedingly well. The key difference is that many of our most expressive words for longing have all but disappeared. Thankfully, 'wistful' still does a lot of heavy lifting. Rather than being full of 'wist', as you might surmise (understandably, given to be 'feckful' is to be full of 'feck' or vigour, and 'ruthful' rests on the beautiful Old English 'ruth', compassion), this is rather different and, perhaps fittingly, rather elusive. The most plausible suggestion is that 'wistful' is a combination of 'wistly', a now-obsolete word meaning 'intently', together with the similar-sounding adjective 'wishful'. To wish intently is what yearning is all about, although there is a dreamy quality to wistfulness, too, as though the object of your regretful longing is as vague and elusive as it is out of reach.

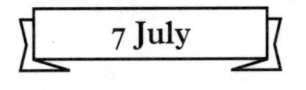

7 July

CERRING

'When is a door not a door?' goes the old joke. Answer? 'When it is ajar.' When a door is 'ajar', it is of course slightly open, but have you ever wondered where a 'jar' actually fits in? The original form of the word was in fact very different, namely 'on char', in which 'char' is rooted in the Old English *cerr* and meant a 'turning'. You will find the same word in the London place name Charing Cross, the site of a memorial cross to Eleanor of Castile, the beloved wife of Edward I, who died on this day in 1307, and which takes its name not from *Chère-Reine-Cross*, 'dear queen cross', as is popularly supposed, but from its position on a 'cerring', or bend, of the River Thames.

8 July

CARRAWITCHET

Shakespeare loved them, Chaucer couldn't resist them: people have enjoyed a good pun since the beginnings of language itself. English lends itself especially well to punning, thanks in part to its many homophones, but it's clear that other languages enjoy them just as much. Bilingual puns are even better: take the famous pun about breakfast that asks, 'Why do French people prefer to have small breakfasts? Because one egg is always un oeuf!'

In the intriguingly titled *A Learned History on Dumpling* from 1726, the prolific poet and balladeer Henry Carey took a satirical swipe at contemporary British politics through the unlikely lens of dumplings, making a comparison between bodily appetites and those for social and political advancement. If that wasn't strange enough, the pamphlet includes several fanciful words that seem very alien to modern eyes, including the 'carrawitchet', mentioned in the line 'Connundrums and Carrawitchets ... at which the King laugh'd 'till his Sides crackt.'

A carrawitchet can be a hoax question as well as a joke, as in this example from a slang dictionary of 1874: 'How far is it from the first of July to London Bridge?' But it is puns that English speakers turn to most readily, amply demonstrated by the carrawitchet that won the comedian Olaf Falafel victory for the funniest joke of the Edinburgh Festival 2019: 'I keep randomly shouting out "Broccoli" and "Cauliflower" – I think I might have Florets.'

9 July

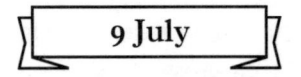

GELASIN

Dimples are designed to be attractive, adding a flourish or exclamation mark to our smile. The deeper the dimples, the greater the perceived happiness of their owner and, by extension, those who behold them. Someone somewhere decided that 9 July was to be National Dimples Day, with a rationale that goes no further than 'celebrating cute adults and babies'. Apparently only 20 to 30 per cent of us have dimples with which to delight, although a commentator in the *Guardian* in 1713 clearly believed they could be acquired through effort: 'The Dimple is practised to give a Grace to the Features, and is frequently made a Bait to entangle a gazing Lover.'

The earliest meaning of 'dimple' was topographical, for the word was once found frequently, with various spellings, in place names from the Midlands and North of England, where it referred to an indentation in the ground, from a deep hole or hollow to a dingle or dell. Historical maps provide evidence, for example, of a farm named Dimple in Bingley, Yorkshire, a field called Kerlingdimpil in Furness, Dumplinton in Lancashire (now Dumplington), and the street name Le Dumple in Scarborough (now Dumple Street).

All in all, it is a sweet name, far cuter than the seventeenth-century 'gelasin', which referred specifically to the dimples that were produced by smiling.

10 July

SEIJAKU

On the most basic level, the Japanese word *seijaku* means 'serenity'. But it remains untranslatable in English because its aesthetic is more nuanced, and more accurately describes an energized calm that can exist even at the heart of chaos. Rather than escaping the never-ending busyness of life entirely, it is about finding relaxation in the midst of it, most particularly within nature, such as a Japanese garden. *Seijaku* allows for stillness and imperturbability at the same time as participation in the hustle and bustle.

11 July

TONGUE-PAD

'Clear your mind of cant,' instructed Dr Johnson of his biographer James Boswell in 1783. Johnson was making a dig at insincere forms of speech. ('You tell a man, "I am sorry you had such bad weather the last day of your journey, and were so much wet." You don't care sixpence whether he was wet or dry.') What concerned him was the contaminating effect of such speech: 'You may *talk* in this manner; it is a mode of talking in society: but don't *think* foolishly.'

This use of 'cant' for affected or insincere speech was the dominant meaning in Johnson's lifetime. The origins of the term, however, go back much further, to a very different class of society than the one the lexicographer occupied. Rooted in the Latin *cantare*, 'to sing', the verb 'cant' is first recorded in the sixteenth century with the sense 'to speak in the whining manner typical of beggars'.

By this time vagrants had long been regarded as outcasts from the mainstream of society. A zero-tolerance Act of 1597 provided for 'the suppressing of rogues, vagabonds and sturdy beggers', in which the latter was 'an able-bodied man begging without good reason, and often using violence'. Contemporary publications recorded much of the tribal shorthand used by such 'rogues', presumably seen as excitingly different from the mode of speech affected by the educated classes, the early equivalents of Johnson and his friends.

By the end of the seventeenth century, *A New Dictionary of the Terms Ancient and Modern of the Canting Crew* provided a collection of the most striking. It includes 'Cog, to cheat at dice'; 'Darkmans-budge, one that slides into a house in the dusk, to let in more rogues to rob'; 'Flash-ken, a house where thieves hang out'; 'Rantipole, a rude wild boy or girl'; 'Sheep-shearers, cheats'; and 'Tongue-pad, a smooth, glib-tongued, insinuating fellow'.

Such slang was still being noted by Dickens in the late nineteenth century. It may even have survived to this day: in 2009, it was reported that Elizabethan slang is being revived in modern prisons as a means of eluding the officers and, no doubt, of establishing a bond between inmates that is as important as the one uniting the early canting crew.

12 July

PANTOFFELN

In *A delicate Diet, for daintiemouthde Droonkardes* from 1576, the Elizabethan poet George Gascoigne mocked the English adoption of foreign fashions, lamenting the English ability to declare something 'vile and villainous', only to copy it within months. Two years later, the lexicographer and royal language tutor John Florio wrote, 'Now let us see, if all the colours you have, are able, of naturall Englishmen, to dye us into artificial Italians.' This was a time of great preoccupation with foreign fashion and manners, which were interconnected with themes of politics and economics.

Florio's Italian-to-English dictionary, entitled *Queen Anna's New World of Words*, featured terms for many fabrics and fashions, including several kinds of 'pantofles'. These included the 'Chianellétte, little or thin pantofles'; 'Buoséga, a wooden pantofle' (also known as a 'loggerhead'); and 'Pianelle, night slippers or pantofles'. By the end of the sixteenth century, a more exotic version had arrived, the 'chopine' or 'shoppini' with raised soles. They were far from popular with everyone; one commentator of the time moaned, 'They have corked shoes, pinsnets, and fine pantofles, which bear them up a finger or two from the ground ... to what good uses serve these pantofles, except it be to wear in a private house, or in a man's chamber to keep him warm?'

To this day, the German for 'slippers' is *Pantoffeln*, albeit of the fluffy, squidgy kind which are indeed confined to private houses and which, it must be said, earn the sound of their name so much better.

13 July

ESTIVATE

Holidays have always been special, particularly for those of a religious persuasion, for a holiday was literally a 'holy day'. A 'red-letter day', one that is particularly memorable, takes its name from the fact that saints' days and festivals were marked in red in the calendar. Sometimes, though, it's worth remembering the benefits of a staycation. We all know about 'hibernation', when we retreat from the harshness of winter, but what do we do when we retire during the summer? The answer is we 'estivate', meaning to spend any prolonged period of hot and dry conditions in a state of torpor or suspended animation.

14 July

CRAPOTER

Today is Bastille Day, which marks the beginning of the French Revolution in 1789. The terms 'left wing' and 'right wing' originated with the political movements of the time, and specifically with the seating plans of the French National Assembly. Here, the anti-Royalist revolutionaries would occupy the seats to the left of the presiding officer, while the aristocratic and more conservative supporters of the king gathered to the right. Many other words were to sweep into view in the wake of the Revolution, from 'aristocrat' to 'regime', 'guillotine', and 'tricolor'.

But it is for its flair away from politics that we largely admire the French language today. Take the word *crapoter*. Although any word beginning with the four letters 'crap' rarely bodes well, it stands as one of many untranslatables that reinforce the ability of French to pack a whole host of nuances into a single metaphor. The basic meaning of *crapoter* is 'to fake-smoke'. Extend that a little and you have someone who may hold a cigarette between their fingers in order to look cool, but who only pretends to inhale. In other words, a *crapoteur* is someone who pretends to be someone they're not.

15 July

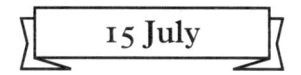

BLUETOOTH

Big companies often think long and hard before choosing a name for their creations, and while you might expect them to dip into a brand-new and shiny lexicon, the opposite is often the case. Starbucks famously borrowed their name from the first mate in Herman Melville's *Moby-Dick*, perhaps in an effort to summon a sense of rousing adventure; their original choice was apparently 'Pequod', a tribute to the book's ship, until the artist commissioned by the founders of the firm pointed out that the suggestion of a cup of 'Pee-quod' might not be the most appetizing.

The technology of Bluetooth, enabling the wireless connection of our electronic devices, was developed by the Swedish firm Ericsson in 1994. This time, its creators went even further back, to the tenth-century Scandinavian King Harald Gormsson, nicknamed 'Bluetooth' on account of a prominent dead tooth. Gormsson had been responsible for uniting various Danish tribes with some of their Norwegian neighbours, and so Ericsson thought him a powerful symbol for a technology that brings connectivity to different industries and products. But they went further still – the Bluetooth logo draws upon Younger Futhark, a runic alphabet that was the primary writing system in the Viking Age. The symbol merges the runes known as Hagall (ᚼ) and Bjarkan (ᛒ) to produce the initials HB, for Harald Bluetooth.

16 July

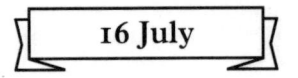

RAMA-RAMA

The naming of insects has clearly proved a joyful exercise over the centuries. 'Caterpillar' was inspired by the Old French word *chatepelose*, literally 'hairy cat', while a millipede apparently has a thousand feet. But no name has attracted quite as much speculation as 'butterfly'; which is variously explained as an alteration of 'flutterby', a reference to the insect's butter-coloured poo; or the folk belief that it will swoop upon butter left unattended in the kitchen. More plausibly, the name is likely a simple nod to the colour of the common yellow or cream species of butterfly.

This fascination with the butterfly is far from exclusive to English speakers: in fact, arguably no other creature has attracted quite as much effort in the search for a suitable name.

In Danish, it is known simply as the *sommerfugl*, the 'summer bird'. In French, it is a *papillon*, the sister word to 'pavilion', whose original canvas awnings reminded people of the outspread wings of a butterfly. In German, beyond the beautiful-sounding *Schmetterling* (from *Schmette*, 'cream'), it is popularly known as the *Molkendieb* ('milk thief'), while the West Flemish dialect of Dutch pulls no punches with *boterschijte*, 'butter-shitter'. For the Italians, the butterfly is the *farfalla*, hence the pasta shape, and the Spanish have added a religious note with *mariposa*, 'Mary, alight!' But perhaps the most expressive name of all comes from Malay, where the insect has invited not just one word of approval but two, in the reduplicated form *rama-rama*, 'lovely-lovely'.

17 July

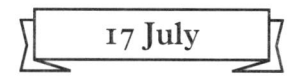

TO DINE WITH DUKE HUMPHREY

Visitors to Old St Paul's Cathedral, before it was destroyed by the Great Fire of 1666, might once have walked down Duke Humphrey's Walk, an aisle that was erroneously named in the belief that its namesake was buried there. The youngest son of Henry IV, Humphrey was made Duke of Gloucester by his older brother Henry V, and took an active role in the Hundred Years War against France. His tomb actually lies in St Albans, but it was in his promenade in the original St Paul's that the poor would loiter in the hope, it was said, of being offered food or invited to dinner. Such was the general futility of these hopes that the phrase 'to dine with Duke Humphrey' became a popular way to describe the act of going hungry.

18 July

ROCKET SURGERY

Linguists revel in the 'eggcorn': a slip of the ear or tongue that very often goes on to replace the original version of the phrase (*see* HAMMER AND THONGS, 31 May). But there are other categories of language blooper that also deserve a mention. Let's not forget the 'malapropism', for example, a term inspired by the character of Mrs Malaprop in Richard Brinsley Sheridan's play *The Rivals* (1775), who is a mistress of linguistic ineptitude, as when she calls one gentleman 'the very pineapple of politeness'.

The latest kid on the block is the 'malaphor', an utterance that manages to combine a malapropism and a metaphor by crunching together two separate expressions and producing a new one. The beauty of a malaphor is that it tends to sound entirely plausible, seducing the brain into believing that it is the standard phrase or expression. Examples of this are suddenly everywhere, as when your boss proclaims, 'It's not rocket surgery!' We might follow said boss 'like lemmings to the slaughter', or 'strike while we're ahead'. Should everything go belly-up, we can then declare that 'the fan is going to hit the roof'. All of which goes to show: you can't teach a leopard new spots.

19 July

SKILLJOY

Alongside the Words of the Year that are chosen annually by dictionary publishers to remind us how accurately words can summarize the mood of an age, one of the most hotly awaited linguistic contests is that run by the *Washington Post*, which invites its readers every year to submit newly invented words to fill a gap in our language. The results are often hilarious as well as useful. 'Percycution' was one suggestion for giving your child a name they will hate for the rest of their lives, while a 'skilljoy' is the would-be friend who is just that bit better than you at everything. 'Crapplause' is a polite but unenthusiastic expression of approval.

The *Post* also invites people to invent new definitions of existing words. Among the past winners are 'abdicate': to give up all hope of a flat stomach (a nice pairing with 'flabbergasted': feeling appalled at how much weight you've gained); 'willy-nilly', with the new meaning of 'impotent'; and 'coffee': one who is coughed upon.

20 July

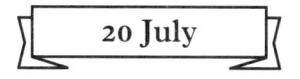

CHURU-CHURU

It is said that in Britain the word for a bread roll changes every hundred miles. From the 'cob' to the 'bap', the 'barm-cake' to the 'stottie', the 'huffkin' to the 'scuffler', such choices take us straight to the language of childhood and of home. The same phenomenon is of course true of many other cultures, but the subjects around which local vocabulary revolves necessarily change. In Japan, it would be hard to find a richer lexicon than the one catering for the making of ramen, the traditional noodle broth served with meat or vegetables. Here, for example, you will find the term *koshi*, which describes the firmness of respective noodle varieties. Within it you will find *yawa*, soft noodles, *futsu*, normal noodles, *kata*, hard noodles, and *barigata*, which are *super*-hard noodles. Most entertaining to non-native eyes are surely the words that relate to the slipperiness of such food. *Tsuru-tsuru* and *churu-churu* both refer to the slurping sound that is unavoidable when eating noodles that are slippery-soft. If that sound comes specifically from a particularly loud sucking of said noodles, then the word you need is *zuru-zuru*.

21 July

GRUGLEDE

Sun, sea, feasting: there's no denying the appeal of foreign climes. But the pessimists among us will also be thinking of the packing, airport queues, and potentially sleepless nights in cramped seats that are equally part of the package. Norwegians have a word for the mixed emotions that accompany many holidays. This is *gruglede*, or 'happy-dread', the *gru* of which has survived in the English word 'gruesome'.

Some say that cynicism is built into the history of the word 'travel' itself. It emerged in Middle English as 'travail', meaning 'painful or laborious effort', and a word that to this day means sheer pain. It gets worse, however, for the ancestor of each is the Latin *trepalium*, an instrument of torture consisting of three stakes. You can make your own mind up, but this fact is worth bearing in mind when your flight is cancelled and you're sleeping on the airport floor.

If you experience real travail on your travels, you might long for the original meaning of the word 'journey', which comes from the French for 'day', because most journeys in the Middle Ages lasted one day before your horse was exhausted and you needed to stop.

22 July

STOPLESSNESS

'The most expensive hyphen in history'. So ran the judgement of science fiction writer and inventor Arthur C. Clarke of events that took place in 1962. The hyphen in question was notable by its absence, omitted by NASA from the coding of instructions given to a probe designed to deliver invaluable data on Venus, and causing the craft to malfunction less than five minutes after take-off.

Rooted in the Latin *punctus*, the 'act of pointing', the word 'punctuation' is first recorded in English in the mid sixteenth century, meaning the marking of the text of a psalm to show how it should be chanted. By the late sixteenth century, today's more familiar meaning had emerged: the insertion of marks into a text to help interpretation, and the use of such marks in the division of a passage into sentences and clauses. The big four

– comma, semicolon, colon, and full stop – were for a long time regarded as precise measurements of a pause: a full stop was worth four commas. Anything devoid of such marks was considered 'stopless'.

Today, social-media norms regularly encourage the omission of a full stop lest it seem passive-aggressive. As astonishing as this sounds, casual messages exchanged rapidly on screen are far more comfortable with emojis and exclamation marks to indicate a positive response. If you wanted to test out the potential aggression of a full stop, think only of an exchange in which you want to congratulate someone on a particular achievement. 'That's great!' shows a shared excitement, while a stopless 'that's great' might be a speedy if underwhelming response, but with 'That's great.' there's no disguising a certain amount of resentment.

The scientist Robert Boyle would not have agreed. By the seventeenth century he was warning that 'if the stops be omitted, or misplaced, it does ... oftentimes quite spoil the sense.' Or, indeed, an entire space launch.

23 July

BREATHING WHILE

English has lost many of its old markers of time, ones which wore their Germanic ancestry lightly. While German retains *vorgestern* for the 'day before yesterday', and *übermorgen* for the 'day after tomorrow', English has somehow lost 'ereyesterday' and the delightfully pithy 'overmorrow', as well as 'yestreen' for 'yesterday evening'.

When it comes to an exact number of hours, we also seem to have made things more cumbersome rather than less. 'Sesquihoral' once had the very specific meaning of 'lasting an hour and a half', while the tides would be counted in 'semidiurnal' terms: every twelve hours. 'Whiles' were measured according to the duration of each task, leading to a 'speech while', the time it takes to make a speech; a 'paternoster while', for the recital of Our Father; and a 'breathing while', the time required to take a slow breath in and out.

What is perhaps most perplexing in terms of English descriptions of duration, however, is that 'next weekend' is still open to interpretation depending on who is using it, and the day of the week on which it is used. Similarly, 'biannually' still carries the dual meaning of 'twice a year' or 'once every two years'. The time has surely come to fix this, perhaps after a little breathing while.

24 July

FORGETTERY

It is an experience universally acknowledged that many of us walk into a room only to forget completely the reason for doing so. To scientists, this phenomenon is less subtly known as the Doorway Effect, which involves a temporary lapse in memory when you go to do something specific but then fail to remember what that something was. The Doorway Effect apparently arises from our brain travelling through different hierarchies of attention requirements, ranging from instinctive tasks where we don't think much about what we're doing, to others that require real concentration. When we shift from one to the other, we can fall into a buffer zone where our brain loses sight of the task at hand. Often the transition involves moving from the mental to the physical and back again: we have gone to the bedroom and met one task, but the rationale for it becomes blurry. Forgetting (or, as they put it in the fifteenth century, 'unremembering') is not necessarily a bad thing. The philosopher and thinker Alan Watts often used the term 'forgettery' as a counterpart to memory, emphasizing the importance of letting go of past experiences and beliefs to experience the present moment fully. 'If you always, and always, and always remembered everything, you see, you would be like a piece of paper which had been painted over, and painted over, and painted over, until there was no space left and you wouldn't be able to distinguish between one thing and another.'

25 July

LION-COLOUR

In 1834, a periodical for the manufacturing industry discussed important ancient legislation, including laws passed during the reign of Edward VI to address a dissatisfaction with 'unnecessary varieties of colours' among those who consequently 'thought it a duty to expunge the superfluous ones'. The result was a complete list of approved cloth shades that included not only standard dyes such as greens, yellows, crimson, orange, etc., but also some rather odd candidates, such as the somewhat vague 'colour of a lion', 'sheep's colour', and even a 'sad new colour', an emotional designation which remains frustratingly unspecified.

Missing from the list is 'turquoise', which was not designated a colour until the middle of the nineteenth century, some time after Edward's bizarre legislation. It had, however, been in use for a precious stone of a bluish-green colour found in Persia, now Iran, even though its name reflects a different geography, for the French *pierre turquoise* meant 'stone from Turkey', because it was transported to Europe from there.

Turquoise is one of several colours which take their names from places that influenced their history. 'Damask', used of a lustrous fabric as well as a greyish red, was associated with Damascus, the 'pearl of the East', while 'eau-de-nil', an adopted French term for a weak green colour which became the height of fashion in the 1870s, was thought to resemble the waters of the Nile.

26 July

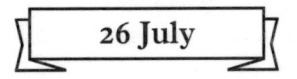

PECKSNIFFIAN

July 1844 saw the publication of the final instalment of *Martin Chuzzlewit*, Charles Dickens's sixth novel. Its story involves an elderly misanthrope of the same name, close to death and surrounded by sycophantic relatives who are eager to inherit his money. Mistrust, greed, and hypocrisy abound as the story charts the fortunes of the old man's grandson and namesake, young Martin Chuzzlewit, who in seeking his own way in the world begins to question his inherited self-interest.

Compared with the author's previous wildly popular works, the story proved something of a flop. It nonetheless contributed two terms to the English language, most famously the word 'gamp', an umbrella, inspired by the character of the drunken and corrupt nurse Mrs Gamp, who always carries one.

Less well known but arguably much more useful today is 'Pecksniffian', another eponym. Seth Pecksniff is a sanctimonious do-gooder who, despite his holier-than-thou attitude and apparently spotless character, will stop at nothing to advance his own interests.

> Mr Pecksniff was in the frequent habit of using any word that occurred to him as having a good sound, and rounding a sentence well, without much care for its meaning. And he did this so boldly, and in such an imposing manner, that he would sometimes stagger the wisest people with his eloquence, and make them gasp again.

Within five years of the novel's final instalment, 'Pecksniffian' had become a pithy description of unctuous hypocrisy and self-serving interference into other people's affairs.

27 July

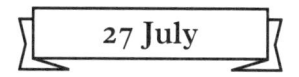

HASTE POST HASTE

In the early summer of 1920, the US Post Office resorted to extraordinary measures to stop a practice that was growing out of control. It involved the posting of young babies and children via the mail service: if they weighed under 50 lb, it was by far the cheapest method of transport for families with little to spare. Photographs of the time show disconsolate postmen carrying mailbags from which equally forlorn children peek out.

The reason we 'post' parcels in the first place is rooted in a time when letters were transported in a relay system that involved several riders on horseback. These riders were 'posted' at set intervals along the route and were themselves called 'posts'. Each rider would pass the letter on to the next fresh horseman at these fixed stages of the journey. If a letter was urgent, it would be marked with the direction 'haste, post, haste', a forerunner of the Special Delivery of today's Post Office. The term was current by the sixteenth century and 'post haste' was soon being used to describe the need for speed in any activity.

The US word 'mail' tells a different story. It came into English from French but is a relative of the Dutch *maal*, meaning 'wallet, bag'. The use of the word for a postal service arose in the mid seventeenth century, thanks to the bag in which letters were carried. The names of newspapers such as the *Daily Mail* and the *Washington Post* still reflect the idea of an 'item delivered' – but preferably not a baby.

28 July

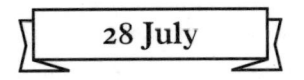

TSUNDOKU

For book-lovers there is nothing quite like the comfort of being surrounded by shelves of enticing stories, as yet unread. As one season turns to another, many of our most recent book purchases still lie unfinished, a fact we seem to forget as we venture into another bookshop and lovingly select a handful of new titles to add to the pile. This, for the Japanese, is *tsundoku*, a word with the literal meaning of 'piled-up reading' and which describes the act of adding to that growing collection of books that you may never quite get round to. Summer might just be the time to kick back, whether by a pool, in a garden or on your sofa, and actually read them.

29 July

SPITTING IMAGE

A popular story about King Umberto I of Italy, who was assassinated on this day in 1900, tells of a meal at a restaurant in the town of Monza, at which the king was astounded to note that its owner was his dead-ringer double. Upon talking to the man Umberto is said to have learned of an astonishing number of connections between their lives, including the fact that the two men had been born not just in the same town, but also on the same day, and had both married on the same date. Furthermore, the king's lookalike had opened a restaurant on the very day of Umberto's coronation. Umberto's assassination is said to have happened on the same summer's day that he received the news that the restaurateur had died in a shooting.

The concept of the doppelgänger (from the German for 'double-goer') has intrigued us for centuries. The first meaning of the term was the apparition of a living person: a wraith considered to be a portent of bad luck. More prosaic is the expression 'spitting image', meaning an exact likeness. It is also found as 'splitting image', which appears at around the same time, and which suggests a similarity so strong that it is as though a person has been split in two. The origin of both phrases is the older expression 'spit and image', which suggests someone so like another that they could have been spat straight out of the latter's mouth. Say 'spit and' fast enough and you will get 'spitten' or, later, 'spitting'.

As for 'dead ringer', contrary to urban legend, this has nothing to do with the tradition of burying people with a bell in case they were still alive, so that they could sound an alarm from underground. 'Dead' here is used in the sense of 'exact' – as in 'dead straight' – while a 'ringer' was a term in racing circles for a horse fraudulently substituted for another.

30 July

FRĒOND-SPĒDIG

'A day without a friend is like a pot without a single drop of honey left inside.' On International Friendship Day, these words from A.A. Milne's Winnie-the-Pooh are worth remembering, together with a term from Old English that once described one of the greatest riches life can offer. *Frēond-spēdig* meant simply 'rich in friends', in which *frēond* is the oldest spelling of 'friend', and *spēdig* means 'wealthy'.

31 July

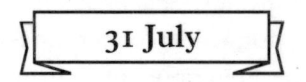

MATRISATE

'Fatherhood is great,' the comedian Jon Stewart once quipped, 'because you get to ruin someone from scratch.' John Betjeman famously provided the perspective from the ruined child's point of view. But like it or not, many of us do end up like our parents, however much we fight against it. 'Twas ever thus, it seems, for in Latin this was known by philosophers as *patrissare*, later to become 'patrisate' in English, meaning 'to take after one's father'. When we 'matrisate', on the other hand, we end up like our mothers, the result perhaps of a 'matricentric' home: one in which the mother is the head of the family.

AUGUST

1 August

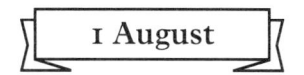

LAMMAS

For all its associations with warmth and idleness, the first day of August traditionally marks the beginning of the gathering-in for winter, and an acknowledgement of the waning of the year.

In Wales, 1 August is the feast of harvest, *Gŵyl Awst*, whose traditions include a 'harvest mare' fashioned from the last sheaf of corn, which is then cut down by the throwing of sickles. Ireland celebrates with *Lughnasadh*, a celebration of Lugh, the Celtic god of craftmanship who is associated with the constellation of Perseus, visible in the north-east sky throughout August. Both are demigods of light.

On this day the early Christian church would celebrate the harvesting of the first ripe corn by consecrating loaves that were made from it. They duly called the day *hlāfmæsse*, 'loaf mass', which evolved into the name 'Lammas', just as *hlæfdige*, used for the mistress of a household or wife of a lord, and literally the 'bread-kneader', became 'lady'. The linguistic origins of Lammas were eventually forgotten, and the custom of bringing a lamb into the cathedral church of York was established as a way of giving a different explanation for the name. In the sixteenth century, 'until latter Lammas' was used in the same way as 'until Doomsday', implying a day that will never come.

2 August

SUPERCILIAN

The lesser-known relative of the adjective 'supercilious', a 'supercilian' is the individual who exhibits haughtily contemptuous behaviour. The word came and went in the seventeenth century, but it offers a good example of the extent to which eyes pop out everywhere in English, especially where you least expect them. 'Supercilious' comes straight from the Latin for 'eyebrow', the implication being that the brows of a supercilian are frequently raised in arrogance.

The Greek word for 'eye', meanwhile, was *ōps* (hence the Cyclops, as well as the family of words that includes 'optician'). The literal meaning of 'autopsy' is 'a seeing with one's own eyes', because careful visual observation is vital in diagnosing the cause of death. A 'synopsis' is a general view or summary: literally a 'seeing all at once', and the toughest of all dinosaurs, the triceratops, was given a name meaning the 'three-horned eye'.

3 August

COMMA

Punctuation is a serious matter, sometimes deadly serious. Take the comma, for example. 'There are people who embrace the Oxford comma and people who don't,' wrote Lynne Truss in *Eats, Shoots & Leaves*, adding, 'and I'll just say this: *never* get between these people when drink has been taken.' Otherwise known as the 'serial comma' (which strongly suggests it belongs in an offenders' institution), the usage has been the preferred house style of Oxford Dictionaries for over a century, hence its name. Put simply, it is the comma that comes before 'and' or before 'or' in a series of three or more items in a list. So 'we ate steak, green beans, and chips' includes an Oxford comma, which in this case changes little and is purely a matter of taste. In other cases, though, the comma avoids costly ambiguity, most famously in the sentence: 'I dedicate this book to my parents, George and Mother Teresa.'

On the other side of the fence are those who consider it to be the fusspot member of the punctuation family, whose clutter and busyness is unwelcome in any text. Not that they are without their own laughs at the Oxford comma's expense. A joke among linguists runs, 'Sam, a semicolon, and an Oxford comma walk into a bar. They both have a great time.'

In 2018, three lorry drivers in Portland, Maine, rested their entire case regarding lost overtime pay on the omission of an Oxford comma in state legislature. The state's law sets out that overtime is not payable to workers involved in 'The canning, processing, preserving, freezing, drying, marketing, storing, packing for shipment or distribution of goods.' The drivers successfully argued that as there was no comma after 'shipment' the implication was that 'distribution' here still related to the packing, and therefore didn't exclude them from overtime pay. They settled for compensation of $5 million.

A comma can also mean the difference between life and death. On this day in 1916 Sir Roger Casement was hanged for treason. A passionate Irish nationalist, his offence had been to try to persuade Irish First World War prisoners in Germany to join the Irish uprising. A critical issue in the case against him was whether the Treason Act of 1351 applied to actions outside the UK. This turned on whether a key provision was modified by a comma. Two of the judges visited the record office to inspect the original document but could not make out whether the mark in question was a comma, bracket, or even a fold in the paper. Unfortunately for Casement, they decided that it *was* a comma and found him guilty. He declared 'I am being hanged on a comma', which was literally (in the traditional sense) true.

4 August

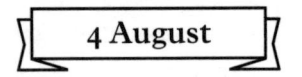

SEABISCUIT

The run-up to any US presidential election is long and arduous. By the summer of the election year the byzantine process of primaries and caucuses has ended, and the campaign trail kicks off in earnest. The lexicon of the process is just as complex, steeped in the history and geography of the country and its peoples. 'Caucus' itself is an anglicization of an Algonquian term for 'he who urges or encourages'.

In the slang of 1930s America, a 'whistle-stop' was a small or remote town which trains would pass straight through unless prompted to stop by a signal from a conductor's whistle. Such places often featured on the campaign trail of presidential candidates, who would stop briefly before moving on to the next. This sense of a series of rapid visits nudged 'whistle-stop' into the more general meaning of something fleeting and superficial.

Elsewhere, there may be talk of 'gerrymandering', the changing of electoral boundaries that takes its name from the salamander shape of a Massachusetts voting district reconfigured by Governor Elbridge Gerry in the nineteenth century, or of a 'seabiscuit', a candidate who comes from behind to win, just like the horse of that name who took part in a race in 1938 that became so dramatic that Franklin D. Roosevelt stopped a cabinet meeting to listen in. Seabiscuit beat all the odds to become a symbol of hope in the Great Depression.

5 August

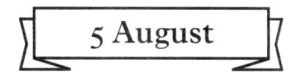

CELLAR DOOR

In a lecture in 1955, J.R.R. Tolkien offered a combination of words that he considered perfect in its entirety, irrespective of its meaning. As a Professor of Anglo-Saxon and a former lexicographer at the *Oxford English Dictionary*, he knew what he was talking about. His chosen pairing was 'cellar door'. 'More beautiful,' he told his audience, 'than, say, "sky", and far more beautiful than "beautiful".'

As it happens, Tolkien wasn't the first to admire the mellifluousness of the two words: writers before him had considered their particular euphony. The subject of such thoughts is known as 'phonoaesthetics', the study of the pleasing quality of words. Tolkien's use of 'cellar door' popularized the idea that certain word combinations can be beautiful simply due to their sound, regardless of their meaning or context.

6 August

BUCCANEER

The word 'barbecue' takes us to foreign climes and Haiti, where a wooden framework used for curing meat over an open fire was called, in the native language of Taino, the *barbacoa*. The term was borrowed into Spanish and passed into English as 'barbecue' in the seventeenth century.

In South America, meat chargrilled over an open fire is known as *churrasco*. In the same way as 'barbecue' moved from the cooking to the social occasion that accompanies it, a *churrasco* is also an outdoor gathering in warm weather at which food is prepared over an open fire. The word is a variant of the Spanish *socarrar*, meaning 'to scorch or singe'.

A similar framework for curing and smoking meat over a pit fire was known as a *boucan*, used by French settlers in the West Indies. A person who hunted for food and cooked meat in this way was known as a *boucanier*, which became 'buccaneer' in English and which was extended to those who 'hunted' on the high seas. Perhaps there is something in the stereotype of male possessiveness over outdoor cooking, as the barbecue buccaneers rub their hands in anticipation of adventure, hunter-gatherers once more.

7 August

GAZEBO

As sunshine lasts long into the night and barbecues are lit, some of us like to add a gazebo to the mix. This can be anything from a highly decorative building with open sides to a more basic canopy erected in the garden. Tomb paintings suggest that as early as 2600 BC the Egyptians were installing gazebos in their gardens, while in ancient Greece, gazebos frequently displayed statues dedicated to the gods. It was wealthy Persians who brought several layers of sophistication to these outdoor structures, adding marble floors, ornate decoration, and elaborate water features to their gazebos.

There is a pretty theory that the name 'gazebo' is a rough anglicization of the French exclamation *que c'est beau!* ('how beautiful it is!'). More likely is that it is built upon the English 'gaze' and the Latin future ending *-ebo*, producing a word that means 'I shall gaze'. If true, this would put 'gazebo' alongside 'belvedere' in the etymological dictionary, a similar structure built to offer fine views and which translates from Italian as 'beautiful to see'.

Less ornate, though not always, is the humble shed, which has been housing people and tools for centuries. Its name derives from the Old English *shadde*, which is related to 'shade'. It is unrelated to the other use of 'shed', meaning 'to cast off', even if the garden shed is where many shed their worries and their partners. That sense derives from an ancient word meaning 'to separate off', which can be the entire point of a shelter that offers peace from the main home and the people in it.

8 August

FOLK-LEASING

It was on this day in 1974 that Richard Nixon announced his resignation from the office of US president as the result of Watergate, the shorthand for the cover-up of a burglary of the offices of the Democratic National Committee by those inside Nixon's administration. Watergate was the name of the complex containing the offices in the Foggy Bottom district of Washington DC. Even by the time of Nixon's resignation, the '-gate' suffix was being attached to other scandals involving deceit and collusion.

Samuel Johnson, in his *Dictionary of the English Language* of 1755, defined 'scandal' with characteristic acerbity. It was, he wrote, 'Offence given by the faults of others.' This was far from the earliest meaning of the word, however, which was entirely religious, involving discredit brought upon a faith by unseemly conduct. Its roots are the Latin *scandalum*, used of both a physical stumbling and the moral kind. It replaced older terms for very public lying, including the Old English 'folk-leasing', which drew on an obsolete use of 'lease' to mean 'issuing falsehoods'.

9 August

NUDDLING

'Nuddling', in Cheshire and in Shetland, is what animals do when they nudge heads while feeding – 'nud' here is a synonym for 'nuzzle'. Cats may thank their lucky owners by nuddling them just before they tuck into their food. And even a building might nuddle if it leans at a certain angle, such as the bell tower in Italy whose construction began on this day in 1173 and which was forever to be known as the Leaning Tower of Pisa.

But there is a more modern sense of the word that is creeping in, thanks to the terrible posture many of us have while bent over our electronic devices. Today's nuddling involves the act of walking or sitting with one's head stooped, as when lost in thought, or – too often – staring at a mobile phone. The result might once have been called the 'dowager's hump' due to its association with elderly women. Today's version is scarcely an improvement: say hello, reluctantly, to the 'tech neck'.

10 August

THE WALLS HAVE EARS

The desire to eavesdrop is as old as time. 'Eavesdropping' itself was the habit of those who stood by their home's 'eavesdrip', the ground onto which water dripped from the eaves, to tune into the conversations of their neighbours. Spy tech may sound more modern, but it is equally steeped in history. Before the invention of recorded sound, most listening devices were an extension of the physical structure of a building. The Renaissance scholar Athanasius Kircher, author of the first detailed study of the science of acoustics, devised architectural systems such as ventilation ducts for courts and palaces that allowed residents to hear sounds in other rooms. Domes in various churches and castles, including St Paul's Cathedral, have 'whispering galleries' that transport sound along their curved surfaces, allowing the softest utterances to be carried from one side of the dome to the other.

On this day in 1793 the Louvre Palace in Paris reopened as a museum, on the anniversary of the fall of the French monarchy. Some of its rooms were said to be constructed, at the behest of Catherine de' Medici, so that what was said in one room could be heard distinctly in another. This was thanks to a contrivance that allowed the suspicious queen to become acquainted with state secrets and plots. These tubes of communication were known as the *auriculaires*. It is thought that devices like these inspired the proverbial warning 'the walls have ears', for listeners may be everywhere.

11 August

GOWPEN

A splash of cold water upon waking up, a scoop of earth while potting a plant, a quantity of biscuits to go with an afternoon cuppa: any or all of these might involve the informal measurement that is a 'gowpen', a word from regional English and Scots that means two hands placed together so as to form a bowl and so, by extension, what you can contain within it – roughly a 'double handful'.

12 August

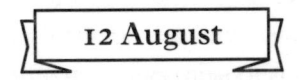

OPACAROPHILE

As the days lengthen, many of us take the chance to renew our awe at the natural world by contemplating its sunsets. There is apparently an evolutionary purpose to finding beauty in such phenomena. The philosopher Denis Dutton believed that the rolling plains of so much landscape art are beautiful to the human eye precisely because they remind us of the savanna of the Pleistocene epoch, when humans were developing aesthetic appreciation. Red sunsets were even more visible across open land, and retreating to the safety of a night-time shelter would allow for a greater appreciation of the vibrant colours of the skies.

For any lover of sunsets, it is nice to know that a name has been invented for us: 'opacarophile' is made up of the Latin *opacare*, 'to darken', and the Greek *philos*, 'loving'.

The Middle East has two lovely words to add to the picture. The Arabic *samar* means to sit together in conversation at sunset, while later into the night a *samir*, from Persian, is someone who converses by moonlight.

13 August

POCHEMUCHKA

'Are we nearly there yet?': five words that can make a parent on a long car journey run the emotional gamut from anxious to zombified, with a spot of murderous intent in-between. English once had a word for such repeated and grating entreaties, namely 'rogitating', which for some unknown reason came and went in the seventeenth century. Russian, on the other hand, has preserved the word *pochemuchka*, derived from the Russian word *pochemu*, 'why?', which is used by parents as a term of endearment. It describes someone (often a child) whose insatiable curiosity leads them to ask far too many questions.

14 August

PLUM RAIN

This is the time of dog-day afternoons – the hottest days of summer when dogs can do little except hug the shade as best they can. Rather than taking their name from our canine friends, however, these times of languorous inactivity are named after Sirius, the Dog Star, long associated with sultry weather in the northern hemisphere because it rises simultaneously with the sun during the height of summer. At this time of year it may be 'a-swullocking' and 'a-sweltering' out there, and many of us will be longing for the relief of rain after a long dry spell.

Japanese has a large reservoir of terms for summer rain, depending on its intensity or effect. There is *teknyuu*, the rain that falls from cloudless skies, and *ryokuu*, the first rain of summer, while the rainy season itself is *tsuyu*, 'plum rain', because this is the time when plums are ripening.

15 August

BLUE PENCIL

The flamboyant raconteur Quentin Crisp defined 'euphemism' as 'unpleasant truths wearing diplomatic cologne'. It's a neat summary of the function of a device whose name comes from the Greek for 'speaking fair'. It doesn't, however, quite allow for the dark humour that many euphemisms inject, something that softens the fear of a subject such as death, or the out-thereness of those such as sex and other bodily activities. From 'popping one's clogs' and 'pushing up the daisies', to 'rumpy-pumpy' and 'siphoning the python', there is a mischievousness to euphemisms that draws attention to the very thing they describe, rather than masks it.

In the Middle Ages, when some of today's strongest taboos were still fair game in everyday conversation, it was religious blasphemy that required the biggest fig leaves. A large lexicon of sidesteps around mentions of God emerged, including 'gorblimey' (God blind me), 'zounds' (God's wounds), 'drat' (God rot), 'Jeepers Creepers' (Jesus Christ), and the gleeful exclamations 'Gadsbudlikins!' for 'God's body' and 'Bejabbers!' for 'By Jesus'.

'Minced oaths' such as these proliferated over the centuries that followed and became a requirement in such arenas as Elizabethan theatre in the face of Puritan opposition to profanity. By the nineteenth century, Charles Dickens was assuring his sensitive readers that he would 'banish from the lips' of all his characters 'any expression that could by possibility offend'. This included the word 'damned', which was represented in novels such as *Great Expectations* simply by its initial 'D'. Not that Dickens was entirely po-faced about the subject, however. In an article on crime, entitled 'On Duty with Inspector Field', he has fun with words that needed bleeping out:

> I won't, says Bark, have no adjective police and adjective strangers in my adjective premises! I won't, by adjective and substantive! Give me my trousers, and I'll send the whole adjective police to adjective and substantive!

It is interesting that the author nonetheless allowed himself the use of the word 'trousers', which offended delicate Victorian ears thanks to the very parts of the male anatomy they covered, leading to such euphemisms as 'unmentionables' and 'sit-upons'.

In Dickens's day, censorship was traditionally carried out by means of a pencil with a blue lead, a tradition that continued well into the Second World War, when newspapers would submit any story containing potentially sensitive information to the censor for scrutiny: all redactions would be marked in blue. There are several theories that explain the choice of blue specifically, from the blue flame of burning brimstone, characteristic of hell, to the blue gown that sex workers were required to wear in prison. There may also be a connection with a category of popular French literature sold in the seventeenth and eighteenth centuries that was aimed at lower-class readers and was known as *bibliothèque bleue*, because it was sold in blue paper covers.

Whatever its origin, 'blue pencil' has survived as a means of crossing something out in order to avoid offence. Perhaps Victorian gentlemen carried one in the pocket of their unmentionables.

16 August

THE DEVIL RIDES ON A FIDDLE-STICK

A singing frog named Flip, who lays on a rousing musical performance for a host of woodland animals, may not be remembered as fondly as Mickey Mouse, but he can at least lay claim to a significant milestone in animation history. Flip the Frog leads the cast of *Fiddlesticks*, the first colour cartoon to be made with synchronized sound, which was released on this day in 1930. His creator was Ub Iwerks, who, with Walt Disney, was to become the inventor of the world's most famous mouse. Seventy years later, *Fiddlesticks* can be seen playing on a TV in the background of an Eminem video for his track 'The Real Slim Shady'.

The earliest use of 'fiddle-sticks' was, unsurprisingly, entirely musical, referring to a violin bow strung with horsehair. Both 'fiddle' and 'violin' descend from the name of Vitula, the Roman goddess of joy. A century after its first use, the expression 'the devil rides upon a fiddle-stick' was used by Shakespeare in his play *Henry IV* to mean 'here's a fine commotion', a reference to both a witch's broomstick and the cacophony that might result from the devil taking hold of a musical instrument. From there, 'fiddlesticks' was added to the already-bulging lexicon for nonsense, to mean at best 'insignificant' and at worst 'nothing at all'. Thanks to its initial letter, it has also become a handy euphemism for a stronger swear word, moving it even further away from the innocence of Flip the Frog.

17 August

OFF THE CUFF

'Travis looks in the mirror.' These bare words are the only stage direction in the script for ninety of the most famous seconds in the history of cinema, given to the actor Robert De Niro, who was born on this day in 1943. In fact 'script' can only be applied very loosely to the scene in the film *Taxi Driver* for which no dialogue was written, making De Niro's now infamous and entirely off-the-cuff words 'You talking to me?' even more remarkable.

Our earliest records of 'off the cuff' suggest that the expression originated in the US just a few decades earlier. The reference is thought to be to the practice of performers of writing notes on their shirt cuffs as a handy backup, in case they forgot their lines. In Charlie Chaplin's 1936 film *Modern Times,* Chaplin's character, a waiter, is required to stand in for a romantic tenor to entertain the patrons. Desperate to keep his job, he is well aware of the stakes after a series of comedic mishaps. To prepare, he writes the song's lyrics on his shirt cuffs as a form of cheat sheet. The plan inevitably goes awry during the energetic performance, when the waiter's cuffs are flung off and he is suddenly promptless.

Chaplin's character delivers a hilarious performance in which he sings in a mix of Italian, French, and total gibberish, but he holds his tune, and the audience is delighted. There is a lot to be said for improvising when there is nothing to lose.

18 August

GALLINIPPER

In the southern states of the US, a 'gallinipper' describes an extremely large mosquito, especially one seen during the 'mafficking', humid days of summer. Most commonly, as the 'shaggy-legged gallinipper', it is used of the *Psorophora ciliata*, a species known for its particularly aggressive behaviour towards humans. The 'nipper' part of its name clearly suggests something capable of taking a hearty bite.

Arguably none of these are as terrifying as the gallinipper of African-American folklore, a species of creatures so large that their bones could surround a 140-acre field. Such was their hold on the imagination they even made appearances in blues songs of the 1920s and 1930s, including 'Mosquito Moan' by Blind Lemon Jefferson.

All of which is a strong recommendation for a mosquito net around your bed, and many before us felt the same. The word 'canopy' comes directly from the Greek *kōnōps*, 'mosquito'.

19 August

LOVE APPLE

Oysters, asparagus, almonds ... the belief that certain foods encourage sexual attraction and arousal is ancient. Few of us might think to throw a tomato in there, but a quick look at the ripe and plump specimens that become available over the summer months might justify its inclusion in the list. In the sixteenth century, this was particularly obvious, for the fruit (yes) went by such epithets as the *pomme d'amour*, as well as the 'love', 'amorous', 'raging', or 'mad' apple. When Spanish colonizers brought this exotic specimen back to Europe, the belief in its legendary powers came with them. And not just as an aphrodisiac: some Europeans were highly suspicious of the tomato, assuming it to be toxic given its supposed membership of the nightshade family. Its scientific name is *lycopersicon*, 'wolf peach': the latter on account of its round form, and the former by association with 'wolfsbane', a member of the nightshade family that was said to be able to summon werewolves.

In the years that followed, the 'love apple' ceded its name to another, borrowed from the Aztecs who had been enjoying the fruit for centuries. In their native language of Nahuatl it was known as *tomatl*, which became *tomate* in French. Since the potato had been introduced some decades earlier, the name evolved in English to mimic the model of 'potato' – hence the spelling 'tomato'. As for its use as an aphrodisiac, there may be some science to it, for research suggests the fruit's acids may stimulate blood flow to the lips and mouth.

20 August

SAN FAIRY ANN

On 20 August 1914 the German 1st Army entered Brussels, while the 2nd Army gathered around the fortified city of Namur, the one remaining obstacle to the Meuse route into France. The Battle of the Frontiers, as the group of engagements became known, involved more than two million troops and was the largest battle of the war.

For all its destruction, wartime can be surprisingly productive when it comes to new vocabulary. During the First World War, the slang of the trenches included a fair amount of mangling of the French phrases overheard by British soldiers on the front line. A few of these survived and made their way home, and 'san fairy (or ferry) ann' is one of them. Used as an expression of indifference or resignation, it is a reworking of the French *ça ne fait rien*, 'it doesn't matter'.

Other phrases that resulted from poorly apprehended pronunciations include 'toot sweet' (from *tout de suite*, 'immediately'), and 'napoo', (from *il n'y en a plus*, 'there is no more'), which was used as an exclamation to mean 'finished!', 'done for!', 'goodbye!'

21 August

KNOCK-KNOCK

On this day in 1879, in Knock in Ireland's County Mayo, an apparition of Mary, Joseph, and St John the Evangelist was allegedly seen by fifteen people – men, women, and children – at the local church. They claimed to have watched the apparition for two hours in the pouring rain, and an official inquiry ruled that their evidence was trustworthy. A shrine built at the site became a place of pilgrimage and a number of miraculous cures are said to have occurred there. So great is the desire to visit, there is even a Knock airport, with regular flights to Rome.

Disbelievers might call this a different kind of knock-knock joke, but they are of course entirely unrelated. The history of the joke's format may surprise, however. The earliest example we have in its current form comes from the 'HeeHaw News' column of an Iowa newspaper in 1936. To today's eyes it would seem quite tame:

Knock – knock
Who's there?
Rufus
Rufus Who?
Rufus the most important part of the house.

Not only does the joke lack any amount of heehaw, but it was far from the first example of the formula. Even Shakespeare manages a look-in in the joke's history, with wordplay that originated in *Macbeth*, when a porter who is still worse for wear from the previous night's drinking hears a knocking and muses aloud how, were he the gatekeeper of hell, he would be kept very busy. With each repeated knock at the door (from Macduff, as we later discover), the Porter ponders various fictional characters who might come visiting. There is little humour here either, for the first is a farmer who has hanged himself because of poor financial prospects. He is followed by an 'equivocator' whose only allegiance is to himself, and finally by a tailor who steals by skimping on the cloth for his customers' trousers. Each character's knock on this fictional stage receives a shouted 'Knock, knock. Who's there?'

Of course, Shakespeare offers none of the pay-offs we can expect from the modern knock-knock repertoire, but as always, his wordplay is rich enough without it. Nonetheless, if we credit him with the invention of the knock-knock exchange, then the tradition of the genre demands we give him the no-bell prize.

22 August

SENT TO COVENTRY

The English Civil War was declared on this day in 1642, when King Charles I formally raised the royal standard at Nottingham. Linguistically, it was to bequeath us many terms, from 'cavalier' to 'puritanical', as well as 'sent to Coventry'. The city was staunchly Parliamentarian, and did not look kindly upon those loyal to the king. All Royalist soldiers sent there were said to be given the cold shoulder by the inhabitants.

Exile has gone by many different names. An Athenian citizen considered unworthy of society would be chosen for expulsion from the city by a ballot system involving a series of votes by *ostrakon*, a pottery shard upon which the person's name would be etched. This is the root of the English word 'ostracize'.

23 August

NEEK

The trajectory of words for those who hold an extreme passion for the intricacies of a particular subject has bucked the usual trend in language, in that they have become progressively more positive over the years; elsewhere, the dictionary tends to reflect a strong pessimism bias as words evolve. 'Nerd', for example, is a word on the move. Originally an American term, recorded from the 1950s, it appeared in the book *If I Ran the Zoo* by the author and cartoonist Dr Seuss: 'I'll sail to Ka-Tro/And Bring Back an It-Kutch, a Preep and a Proo/A Nerkle, a Nerd, and a Seersucker, too!' This may be the origin of the word, although the leap from an imaginary animal to an obsessive and boring fan seems quite bold. Alternatively, its story may have begun with Mortimer Snerd, a dummy used by the American ventriloquist Edgar Bergen in the 1930s. Whatever its origin, being a 'nerd' is no longer a thing of shame, but rather a marker of knowledge and expertise.

The same is true of 'geek', which has achieved even greater heights, quite astonishingly given it was once a label applied to performers at freak shows who would undertake such intense acts as biting the heads off live snakes in front of a gasping crowd. The idea of extreme and obsessive behaviour eventually attached itself to computer-related tasks or niche subject areas. Today, it is a word largely worn with pride.

Not so, as yet, for the 'neek', the latest kid on a block that combines 'geek' and 'nerd' to describe a dull or unlikeable person, once more with an extreme interest in one particular subject. Linguistically it's predictable: a portmanteau or mash-up that has become the most popular form of word-coining. But its predominantly negative uses suggest it is very much at the bottom of the likeability ladder. Everyone loves a geek; no one wants to be a neek, even on Find Your Inner Nerd Day.

24 August

FINIFUGAL

Whether it's the summer holiday, your favourite box set, a book which keeps you reading into the small hours, or a relationship that begins to splutter, there is an underused word to describe the fear of something coming to an end. 'Finifugal' is an adjective based on the Latin for 'end-flight', and it simply involves our shunning the end of something because we want it to go on for ever.

25 August

INTERDESPISE

There is little comfort in the knowledge that English offers a word for despising someone as much as they despise you. Yet there is no doubt that 'interdespise', from the nineteenth century, can come in useful, as bitter feuds between rivals and lovers have proved for centuries, from Gladstone and Disraeli to Tony Blair and Gordon Brown, Michelangelo and da Vinci to Ernest Hemingway and William Faulkner.

Mutual loathing certainly characterized the relationship between Gore Vidal and his nemesis Truman Capote, who died on this day in 1984. Vidal, a brilliant writer and public intellectual known for his excoriating pronouncements on society and politics, and those who strutted their stage, was easily rattled when others stood in the limelight he felt belonged to him. Capote was one such individual, winning plaudits for his novel while Vidal's own faltered. When the two men eventually met, Vidal's friend Jay Parini recorded Vidal's memory of it:

> I first met Truman at Anaïs Nin's apartment. My first impression – as I wasn't wearing my glasses – was that it was a colourful ottoman. When I sat down on it, it squealed. It was Truman.

The two men squabbled continually under the public gaze, openly criticizing each other's writing style with swipes that ranged from catty to bitter. Their interdespising continued until Capote, ill from addictions to drugs and alcohol, died. Vidal was informed of his rival's death by his editor over the phone and, after only the briefest pause, remarked, 'A wise career move.'

26 August

GROPING A GULL

The act of scamming has attracted as many descriptions over the centuries as its perpetrators, ranging from 'groping a gull' and 'plucking a pigeon' in the sixteenth century, to 'licking another's fingers' and 'living upon the shark' in the seventeenth. These were a lot more vivid than today's 'phishing' – the umbrella term for impersonation scams and a simple respelling of 'fishing', because the fraudsters try to reel us in. But their hooks are as lethal as ever, and their spiel is just as seductive.

In August 1835, the New York *Sun* published a series of articles that claimed to have found life on the moon. The paper attributed the discovery to the astronomer Sir John Herschel and a fictional companion, Andrew Grant, who it related had used an immense telescope built on entirely new principles. The articles described a lunar landscape with forests and seas, populated by humanoid creatures. Herschel, initially amused by the hoax, grew increasingly irritable when he realized many readers took it seriously. The articles were not exposed as bogus until several weeks later, when they were duly dubbed the Great Moon Hoax.

The word 'hoax' is believed to be a shortening of the 'hocus pocus' of old-time charlatans, which took its name from a sham Latin formula – *hocus pocus, tontus talontus, vade celeriter jubeo* – that was used by conjurors to distract from their sleight of hand. Thanks to the deliberate deflection by such 'patter' (from another rapid recitation, this time of the 'paternoster' prayer), the idea of trickery was born. As for groping a gull, this thankfully involved no seabirds: rather a 'gull' was someone who was easily duped, and the sister word to 'gullible'.

27 August

LAGOM

The 'umbles' that originally went into 'umbles pie', later playfully converted to 'humble pie', involved the entrails of deer, given to lowlier guests at a grand dinner while those of higher status were served the best cuts of meat. This idea of simple sufficiency may have inspired the word 'umblement', which once belonged to the dialect of Kent, and which meant 'the minimum required'. If you put a slightly more positive spin on it you end up with the Swedish *lagom*, a Goldilocks word that means 'exactly the right amount; no more, and no less'.

28 August

GADWADDICK

These are the days of wander. And what better approach to a free day than going on an extended gadwaddick? This appropriately bouncy word from Norfolk dialect means simply going on a jaunt or pleasure trip. It is probably based on the sense of 'gadding about' by moving from one location to another in a frivolous and happy manner. Best not to focus on its likely etymology, which was a stick used to spur oxen. Gallivanting and gadwaddicking beneath the sunshine is what it's all about.

29 August

AFTERMATH CHEESE

> Whan the sunne shinth make hay
> Whiche is to say
> Take time whan time cometh
> Lest time steale away

Like all proverbs, this example from the Middle Ages holds an important truth: that dry days in late summer offer the perfect conditions for the cutting of meadows and grasslands and for the harvesting of hay for winter fodder. In the Middle Ages, that cutting would be done by scythe over several days, when teams of farmhands would painstakingly sweep their long blades over the grass in stages. Afterwards, the hay would be left on the surface to dry out before being gathered into haystacks.

In English dialect, a mowing was known as a 'math', a word of Germanic origin that is unrelated to mathematics. In his novel *Castle Gay*, John Buchan wrote of 'meadowland from which an aftermath of hay had lately been taken'. This was the original meaning of our word 'aftermath', used for the crop of new grass that springs up after a field has been mown in summer. Only later did it take on the sense of the set of conditions that arise in the wake of a particular event. 'Aftermath cheese', meanwhile, was cheese made from the milk of cows fed on the aftermath, making it particularly rich in flavour.

30 August

AUNT POLLYS

'Twiddle-diddles', 'jellybags', 'nicknacks', 'gingmabobs', 'whirligigs', 'gonads', 'tallywags', 'nutmegs', 'plums': the lexicon of terms for the testicles positively bulges at the seams. Perhaps it is because of the perceived need for euphemism when approaching such a sensitive subject. But in the realm of 'bollocks' (an entirely neutral term from Old English right up until the seventeenth century), one of the most affectionate synonyms is surely 'Aunt Pollys', defined in *Green's Dictionary of Slang* as 'very, very small testicles', alongside the example 'Geez, yo ant pollys are smaller than chick pees.'

Every year in the final days of August, Serbia hosts the World Gonad Cooking Competition (the Balls Cup for short), when people travel from across the world to compete to cook the most innovative recipe involving testicles. The festival also includes an award for 'ballsy' newsmakers: past winners include US President Barack Obama and pilot Chesley Sullenberger, who landed his plane on the Hudson river after his engines packed up and who must have been flying by the seat of his twiddle-diddles.

31 August

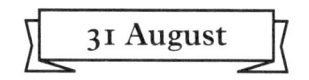

PAGAR A LA INGLESA

One of the many linguistic repercussions of the Anglo-Dutch wars in the seventeenth and eighteenth centuries is the expression 'going Dutch', an idiom that neutrally describes the sharing of a cost today, but which originally implied miserliness on the part of a host. It joins 'Dutch courage', 'double Dutch', and the lesser known 'Dutch consolation' (another way of saying, 'thank God it's not worse') and Dutch wife (a pillow).

None of this is unusual in language wars, when each nation will happily take a pop at another in the form of sarcastic or snide turns of phrase. While English has 'take French leave' for going AWOL without permission, the French like to say *filer à l'anglaise*, 'to leave the English way'. Going Dutch also has a Spanish equivalent, which takes a dig at our very own nation, for they speak of *pagar a la inglesa*, 'to pay the English way'.

SEPTEMBER

1 September

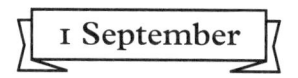

LA RENTRÉE

In France the summer kicks off a national phenomenon whereby entire sections of the population holiday at the same time. The French take their summer break very seriously. Schools are closed, most businesses (unless involved in the tourist industry) adopt shorter opening hours or simply shut up shop for the whole of August, and every man and his dog heads off on their hols. September brings it all crashing down, when *la rentrée*, 'the return', describes the frantic rush of students back to school, businesses reopening, and tanned politicians returning to parliament. This period of frenzied activity in September, when life returns to normal, is known by the same name in Italy, in the form of *il rientro*.

2 September

TIDSOPTIMIST

On 2 September 1752, eleven days were effectively deleted from the year. The Julian calendar, used since 45 BC, had a leap year every four years, which overestimated the solar year by about eleven minutes annually. By the sixteenth century, this had accumulated to roughly ten days of drift, misaligning the calendar with the seasons. The Gregorian calendar, introduced in England in 1752, much later than many other countries, corrected this by refining the leap year rule: a year is a leap year if divisible by four, unless it's a century year, which must be divisible by 400.

Of course, even eleven days might not be enough for those who are notoriously bad at timekeeping. At the less extreme end, there is the person who is habitually a little bit later because they are convinced they have more time than they actually do. Sound familiar? The Swedes have a word for such a person: a *tidsoptimist*, 'time optimist'.

3 September

UMBRAPHILE

September marks the beginning of eclipse season. In 585 BC, the Greek historian Herodotus observed the prolonged and bloody war between the Medes and the Lydians, and surmised it would take an eclipse to end the slaughter. But then, he wrote, 'just as the battle was growing warm, day was on a sudden changed into night ... The Medes and Lydians, when they observed the change, ceased fighting, and were alike anxious to have terms of peace agreed on.'

Throughout much of history, supernatural beliefs have surrounded the phenomenon of the eclipse, when some cultures believe the sun is being devoured by the gods or by monsters as a result of evil or avarice.

A sense of similar failure or deviation hangs around a word that reflects the fading of light during a partial or total eclipse: 'deliquium', which beyond the planets can also describe a loss of consciousness during a fainting spell. Its roots are the Latin *deliquium*, 'eclipse', from *delinquere*, 'to fail, be lacking', which was also the source of the seventeenth-century rarity 'delinque', meaning 'to leave or abandon', and today's much more common 'delinquent'. Meanwhile the edge between night and day on the moon is known as the 'terminator'. At the other end of the spectrum are 'Baily's beads', diamond-ring flashes of light that can often be seen around the circumference of the moon's blackened disc shortly before the total solar eclipse. Then the world goes dark, and birds fall silent. No wonder eclipse-chasing has become such an obsession for 'umbraphiles' (literally 'shadow-lovers') who criss-cross the globe to see them. If you're willing to go anywhere on earth – and many umbraphiles are – a total solar eclipse is visible somewhere in the world every eighteen months.

4 September

SUSPIRE

If we're lucky, the soft zephyrs of summer might linger into September, taking their name from the god of the west wind in Greek myth whose breezes were far more clement than the other wind gods, the Anemoi. For the ancients, however, the winds could affect a person's emotions as much as their physiology. The word in classical Greek for 'breath' and for 'wind' was one and the same, *pneuma*. This was the vital principle of health and strength: a person's very life force, which in turn was 'pneumatic', operated by wind or breath, and, in its earliest sense, related to one's spiritual existence.

For the Romans, too, the human 'spirit', from the Latin *spirare*, 'to breathe', was breathed into the body. *Spirare* inspired a host of other words, including 'aspire', to breathe upon; 'conspire', to breathe together; 'perspire', to breathe through; and 'inspire' itself, which carries the metaphor of breathing hope and ambition into another's soul. Perhaps the most beautiful of all, however, is 'suspire', a verb from the Middle Ages that means to let out a long, deep sigh of emotion.

5 September

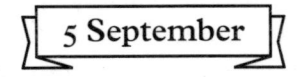

SHTURMOVSHCHINA

A last-minute panic, as the clock ticks down to an inexorable deadline, was known in nineteenth-century English as a 'fit of the clevers'. In Russia's Soviet times this was the *shturmovshchina*, the panicked overtime that proved necessary at the end of a work schedule if the planned production targets were to be met. It was said to involve three stages, each of which would still be familiar to modern workers. First comes *spiachka*, 'hibernation', when workers are not as efficient as they might be. That is followed by *raskachka*, or 'build-up', when things are still fluid, and time still seems sufficient. Finally, *goriachka* arrives, a stage whose name translates to 'fever' and which brings us to the frenetic and panicked attempts to meet a deadline that only now sinks its teeth into us. It is also, as most of us know, the time when productivity is necessarily at its peak.

6 September

I BEFORE *E* . . .

As lexicographers know, the clamour for strong linguistic government never goes away. When the verification of a word is required, a dictionary is the obvious resource, but it is also relied on for much more, namely confirmation of whether a word even exists (if it's not in there, it is deemed to be illegitimate) and how it should be used. In the absence of any academy or other linguistic authority presiding over our language, the dictionary is felt to be the only arbiter there is. It is the lawmaker, the rule-giver, the government of words, the 'logocracy'.

It is always surprising, therefore, to learn that those rules that are routinely applied to English, from the split infinitive to ending a sentence with a preposition, are rarely useful. Calculating whether the 's' sound at the end of a word should be spelled 'ce' or 's' requires six different rules, which only help with half of our vocabulary anyway.

An episode of *QI* famously revealed that a huge number of words fail the only spelling rule any of us were taught – '*i* before *e*, except after *c*'. All of this means that we can be utterly forgiven for misspelling 'seize' and 'caffeine', 'science' and 'ancient'. The '*i* before *e*' rule was created after the majority of these exceptions. There are in fact almost a thousand words that break the rule. And rather brilliantly, the editors of the Merriam-Webster dictionary have put together the jingle we *should* be using in school instead:

I before *e*, except after *c*
Or when sounded as 'a' as in 'neighbour' and 'weigh'
Unless the 'c' is part of a 'sh' sound as in 'glacier'
Or it appears in comparatives and superlatives like 'fancier'
And also except when the vowels are sounded as 'e' as in 'seize'
Or 'i' as in 'height'
Or also in '-ing' inflections ending in '-e' as in 'cueing'
Or in compound words as in 'albeit'
Or occasionally in technical words with strong etymological links to their parent languages as in 'cuneiform'
Or in other numerous and random exceptions such as 'science', 'forfeit', and 'weird'.

That's that, then.

7 September

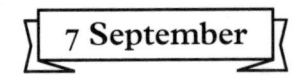

QUIDNUNC

No one likes a 'nosy parker', a 'stickybeak', a 'curtain-twitcher', or 'prodnose'. These and many more populate the vocabulary for interfering, inquisitive, and prying individuals who are always chasing down the latest developments in the affairs of others.

The identity of the original nosy parker is a matter of conjecture. It's often said that the inspiration for the name was Matthew Parker, the nasally blessed archbishop of Canterbury in the reign of Elizabeth I, who seems to have been well known for sending out detailed enquiries relating to the conduct of his diocese and was consequently regarded as a bit of a busybody. He was so unpopular that his bones were dug up during the English Civil War and flung on a dung heap.

Annoyingly, the chronology of the word is against him, since 'nosy Parker' is not recorded before 1890, some 300 years after Parker was sticking his nose in. The phrase was certainly popularized by the caption of a series of early twentieth-century postcards 'The Adventures of Nosey Parker', featuring a peeping Tom in Hyde Park.

An alternative term for an inveterate 'stickybeak', someone who has to know all the latest gossip immediately, is 'quidnunc', from the early eighteenth century. It is formed appropriately from the Latin for 'what now?'

8 September

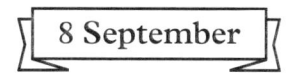

BAFFLEGAB

'The problem's communication ... too much communication.' Homer Simpson, as so often, has it right, for life today is overly full of 'bumf'. This word, which originated in military slang for toilet paper – 'bumfodder' – describes much of the communication that shoves its way into our homes and inboxes. And more often than not, it is written in language that is designed to obfuscate rather than enlighten.

In 1952, the *Daily Telegraph* announced a new word for officialese and jargon. It described it as the invention of Milton A. Smith, assistant general counsel for the American Chamber of Commerce, who reportedly won a prize for both the word and its definition. His creation was 'bafflegab', and its definition 'Multiloquence characterised by a consummate interfusion of circumlocution ... and other familiar manifestations of abstruse expatiation commonly utilised for promulgations implementing procrustean determinations by governmental bodies.' 'Bafflegab', in other words, is incomprehensible bureaucratic verbiage of the highest order. Its two elements are fairly easily understood: 'baffle' as in perplex, and 'gab' as in chatter or prattle – both of which flow from the 'gob', a word from the same family. If 'bumf' is intended for the bottom end, 'bafflegab' clearly spouts from the top.

9 September

DEBUG

The first 'bugs', in the Middle Ages, were objects of intense fear and dread, akin to a bogeyman. And that indeed is the likely etymology of the word, with relatives in the regional

English 'buggart', as well as the Irish *bocánach*, a kind of supernatural being associated with battle, and the Welsh *bwgan*. The 'bugbear' comes from the same family, and originally described a monster invoked by parents to scare their children into obedience (*see* SNOLLYGOSTER, 18 April).

By the sixteenth century, a different sense of 'bug' had emerged, descended it seems from this idea of something undesirable. A medical manual from 1594 speaks alarmingly of a medicine which 'caused many times, a certaine blacke bugge, or worme to come forth which had many legs, & was quicke'.

Perhaps inevitably, the idea of a human bug eventually emerged in the form of a contemptible or dishonest person as well as a harmful microorganism that makes us ill. A 'bug-word', first used in 1560, was one 'meant to irritate or vex'. But on this day in 1947 the only bug being talked about was in a computer, when a team of engineers in Cambridge, Massachusetts, reported that a moth had been caught between the relay contacts of the Harvard Mark II computer. The body of the offending insect was even taped into the computer's logbook, alongside the statement 'First actual case of bug being found.'

Clearly, the computer scientists saw the punning potential in a very literal example of a word they had been using for a glitch for some time. The first use of 'bug' in this context is thought to have originated many decades earlier, when Thomas Edison drew on the idea of an imaginary 'bogeyman' messing with his telegraph system.

10 September

PASSEGGIATA

'It was an agreeable habit, the late afternoon *passeggiata*, that Americans easily fell into.' In the spirit of bringing back good habits picked up on holiday, here is one souvenir guaranteed to make your day better. Tennessee Williams was the first to record in English this uniquely Italian custom of going for a walk around town at the end of the working day. Our closest equivalent is a 'constitutional', but rather than a brisk solitary walk with the aim of improving your health, the *passeggiata* is a deliberately sociable amble. Whole families dress up for the occasion and step out to greet friends or to appreciate the colourful window displays in the piazzas.

The *passeggiata* is all about engaging with others. If too old or infirm to walk, older people put out a chair in front of their house and sit there to chat with passers-by. This they know as *prendere il fresco* ('taking the freshness'). It is said that one of the original purposes of the *passeggiata* was for the unattached to scope out potential partners and to *fare una bella figura*. Although *bella figura* literally means 'beautiful figure', the phrase has the extended sense of maintaining a good appearance and being well-put-together.

Whatever the motivation, this is far more than a casual stroll: the goal is to see and, above all, to be seen, but in the best possible way.

11 September

POLYTROPIC

When a plant or tree encounters an obstacle, you may notice how it grows around that obstacle as a way of overcoming it. This is a curiosity said to have been discovered by Charles Darwin who conducted experiments on the radicles of such plants as peas and beans by attaching a piece of card to their tip. He noticed how the plants would move away from the vertical position and even make complete circles in order to circumvent the card and grow away from it.

'Aphercotrophism', the name for this phenomenon, is made up of the Greek *apo*, 'away from', *tropos*, to 'turn', and *herkos*, 'a fence or barrier'. It is a relative of the more pronounceable 'polytropic', which describes a thing or person who is capable of taking various courses of action and is therefore highly versatile. In its early uses it was often used to describe Odysseus in Homer's *Odyssey* thanks to his resourcefulness and endurance.

Next time you see the roots of a tree wind a route around paving stones that would otherwise restrict their growth, you might recognise it as a poignant metaphor for human adaptability to situations that might otherwise floor us completely.

12 September

BEGGAR'S VELVET

John Camden Hotten, born on this day in 1832, was one of the first to give proper lexicographical attention to the argot of the street and the criminal underworld. His definition of 'slang' remains one of the best, namely that it is a category of speech that 'represents that evanescent, vulgar language, ever changing with fashion and taste . . . spoken by persons in every grade of life, rich and poor, honest and dishonest.'

In his *Dictionary of Modern Slang, Cant, and Vulgar Words*, Hotten recorded the coded slangs that arose from the 'congregating together of people in cities [. . .] the result of crowding, and excitement, and artificial life'. Much of it is inevitably gritty, but it is not without charm. His lexicon includes the term 'beggars' velvet', defined as 'downy particles which accumulate under furniture from the negligence of housemaids. Otherwise called sluts' wool.' It's worth saying that 'slut' here did not carry the judgement it does today: in Hotten's time, it implied simply slovenliness, so that the worryingly named 'slut's hole' was nothing more than a corner of the room to which things were jettisoned to gather dust.

Today, beggar's velvet is more popularly known as a

collection of 'dust bunnies'. Astrophysicists use these particles, held together as they are by static electricity and felt-like entanglement, to explain how planets form.

13 September

SHIVVINESS

This is the time of year when we are often breaking in smart clothes or new school uniforms. The Spanish call this *estrenar*: strutting one's stuff when wearing new clothes. Which is fine, of course, as long as the clothes are comfortable.

When harvesting is under way and only stubble remains on the fields, beware the 'shive', a sharp splinter from a husk of harvested flax, hemp, or other crops. A word with Germanic roots that mean 'split', and a relative of 'sheave', 'shive' can be used for other leftover material too, such as a dark particle in a sheet of finished paper, or a piece of trailing thread on the surface of cloth. The theme throughout is of something irritating and in the way, which surely reaches its zenith in the word 'shivviness', defined simply in the *English Dialect Dictionary* as 'the feeling of roughness caused by a new undergarment'.

14 September

VÄNSKAPSKAKA

On this day in 1985 *The Golden Girls* made its debut on US television, introducing the laughs and struggles of four older women sharing a house in Miami. Running for seven seasons, it remains one of the best-loved sitcoms across the world. The character of Rose, played by Betty White, is a Norwegian-American from St Olaf in Minnesota who boasts a bespoke Scandi-style lexicon that combines real words with the comedically fictional. In the latter camp is 'ugelflugel', hide-and-seek for adults, and 'tutenbobbels', a byword for the buttocks. But of her genuine usages, one stands out: the *vänskapskaka*, a real Swedish name for a friendship cake. The making of it is a collective experience among friends as a yeast starter is passed on like a chain letter and fed flour, milk, and sugar by each person over several days, until it is divided among the group, whereupon each bakes their own delicious cake.

It's a wonderful idea, as Rose knows. But then, as she also assures her three roommates, 'I'm not one to blow my own vertubenflugen.'

By the way, in Sweden itself *The Golden Girls* was retitled *Pantertanter*, a term for active elderly women which literally and very appropriately means 'panther aunts'.

15 September

CLOBBER

Today is Battle of Britain Day, marking the date in 1940 when the German Luftwaffe launched a large-scale aerial assault of the skies over Britain. After a day of fierce fighting, the Luftwaffe were heavily defeated.

Pilots of the Royal Air Force at the time were the first to throw around the word 'clobber'. If a plane was badly damaged by gunfire in a bombing raid it was said to be 'clobbered'. This went on to inspire the use of the word for other poundings, both literal and metaphorical. No one quite knows the origin of this sense of 'clobber', which is just one of many expressions born in the skies. They include such aeronautically inspired phrases such as 'pushing the envelope', relating to graphs of aerodynamic performance, and the more wistful 'gone for a Burton', a dark phrase that emerged in the days before the Battle of

Britain which invokes the name of the popular Burton's Ale, produced in Burton upon Trent, to explain that a plane has crashed into the ocean and gone 'into the drink'.

16 September

APPLE-CATCHERS

Gala, McIntosh, Honeycrisp, Cortland, Jonathan, Fuji, Granny Smith: all of these apples come into season somewhere in the world in the month of September.

Originally, the Old English word *æppel* could be used to describe any fruit: the forbidden fruit eaten by Adam and Eve in the Garden of Eden is generally thought of as an apple, but the 1611 King James Version of the Bible simply calls it a fruit. As the predominant fruit of northern Europe, apples populate English expressions in dozens of ways. The 'apple of one's eye' was once a term for the pupil, which people used to think of as a solid spherical ball and which they later extended as a symbol for anyone who was particularly cherished. Such positivity runs through the Australian expression 'it's apples', used to mean that everything is just fine and there is no need for worry.

But trust English dialect to bring us back down to earth. In Norfolk, large knickers were traditionally referred to as 'apple-catchers': they were so big that they might be employed during the harvesting of apples.

17 September

ALGEBRA

Many words in English begin with the two letters 'al-', yet they seem to have little in common. They include 'algebra', 'alcohol', 'alcove', 'Allah', 'alchemy', and 'algorithm'. They are nonetheless tied by a common thread, now invisible, which is Arabic, for all these words involve the Arabic definite article *al-*, 'the'.

The enormous contribution that the Islamic Golden Age made to civilization has been downplayed by Western history until relatively recently. Baghdad was one of the main centres for medicine, science, and astronomy; as a result, Arabic became the main language of study in the fields of science. Along with cultural elements, traditions, and religious beliefs, Arabic was one of many languages that moved along the Silk Roads thanks to travelling Arab merchants and scholars.

Much of this is demonstrated in the Arabic words that became naturalized in English, many of which retain the *al-* prefix. 'Alcohol', for example, came from *al-kuhl*, 'the eye kohl', and by extension referred to any powder or liquid obtained by distillation. 'Alcove' began as *al-qubba*, 'the vault'; 'Allah' is a contraction of *al-'ilāh*, 'the god'; and 'alchemy' is from *al-kīmiyā*, 'the art of transmuting metals'. The word 'algorithm' is based upon *al-kwārizmī*, 'the man of Kwārizm' (now Khiva), an alternative name for the ninth-century mathematician Abū Ja'far Muhammad ibn Mūsa, who was an author of widely translated and highly influential works on algebra and arithmetic.

Most colourfully of all, 'algebra' was a word that belonged to the medical ward, where it comes from the Arabic *al-jabr*, 'the reunion of broken parts'; it was originally used for the surgical treatment of fractures and bone-setting. Algebra is after all about putting letters and symbols in their rightful place.

18 September

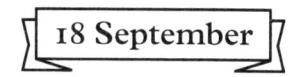

TWITTLE-TWATTLE

Samuel Johnson was born on this day in 1709. His *Dictionary of the English Language*, published in 1755, was the first to attempt to chart a language's meanings according to democratic usage rather than committee. He sought such consensus in the most important writers of his time, from whom he selected his examples. His selection of literary sources was occasionally a little quirky – the traveller Thomas Coryate is one of them, included under his nickname Furcifer on account of his having alleged he was the first Englishman to eat using a fork. Nonetheless, Johnson's approach to lexicography remains broadly the same principle that is applied today: a word is defined by its use, even if the works of Pope, Swift, and Shakespeare have been swapped for the output of chat rooms, blogs, and newspapers.

Not that Johnson's *Dictionary* is entirely objective by modern standards: it was written in a voice that is for the most part both modest and candid, but that is interspersed with the occasional stinging reproof or cheering approval. Famously so in the case of the adjective 'dull', which he defined as 'Not exhilaterating [*sic*]; not delightful; as, *to make dictionaries is* dull *work.*' The noun 'twittle-twattle' he defines as 'A ludicrous reduplication of *twattle*. Tattle; gabble. A vile word.'

Johnson's *Dictionary* became a symbol of Britishness elsewhere, but sometimes its influence could have startling results. In the summer of 1775, the toast of British high society was Omai, a young man brought back from Tahiti by Captain Cook's party. Quick to learn chess, Omai was rather less successful in his command of English, and apparently, having gathered from Johnson's *Dictionary* that 'to pickle' meant 'to preserve', he saluted Lord Sandwich, the Admiral of the Fleet, with the hope that 'God Almighty might pickle his Lordship to all eternity'.

19 September

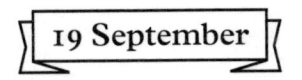

QUOCKERWODGER

If you were to ask an alien to guess the meaning of 'sleaze', they'd probably have a good go at it. The sound of the word is a perfect match for its definition – it is unctuous, slithery, and suggestively seedy. It is also extremely versatile, encompassing jobbery and nepotism, cronyism and straightforward lying. It has become a multi-purpose shorthand for corruption.

In its earliest days the word 'sleaze' was much more about flimsiness than filth. 'Sleazy cloth' was a light fabric from Silesia, an area now in south-western Poland that was once famous for producing fine textiles. 'Silesia' itself became a generic term for high quality, and 'sleazy' cloth was therefore originally anything but sordid. Its reputation was not to last, however, and it was discounted knock-offs that did for the word in the end. 'Sleazy' eventually became attached to cheap imitations of the real thing: 'seamy' in every sense.

Sleaze often involves the capitulation of integrity to personal gain. In his slang dictionary of 1859, John Camden Hotten includes the word 'quockerwodger', which he describes as a wooden toy figure which jerks its limbs about when pulled by a string. It had also, he noted, acquired an additional meaning: 'A pseudo-politician, one whose strings of action are pulled by somebody else, is now often termed a quockerwodger.' The word certainly conjures up the image of a sleazy public figure flailing about in subservience to another.

20 September

WHEN IN ROME

On 20 September 1870, Italian troops snatched Rome from the Papal States and kick-started the process of incorporating the city into the kingdom of Italy, marking the final stage of Italian unification. The event is still widely commemorated in the country and in street names such as 'Via Venti Settembre'.

The history of Rome as the ancient seat of power was by this time already well reflected in language. The notion that 'all roads lead to Rome' is recorded as far back as the fifteenth century, with 'Rome was not built in a day' hot on its heels. It was also seen as a place of decadent morals and behaviour. Long before Audrey Hepburn and Gregory Peck cavorted around the Trevi Fountain, Byron's expression 'Roman holiday' cast a backwards glance at gladiatorial combat in ancient Rome, originally describing a violent or bloody spectacle before moving on to mean one at which entertainment is had at the expense of others.

In the second half of the eighteenth century, Pope Clement wrote a letter to one of his priors with a nugget of advice: 'The *siesto*, or afternoon's nap of Italy, my most dear and reverend Father, would not have alarmed you so much, if you had recollected, that when we are at Rome, we should do as the Romans do.' The proverb he was referencing was far from new: in fact its beginnings can be traced back to the early Christian church and another letter, this time from St Augustine to the bishop of Naples from circa AD 390, while staying in Milan:

> *Cum Romanum venio, ieiuno Sabbato; cum hic sum, non ieiuno: sic etiam tu, ad quam forte ecclesiam veneris, eius morem serva, si cuiquam non vis esse scandalum nec quemquam tibi.*

When I come to Rome, I fast on Saturday, but here I do not. So you also follow the custom of whatever church you attend, if you do not want to give or receive scandal.

For those who wanted to avoid being the entertainment at any kind of Roman holiday, this was surely solid advice.

21 September

MICROMORT

A general anaesthetic has 10, travelling 200 miles by car involves 1, as does scuba-diving, and hang-gliding gives 8. There is as yet no number attached to having a red-hot poker and then a ram's horn forcefully pushed up your backside, as is popularly believed to have caused the torturous demise of Edward II on this day in 1327, but then he lived and died some 600 years before the birth of the 'micromort': the one-in-a-million chance of sudden death which is used by scientists and insurance companies to measure risk.

The notion, and its name, were the brainchild of Stanford University professor Ronald Howard, on the basis of 'micro-', 'one in a million', and 'mortality'. In 2010, a study showed that the most hazardous profession in both the UK and the US in the decade ending 2005 was far from predictable: it was commercial fishing, with an average of 1,020 micromorts per year. Worldwide, the most micromorts are attached to climbing Everest, with a phenomenal risk factor of 40,000 micromorts per ascent.

If your hobbies are less adventurous, don't get too complacent, however, for even getting out of bed in the morning carries a risk of 2.4 micromorts. Perhaps we should focus instead on the 'microlife', another unit of risk that involves changes to life expectancy. Effectively it is much the same thing – it just sounds better.

22 September

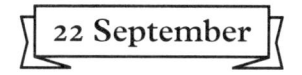

GATTARA

On this day in 1692, Martha Corey, Mary Eastey, Alice Parker, Mary Parker, Ann Pudeator, Wilmot Redd, Margaret Scott, and Samuel Wardwell were hanged, the last of those to be executed in the Salem witch trials. In the medieval and early modern eras, many religions, including Christianity, taught that the devil awarded certain people the power to harm others in return for their loyalty. These were the devil's witches, and over the course of the so-called 'witchcraft craze', which rippled through Europe between the fourteenth and seventeenth centuries, tens of thousands of supposed companions to the devil – mostly women – were executed.

Some might say that the term 'crazy cat lady', used by the US Vice-President J.D. Vance among others, is not a million miles away from the epithets that were thrown at the likes of Martha Corey, the very last woman to be hanged in Salem. In Italy, the word *gattara* is used of a woman who devotes herself to looking after stray cats, an animal long associated with witchcraft. The term can be used affectionately depending on the speaker, but in many cases the inference is clear: this is the kind of woman whom communities would once single out for their witchy differences, and try to expunge from society.

23 September

ANATOMICAL SNUFFBOX

There is a word for almost everything. The small divots in our lower back, for example, were once known as the 'dimples of Venus', named after the Roman goddess of beauty.

The slight hollow overlying the lower end of the breastbone, meanwhile, was known in the Middle Ages by the beautiful name of 'heartspoon'.

These are far from the only parts of the human anatomy that have attracted a colourful name. None more so perhaps than the 'anatomical snuffbox', a term commonly used in medical circles for the radial fossa of the hand, a triangular depression just beneath the thumb which can be seen if you hold your hand up with the palm facing down and spread your fingers. When snuff was a popular stimulant, people would place it in this small groove before sniffing it.

24 September

SCREAMER

How many times do I have to tell you? Who's to say? Are you kidding me? If adding a question mark to rhetorical questions like these makes you wince, you are not alone. In fact, generations of writers before us have felt the need for a distinct punctuation mark for questions that neither need nor deserve an answer. In the sixteenth century, an English printer named Henry Denham proposed a reverse question mark to indicate sarcasm or irony. This he called the 'percontation mark', from the Latin *percontari* for interrogate, in which *contus* means a 'bargepole'. Despite Denham's best efforts, his proposal never quite caught on, and it's a curious fact that despite other changes in modern punctuation, such as the shoving aside of colons and semicolons by dashes and full stops, the rhetorical question mark has never quite become a thing, relegated to discussions on days like today, National Punctuation Day.

In the 1960s, a further attempt was made in the form of an 'interrobang', a hybrid of the question mark and exclamation mark – ‽ – to be used to express incredulity. To date, this too has failed to gain space on the standard keyboard.

All of which is enough to encourage a pile-on of exclamation marks as a measure of frustration. There is no sign of this punctuation mark going anywhere – the opposite, in fact. It has long been the star turn of punctuation, earning itself many names over the centuries, including the 'gasper', 'bling', 'pling', 'shriek', 'Christer', 'startler', and, best of all, 'screamer'. All of which put the subtlety of the rhetorical question rather in the shade.

Need I say more?

25 September

DOOFER

There is formal language, there is local language, and there is family language, and as born code-switchers we can slip into each as circumstances dictate. Family language – the lexicon of home, which we shrug on like a warm and familiar jumper – consists of those words and expressions that only we and our relatives can truly understand. When it comes to the subjects it dedicates itself to, one invariably sits at the top of the list: the 'whatchamacallit', 'doofer', 'gizmo', 'dipper', 'doodah', 'zapper', or 'bleeper' – aka the remote control, the gadget that can inspire a family brouhaha like no other. Many of them are fanciful in origin – no one quite knows who first invented the 'gizmo', for example – but we can guess that one of the most popular, 'doofer', sprang from the sense of 'that'll do fer now'.

26 September

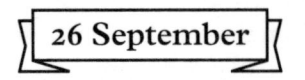

TITTLE

Describing someone as 'selfish to a T' might leave the recipient wondering what on earth the 'T' represents in the first place. The phrase 'to a T', which means 'exactly', 'to a perfect degree', is first recorded in 1693, but its roots appear to lie in an even older expression involving a different letter of the alphabet altogether.

For the ancient Greeks and Romans, the smallest letter in the alphabet, ι or 'iota', was used to represent the least part of anything, hence the modern use of 'iota' in English to mean the tiniest amount ('not one iota of respect'). The anglicized version of 'iota' was 'jot', which we also use to mean 'the least', as in 'I don't care one jot'. The dot above the letter 'i' was of course even smaller and became known in English as a 'tittle'. In the same vein, 'to a tittle' came to mean 'to the finest point' of something. It's very likely that the 'T' in 'to a T' is simply short for 'tittle'.

27 September

CODGER

In late September 1066, William the Bastard, illegitimate son of Robert I, Duke of Normandy, set sail from the mouth of the Somme in Picardy, marking the first day of what was to become the Norman Conquest. The impact of William's ascension to power upon society, law, and government was profound, but the Norman influence upon language was arguably even more dramatic. The conquerors brought with them a dialect of Old French that eventually merged with Old English to form a hybrid known as Anglo-Norman, but the separation between the privileged words of French origin and those English terms considered to be of lower status can still be seen in such doublets as 'swine' and 'pork', 'cattle' and 'chattel', 'begin' and 'commence', and 'rood' and 'cross', from English and French respectively.

The vocabulary of the nobility, and of their pursuits, was particularly affected. Falconry, for example, a sport long favoured by the French aristocracy, handed down such terms as 'haggard' (once used of a wild and untamed bird caught for hawking), 'mews' (the cages in noble and royal households where falcons were kept during moulting season), and 'codger'. This last was a riff on 'cadger': a man, usually elderly, who assisted the falconer, but the word took a definite downward turn in the centuries that followed, so that a codger became 'an unpleasant (old) man, especially one who is mean, miserly, irritable, short-tempered, or strange in behaviour or appearance'. Today, you will rarely find a codger without an 'old' tacked on to it.

28 September

CRAP

Contrary to popular belief, the word 'crap' has nothing to do with the fact that Thomas Crapper, baptized on this day in 1836 and apparently obsessed with water and plumbing from that moment on, helped invent the flushing lavatory.

Crapper certainly was responsible for multiple improvements, even if not all of them were hits. One of his toilet creations was a self-raising seat, but its functionality was apparently so hit-and-miss it became known as the 'bottom slapper'. More importantly, Crapper lifted the taboo on talking about toilets – euphemistically termed 'sanitary ware' – at all. He is credited with opening the first bathroom showroom in the world in London's Chelsea (inducing, it's said, such shock in passers-by that the most vulnerable fainted on the spot).

All of this was no doubt helped by Crapper's name, which you might still spot on toilet cisterns today. But he did not give us an eponym in the language for the contents flushed down those toilets: rather 'crap' is a word with a much older history, with the original meaning of chaff, the outward husks of grain. These would be unwanted and thus discarded, which is how the word was transferred to a human by-product that needs to be got rid of.

Today, 'crap' is also a placeholder for anything of little or no value, as well as downright rubbish. Thomas Crapper is perhaps lucky he got out before things took a tumble.

29 September

SILLY GOOSE

Today is Michaelmas, the festival of the archangel who threw the devil out of heaven. It was one of the four quarter days of the year and the time at which new servants were hired or land was exchanged and debts were paid. This is how Michaelmas came to be the time for electing magistrates, as well as the beginning of legal and university terms. It was also known as 'Goose Day' – as the saying goes, 'Eat a goose on Michaelmas Day,/Want not for money all the year' – when every family who could afford it would feast on a well-fattened goose, fed on the stubble from the fields after the harvest and consequently known as 'green geese'. Goose fairs were held around this date all over Britain and Europe, and to this day, the famous Nottingham Goose Fair is still held on or around 3 October.

Though revered in classical times, thanks to the legend that a flock of them had saved Rome from a night-time barbarian attack thanks to their noisy honking, by the fifteenth century geese were seen in a rather different light. Dr Johnson defined them as 'a large waterfowl proverbially noted, I know not why, for foolishness'. Someone who behaved in a stupid way was referred to as a 'silly goose' or as 'gooseish'. Like Johnson, people have been wondering why ever since, suggesting that this might be due to their ungainly waddling walk or their aggressive hissing and honking at any perceived predator ('taking a gander' at something describes the behaviour of a male goose). To goose someone is to poke them in the bottom. All in all it's a bit of a comedown for a bird once celebrated as the saviour of an entire city.

30 September

TAMALOUS

There comes a point in a person's life when they join a club they rather wish they didn't have to. Its members share one defining characteristic: they have all reached the age when the only news of any interest revolves around their various aches and pains and prospective doctor's appointments. Welcome the *Tamalous*, a French name based on the greeting, not of 'How are you?', but rather *T'as mal où?*, 'Where does it hurt?'

In Liverpool, older citizens go by a different nickname, thanks to their habit of arriving at the bus depot with their pensioner's pass for nine o'clock, when free off-peak travel begins. Or rather, in their enthusiasm, some considerable time beforehand, leading to the sobriquet 'Twirlies' – because they are always 'too early'.

OCTOBER

1 October

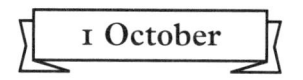

HARVEST SWAIN

'Come Sons of Summer, by whose toil/ We are the Lords of Wine and Oil'. October marks the second of the months traditionally regarded as autumn, although its precise boundaries have proved pretty fluid over the centuries. In astronomy, autumn is defined as the period from the autumnal equinox to the winter solstice. This is a season which in Old English was known first and foremost as *hærfest*, the forerunner of our modern 'harvest'. It was the time for reaping and gathering ripened grain, when 'harvest wenches' and 'harvest swains' would spend long days in the fields accompanied by the 'harvest bells'.

Our modern term 'autumn' only supplanted 'harvest' in the fifteenth century, thanks to the linguistic and social influence of the Normans and their name *automne*. By then another name for the season was well and truly in the mix: 'fall'. This was a shortening of 'fall of the leaf', which formed an annual symmetry with 'spring of the leaf', the full name for 'spring'. For a time, both 'autumn' and 'fall' coexisted, but 'fall' eventually fell out of British use, and is now looked (or frowned) upon as being uniquely American.

Harvest swains and wenches may still rejoice at this fruitful time of year. And celebrations once work was completed were guaranteed: Robert Herrick writes how the reapers would 'bound For joy, to see the Hock-cart crown'd'. The 'hock-cart' in question was the wagon which carried home the last load of the harvest.

2 October

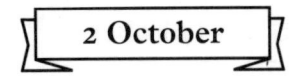

HUMUSK

There is a distinctive aroma that greets the nostrils as the days begin to wane, marking the threshold between two seasons. If scents carry emotions, it is a slightly melancholy, wistful one. Unlike the equally unmistakable smell of rain in summer, known as 'petrichor', we have no single word for the smell of autumn: the damp, musty perfume of leaves beneath the feet, of cedar, maple, apples, and forest mushrooms. The closest we have perhaps is 'humus', the decomposition of leaves and other plant material by microorganisms in the soil. This led one muser to the word 'humusk', which has the bonus of a sense of musk and mustiness to accompany it.

The lack of a word is particularly strange because English typically does quite well when it comes to highly distinctive scents. 'Mundungus', for example, from the seventeenth century, described the unpleasant whiff you might get from foul-smelling tobacco, while the thankfully rare 'nidorosity' is defined in one dictionary as belching 'with the smell of undigested meat'. Other forgotten descriptors include 'alliaceous', smelling like garlic or onions, and 'hircine', having a distinctly goaty smell. There is some disappointment on learning that the eighteenth-century 'stinkibus' describes cheap alcohol rather than someone who reeks of it.

Other words are embedded in the culture of their speakers. The Jahai, a group of nomadic hunter-gatherers in the mountain rainforests of Malaysia, are said to have a vast lexicon for certain smells. It includes 'itpit', used for ripe fruit, and 'cnes', the smell of bat droppings in bat caves.

With such riches already out there, the search must go on for a description for autumn's perfume – one that promises pumpkins, bonfires, pine resin, blackberries, and woodland walks. It's an intoxicating concoction, and surely deserves a name as magical as 'petrichor'. Humusk is down as a marker for now, but the search goes on.

3 October

TATTOO

The Bavarian Oktoberfest is the largest festival in the German-speaking world, held annually in Munich and coming to a peak in the opening days of this month. Most of us know it not for its (considerable) entertainments and status as a folk festival, but for the vast quantities of beer consumed every year (over eight million litres at the last count). The festival always opens with the same ritual: a twelve-gun salute, followed by the tapping of the first keg by the mayor of Munich and the famous words *O'zapft is!*, which in Bavarian dialect means 'It's tapped!'

Their signal for the stopping of drinking is unrecorded, but the Bavarians might like to borrow a bugle and drum and adopt a military 'tattoo', when soldiers are recalled to their quarters. This tattoo – unrelated to the skin tattoos, whose name comes from the Polynesian languages of the Pacific Islands and entered English courtesy of Captain Cook – was originally spelled 'taptoo', and began with the Dutch command *doe den tap toe*, 'close the tap'. Just like the vast numbers of taps in Munich at this time, the tap in question was on a cask, and closing it signalled that the time for drinking was over and soldiers should go home.

4 October

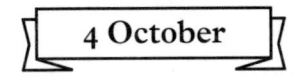

TIME AND TIDE WAIT FOR NO MAN

On this day in 1675, the Dutch physicist and astronomer Christiaan Huygens patented his pocket watch. Huygens used a balance spring analogous to the mechanism in a pendulum clock, having observed that two pendulums, when placed side by side, would synchronize and swing in opposite directions. When he reported the discovery to the Royal Society, he described the two sharing 'an odd kind of sympathy'.

The word 'horology' refers to both the measurement of time and the art of making clocks and watches. The importance of each ripples through English in hundreds of ways and is preserved in many a proverbial expression. 'The tide tarrieth for no man' is one, recorded since the fifteenth century and surviving today as the familiar 'time and tide wait for no man'. If the 'tide' seems curious, it is explained by the fact that in Old English it meant a period of time or a season, still found in such words as 'eventide', 'Eastertide' and 'Yuletide'. Only later, in the Middle Ages, did it become connected to the swelling and the ebbing of the sea. 'Time and tide' therefore meant the same thing, repeated to emphasize that no human intervention can ever slow the inexorable march of time.

5 October

CIRCUMBENDIBUS

'Now you're beginning to talk in a roundabout way,' says a TV host to his interviewee, Mr Pudifoot, in a sketch from the TV show *Monty Python's Flying Circus*, the first episode of which aired on this day in 1969. Mr Pudifoot eventually objects to being treated like a freak on account of his circumlocutory habits and walks off the set, leaving him little time to deliver anything particularly 'circumbendibus'. Rather than an articulated slinky bus with a flexible middle, this seventeenth-century term neatly describes any roundabout process or method.

6 October

MACULATE

The devastating pandemic of bubonic plague known as the Black Death arrived in Europe in October 1347, when a dozen ships from the Black Sea docked at the Sicilian port of Messina. Among its cargo were rats, which had already infected many of the sailors on board. Those men still alive were in grave condition, covered in oozing boils. Despite the frantic efforts of Sicilian authorities to move the fleet of death ships from the harbour, it was too late. In the coming years, the Black Death would kill one-third of the continent's population.

The lesions on the plague's victims were known as 'bubos', a term with roots in the ancient Greek for 'swollen glands', for the nodular swellings were often groups of lymph nodes. 'Bubonic' takes its name from them. Those infected were 'maculate', an adjective meaning 'spotted' or 'stained' that has the same root as both the 'macula' of the eye – a spot or scar in the cornea – and 'immaculate', whose literal meaning is 'unstained'. As for the Black Death on the waters of Italy, it was also the catalyst for 'quarantine', for the ports of Venice and Ragusa came to require ships from plague-stricken countries to lie at anchor for forty days before they were allowed to enter port. The Italian for forty is *quaranta*.

7 October

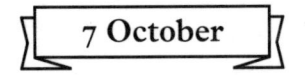

CUT TO THE CHASE

The US crime thriller *The French Connection* premiered in New York City and Los Angeles on this day in 1971. It proved a box-office smash hit, thanks in no small part to one of the most dramatic car chases in the history of cinema, in which Popeye Doyle (Gene Hackman) commandeers a car and chases the villain who has just tried to kill him. The director William Friedkin opted to film the chase in real city traffic on the streets of Brooklyn, and insisted on minimal safety precautions, so that when cars seemed to collide, they really did.

Some fifty years before the film was made, a Hollywood script had carried the simple direction 'Jannings escapes ... Cut to chase'. The phrase was to become well established within film-making for moving swiftly to a fast-paced action scene in order to keep the film's momentum and the audience's attention. The phrase eventually slipped its moorings to encompass much more in life than cinematic car chases.

8 October

OMPHALOPSYCHIC

In 1944, the corridors of the US Congress were abuzz with controversy surrounding a subject more suited to theologians than politicians – whether or not Adam and Eve had belly buttons. The catalyst for the kerfuffle was a public-affairs booklet intended for issue to US servicemen, in which an illustration of Adam and Eve included small black dots representing navels. Opinions, each rooted in deep religious belief, differed over whether God intended the pair to have the appearance of mortality, or whether the booklet was blasphemous in its depiction. The committee ruled that to include navels would be misleading to the soldiers.

This was far from the only controversy surrounding the depiction of belly buttons. Michelangelo was accused of heresy for depicting Adam and Eve with navels on the ceiling of the Sistine Chapel. Previous artists had ducked the issue by strategically painting foliage or long hair to cover the pair's abdomens.

While these discussions involved matters far beyond the scope of earth and mankind, 'navel-gazing' today is all about contemplation inwards, notably of a complacent, self-obsessed, or useless kind. The term is recorded from the latter decades of the nineteenth century, when it referred to the navel-gazing monks of Mount Athos centuries earlier, who would stare fixedly at their belly buttons during prayer in order to enter a mystical state. These were the Omphalopsychics who, according to one historical journal from 1892, 'habitually threw themselves into ecstatic catalepsy by gazing at their navels until cerebral exhaustion produced marked changes which finally resulted in deep hypnosis'.

9 October

YEOUBI

In the seventeenth century, weather would be described as 'foxy' if it misled people into thinking it was warm outside when in reality it was extremely chilly. The fox was invoked because of its reputation for craftiness and cunning.

In Korean, *yeoubi* refers to the phenomenon of a 'sun shower', when the sun shines through the rain. This time the name, literally 'fox rain', involves a bittersweet tale of love from Korean folklore. In the story, a cloud falls in love with a fox, only to see the fox get married to a tiger. The marriage takes place on a bright sunny day, but the cloud cannot help but weep for its unrequited love. Its teardrops are transformed into rain, until the cloud realizes that the sun shines regardless, and so it stops crying and gives instead its best wishes to the fox, wishing the animal joy in the future, even though it will be with someone else. It is one of many stories to celebrate on this day, which commemorates the creation of Hangul, the Korean alphabet.

In South Africa the equation between animals and weather is taken in an even stranger direction, for here a mixture of sunshine and rain is known as a 'monkey's wedding', for reasons no one can quite explain. The same phenomenon features in a Polish saying: *słońce świeci, deszczyk pada, baba jaga masło składa*, 'when the sun is shining and the rain is raining, the witch is making butter'.

10 October

DEPOOPERIT

If the vocabulary of drunkenness can be extended willy-nilly by simply taking a noun and adding the flourish of an '-ed', the lexicon for tiredness seems similarly elastic. Given enough oomph, an emphatic 'I am', and a hyperbolic opening like 'utterly' or 'totally', then any past participle will serve its purpose to render a sense of being entirely 'faldered', 'paggered', 'bellowsed', 'spunned up', 'pootled', 'razzored', 'blethered', 'jiggered', 'maggled', and 'creased'.

Scots does exhaustion particularly well. 'Forjeskit', for example, a riff on 'disjasked' (dejected), means 'broken down', 'dilapidated', and 'decayed'. But topping the list is surely 'depooperit', meaning feeling entirely depleted or 'paupered' by tiredness. Say it with as long an 'o' as you dare, to up the tiredometer.

11 October

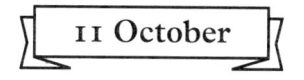

SCRUMPING

If we are to believe English folklore, this is the last day blackberries can be picked. It is said that when St Michael expelled Lucifer from heaven, the devil tumbled from the skies and landed in a prickly blackberry bush. Satan cursed the fruit, and then proceeded to spit on it, scorch it with his fiery breath, trample it underfoot, and finally urinate on it, all in order to render its fruit unfit for eating. As a result, it is considered a very bad idea to eat any blackberries after 11 October, Old Michaelmas Day, and a Michaelmas pie is made from the very last berries of the season.

For those who stick to the rule, they might wish to dispel the bleakness of blackberrylessness by scrumping for apples. The original sense of 'scrump' was simply to capitalize on the windfalls of small apples left on the trees after harvesting. Today, it has a distinct edge of illicitness about it, and suggests climbing over fences or even up trees in order to reach the booty. The origin of 'scrump' itself is not entirely appetizing, for it may lie in an old dialect word for something shrivelled and dried up: not what you wish for when drinking 'scrumpy', a related word for a particularly rough and strong cider made with the apples from the tree. Some who drink too much of it may wish they'd risked picking those late blackberries after all.

12 October

TWITTEN

Alleyways hold a special place in English dialect. They, and our names for them, are strong reminders of playing as children, and of home. They also hold an intrinsic kind of magic: existing in the boundary between home and outside, private and public space, light and darkness. They are escape routes, shortcuts, meeting places, and romantic venues: an alley is always somewhere you 'duck down'.

In terms of their linguistic productiveness, alleyways are the urban equivalent of the brooks and streams that fill our countryside. 'Alley' itself is first recorded in the sixteenth century in descriptions of the narrow backstreets of London; its roots are French and the verb *aller*, 'to go'.

But this was just the start. From the 'ginnels' and 'snickets' of Yorkshire and Lancashire, to the 'twitchels' of the East Midlands, the 'twitten' of Sussex and on to the 'ennogs' and 'jiggers' of Liverpool, local alleyways are embedded in the culture of the industrial towns and cities of northern England.

Our vocabulary for narrow walkways doesn't end at the boundaries of a town or city, where the winding country lanes begin. The 'loanings' of Scotland and northern England and the 'lokes' of East Anglia are some of them, but you might also discover a 'gang-boose', one that leads from the cowshed to the barn. These are the Old Ways, the ancient paths and tracks that people have trodden for centuries, and which connect people and places just like the alleyways of childhood.

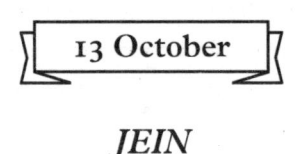

13 October

JEIN

Hedging your bets can often lead to excessive circumlocution in language, to avoid having to commit. English has, traditionally speaking, not offered much in terms of concise words that keep an escape route open. Those that its users have devised tend to belong in the humorous category. 'Probsolutely', for example, is one means of expressing a definite maybe. The

Germans have surely sussed it, however, with the slang term *jein*, another portmanteau which neatly conveys indecision and hesitation, as well as the potential sense of 'technically, yes, but not really'. A mixture of *ja* and *nein*, 'yes' and 'no', it is the multitasker that English currently lacks.

14 October

LUBBERLAND

In the Middle Ages, any frustrated parent might accuse their teenagers of living in 'Lubberland': an imaginary land of plenty where every desire is catered for and laziness is a given. The name of this notional country was based on the much earlier use of 'lubber' to describe 'a big, clumsy, stupid fellow', as well as 'one who lives in total idleness'. Its applications were broad: 'abbey-lubber' took a swipe at the stereotypical monk, while the more familiar 'landlubber' was a favourite insult among sailors for those unused to the high seas and who didn't (quite literally) know the ropes.

English is far from alone in having a large lexicon for lazybones. Spanish has a variety of insults to throw at them, including *Trabajas menos que el sastre de Tarzán*, 'You work less than Tarzan's tailor.' Any German who dares rest on their laurels might be asked *Erwartest du, dass dir de gebratenen Tauben in den Mund fliegen?*, 'Do you expect fried pigeons to simply fly into your mouth?'

15 October

NUCULAR

'"Nucular", it's pronounced "nucular",' insists Homer Simpson when he's told he's assigned to a 'nuclear sub'. It's tempting to assume that it was this correction of the 'correct' pronunciation that propelled 'nucular' into popularity, but English speakers have been having this debate for some time, and the first records of 'nucular' in the *Oxford English Dictionary* are from fifty years earlier.

While language liberals see it as an inevitable shift to something more comfortable on the tongue, for others it is an abomination. The objective observer can at least tell you that this is an example of 'metathesis', a linguistic process by which speakers swap sounds around. The word 'thrill', for example, comes from 'thirl', an 'opening' (*see* EYETHIRL, 27 May). Similarly, a 'wasp' was a *waps*, a 'bird' a *brid*, a 'crocodile' a *cocodrilo*, and a 'horse' a *hros*. In most cases, the change happens because the new sound is more familiar or just easier for the speaker – in the case of 'nuclear', there are few current examples of the 'lear' sound, other than 'cochlear', and far more of the '-ular' sound, as in 'molecular' or 'secular'. Perhaps the most obvious example of metathesis today is the use of 'aks' or 'ax' instead of 'ask', popular in many varieties of English and documented in the language as far back as the eleventh century.

Children are particularly good at metathesis, opting for sound swaps that simply feel easier to say, giving us 'aminal' for 'animal', or the charming 'pa-sketti' instead of 'spaghetti'.

16 October

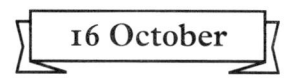

TUNG

'Tung', 'soop', 'dawter', 'iland', 'thum', 'spunge', 'bilt', 'beleev' ... It would be hard to argue that these reinventions of common English words are not easier to spell. Each of them was the creation of the lexicographer Noah Webster, born on this day in 1758. Webster was a revolutionary, growing up against the backdrop of the American War of Independence. After his father mortgaged the family house to send him to Yale, he fought in the Connecticut Militia against the British and later became determined to forge a separate American language from the one spoken across the Atlantic. Writing his *American Dictionary of the English Language* became a war of linguistic independence too.

Webster wanted to rescue American children from being forced to follow Cockney intonations and from the unnecessary extra letters that scholars had scattered through English spellings to show off their heritage – especially the silent kind. It is thanks to Webster that US English has 'color' rather than 'colour' (which is in fact closer to the word's Latin roots, while British English went with the more fashionable French spelling). Similarly, 'centre' became 'center', 'plough' became 'plow', and 'defence' became 'defense'. In every case Webster sought to smooth the considerable creases in English spelling and remove the obstacles to its mastery.

While it is indisputable that Webster gave his native tongue a vitality and dignity of its own, not all of his respelling suggestions made it, including each of those in the first paragraph. Today's proponents of spelling change – part of a long line of reformers who have tried and failed to simplify it – might regret that Webster's respelling of 'tongue', 'tung', never quite caught on.

17 October

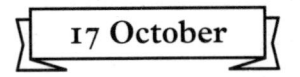

MACARONI

Today is World Pasta Day, when we need no other reason to tuck into one of the best comfort foods on earth. The inspiration for the Italian names of different types of pasta ranges from the straightforward to the bizarre. The simplest are based on shape: *fusilli* is regional Italian for 'little spindles', while *penne* means 'quill pens' or 'feathers'. *Spaghetti* translates as 'little strings', and *vermicelli* as 'little worms'. Ribbons of *tagliatelle* take their name from the Italian *tagliare*, 'to cut', while *cannelloni* is the descendant of a Latin word meaning 'pipe' or 'tube'. Other names are a little more unexpected. The literal meaning of *strozzapreti* is 'priest choker', perhaps because they look a little like discarded clerical collars, although various legends will tell you the name began with greedy priests who would invite themselves to dinner after Mass too often, provoking the irritated host to show their displeasure on a plate.

Tortellini are said to have been inspired by a voyeuristic innkeeper who spied on a naked Venus through a keyhole and was transfixed by her beautiful torso: hence its more highfaluting name *ombelico di Venere* – the navel of Venus. But it is *lasagne* that wins the prize for the most unappetizing beginnings, for they lie in the Latin *lasanum*, 'chamber pot'. The name thankfully broadened to mean a pot used for cooking, although it's tempting to think that the shift was the result of a jibe towards a particularly poor chef.

Traditional pasta sauces can be equally surprising: the spicy sauce known as *arrabbiata* gets its name from the verb *arrabbiare*, 'to get angry': a nod to the heat of the chilli peppers in the sauce. And *puttanesca*, famously, derives from the Italian for 'sex worker', a reference, it is said, to the speed with which it can be made, allowing for it to be cooked quickly between clients.

But few pastas have travelled as far as *macaroni*. In the eighteenth century, wealthy young British men traditionally took a trip around Europe, known as the Grand Tour. Italy was the key destination, so much so that the Macaroni Club was founded in London in 1764 by those returning. Here they would refer to anything that was fashionable or *à la mode* as 'very maccaroni'. The real 'macaroni' was a small tricorne hat placed on top of a teeteringly high wig, and it soon became an insult towards dandies, fops, and those considered overdressed. In the nursery rhyme, Yankie Doodle Dandy 'sticks a feather in his cap and calls it macaroni'. As for the pasta? That was so named because, to those outside Italy, it seemed highly exotic, and so fitting for the stylish Macaroni Club's members.

18 October

CHUGGYPIG

In autumn, certain creatures who have been less visible during the summer months begin to reappear. Should a woodlouse be among them, it might be one of over forty different varieties common to the British Isles, out of a staggering 3,500 or so worldwide. No matter which it is, each of us will probably apply just one name to it: the one we learned as a child. But what is that exactly? It turns out that the vocabulary for woodlice is one of the richest in the entire lexicon of British dialect.

To start with Cornwall, here it will often be known as a 'grammersow', part of a mystifying theme that equates woodlice to pigs and which also manages to add a grandparent to the mix. Perhaps the reference is an affectionate dig at the elderly, who might keep a woodlouse as a pet pig because they are too frail to look after the real thing. The theme continues through Dorset and Somerset further north until Gloucestershire, where you might encounter a 'chiggypig', 'chuckypig', 'charliepig', or 'chiggywig'. Linger awhile in Bristol, and you could pick up a 'slunkerpig' or even a 'penny sow', and in Wales, *moch y coed* will give you a 'treepig'. The Isle of Man, confusingly, makes them a 'parson pig'. Nor do animal analogies stop there, as monkeys get a look in too, with 'monkeypede' and, just to make things equal, a 'monkeypig'.

Grandparents return when it comes to particularly large specimens of woodlouse, known in some places as a 'granfy crooger', while standard-sized ones range from 'granddad gravy' to 'granny granshers'.

You might hope to wrap it up there, but the south-east has somehow managed to add in a dairy theme. Here, creepy-crawlies can be a 'cheeserocker' or 'cheeselog', a 'cheesybob' or plain 'cheeseball'.

19 October

STEPMOTHER'S BREATH

The fifteenth-century English word 'novercant' is included in the *Oxford English Dictionary* with the definition 'having characteristics attributed to a stepmother'. But that is not all: the same definition is followed by an adjective that lurks in many popular representations of the stepmother in fairy tales, folklore, and literature: 'hostile'. So entrenched is this belief in the wicked stepmother that even the weather became involved, for in the nineteenth century a 'stepmother's breath' was a sudden and unexpected cold snap or a bitingly cold wind. In the same century, a 'stepmother's blessing' might also crop up, but lest you assume this brings some warmth into the equation, it actually described a small patch of partially detached skin near a fingernail – something that can be extremely painful and most definitely 'hostile'.

20 October

JACHELT

As the poet Robert Frost knew, the paths less travelled often make all the difference. An impromptu footpath or walkway that has been imprinted into the earth by the footfall of passers-by was once known rather beautifully as a 'desire path'. Many of them, by dint of offering a short cut, will take the traveller across exposed hilltops and mountain tree-lines which bear the brunt of the wind. The traveller of a desire path may then witness many 'jachelts', a word from Scots that describes trees that twist and contort in the direction of the wind, appearing as though frozen in a deep bow towards the elements. In Newfoundland English, these gnarled and grizzled trees are known as 'tuckamores'.

21 October

NACHO

Etymology can be a slippery beast. Some of our most everyday words have origins we have yet to discover. There are, however, some mysteries that have been cracked by informal or spontaneous sleuthing by lexicographers who decided to don their deerstalkers and set off for a bit of independent research.

The story of 'nacho' is one of these. For years the *Oxford English Dictionary* could offer little explanation for the name of one of the most popular Mexican tortilla chips, hinting only that, possibly, it might be rooted in a Spanish word that means 'flat-nosed'. That was before one etymologist from the dictionary, doing research at the Hispanic Division of the Library of Congress, was approached by another user of the library, who explained that she was from a small town in Mexico, just across the border from Eagle Pass in Texas. There, only one meaning of 'nacho' was popularly understood: as the nickname of a local boy named Ignacio, or 'Nacho', Anaya, who had gone on to become a chef. It was he, the woman explained, who should be credited with making the first nachos in 1940 at the Old Victory Club in Piedras Negras, when he was asked by a group of customers for a snack to accompany their cocktails. The problem was that it was already a few minutes past closing time and there was little left in the kitchen. Ignacio was forced to improvise, and put together a conglomeration of what he did have: a few tortillas, some shredded cheese, and some pickled jalapeño peppers. These he cut up and baked for a few minutes for the cheese to melt. His customers greatly enjoyed this little snack, and when they asked Ignacio what it was called, he answered, 'Nacho's Especiales.'

Word travelled fast, and the Moderno Restaurant in Piedras Negras serves the original recipe to this day, while Ignacio Anaya was honoured with a bronze plaque. It was he who consequently gave his name to the dish, as is now acknowledged (albeit with a 'perhaps'), in the *OED*. What's more, 21 October has been formally designated the International Day of the Nacho.

22 October

BEARN-LUFU

Old English, like Greek, had several words for love. Far from relying on the single word to cover every variety of the emotion – whether it's loving hot dogs, one's pet, siblings, partner, or many more – it offered a range of specific love combinations whose name ended in *lufu*, the ancestor of 'love'. *Sib-lufu*, for example, was 'kin-love', the love for one's family, and *frēond-lufu* was 'friend-love'.

Perhaps most lacking from English today, however, is *bearn-lufu*, the love a parent feels for their child. There is a myth that the emotion is so universally powerful that, *in extremis*, pelicans will keep their young alive by piercing their own breasts so that their chicks may drink their blood. For the ancient Greeks, *storgē* was the precious and unparalleled love between parent and child. They also gave us the roots of the strange word 'antipelargy', which describes a child's support of their parent in old age. Its name reflects classical legends in which young storks (*pelargoi*) bear the weight of their parents in flight.

23 October

LICKSPITTLE

The term 'lickspittle' was never going to end well. From its very first appearances in the 1600s it has described a sycophant or obsequious acolyte – one who is prepared to go to extreme lengths to ingratiate themselves with those in power. In this it resembles the 'catchfart' – another seventeenth-century epithet for a fawning servant or follower of the political wind, but in this case one who followed their master or mistress a little too closely for comfort.

The story of 'sycophant' is much less obvious, involving as it does the Greek word for the fig, a fruit that begins to grow in spring and ripens over the summer. It seems an unlikely focus for a historical profanity, but showing someone 'the fig' involved wedging the thumb between two fingers, presumably to represent female genitalia. 'Sycophant' is Greek for 'fig-shower', the implication being that a deceiving flatterer may be saying and doing very different things behind the flatteree's back.

24 October

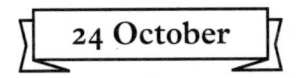

PLINIAN ERUPTION

About one in the afternoon, my mother desired [my uncle] to observe a cloud which appeared of a very unusual size and shape ... he immediately arose and went out upon a rising ground from whence he might get a better sight of this very uncommon appearance. A cloud, from which mountain was uncertain, at this distance (but it was found afterwards to come from Mount Vesuvius), was ascending, the appearance of which I cannot give you a more exact description of than by likening it to that of a pine tree, for it shot up to a great height in the form of a very tall trunk, which spread itself out at the top into a sort of branch.

Such was the description by Pliny the Younger, a magistrate of ancient Rome, of his uncle Pliny the Elder witnessing an impending volcanic eruption from Mount Vesuvius. His description, remarkable in its objectivity, was found in two letters to the renowned historian Tacitus. He goes on to explain how his uncle urged him to accompany him on a galley across the Bay of Naples to observe the cloud at closer hand, an offer the nephew declined, preferring to remain with his books. It was a fateful decision, for Pliny the Elder and thousands of others in Pompeii and Herculaneum were killed by the eruption. Recent archaeological discoveries have conclusively confirmed the date of the eruption as 24 October AD 79 rather than the 24 August it was long assumed to be.

Volcanic eruptions are classified according to seven levels of increasing explosivity. As a result of his account of the catastrophic eruption, Pliny's name was given to the most violent, at numbers six and seven, which are known as Plinian and Ultra-Plinian eruptions respectively. They are the most devastating examples of volcanism, marked by colossal clouds of volcanic ash that rise up from a giant cinder cone, just as Pliny described. Notable examples include Krakatoa in 1883 and, more recently, Mount Pinatubo in the Philippines.

The loss of Pliny the Elder was a significant one. As he set off for Vesuvius with his fleet, he is reported to have used a phrase that has become a motto of many military and civilian institutions: *Fortes fortuna iuvat*, 'Fortune favours the brave.'

25 October

LIBROCUBICULARIST

Readers come in many varieties, from those who casually borrow the latest novel from a friend and somehow forget to give it back (the 'biblioklept'), to those who are so drunk on books they read at the dinner table or at the expense of conversation (the 'bibliobibuli'). Of all reading types, however, most of us can probably relate to the 'librocubicularist'. This mouthful of a label describes something very familiar, being made up of the Latin *liber*, 'book', and *cubiculum*, 'bedroom'. In other words, a librocubicularist is someone who reads in bed.

The word is thought to be the creation of the American writer Christopher Morley in his 1919 novel *The Haunted Bookshop*, in which a rather eccentric antiquarian bookseller suggests to his young lodger that she take a book up to her room, posing the question, 'Are you a librocubicularist?' The lodger is clearly alarmed until another character offers her an explanation: 'He only means are you fond of reading in bed. I've been waiting to hear him work that word into the conversation. He made it up, and he's immensely proud of it.' The rest of us can be equally grateful that it exists.

26 October

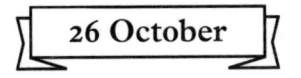

NÜSHU

For all its gawkiness, the word 'mansplaining' was clearly so necessary a gap-filler in our language that it has thrived ever since it began to emerge in online forums in the late noughties. A decade later, a new kid was enthusiastically welcomed to the block in the form of 'hepeating'. It was introduced to the wider world by Nicole Gugliucci, Associate Professor of Physics at Saint Anselm College in New Hampshire, who was clearly familiar with the experience of putting forward an idea to a group and receiving little response, until a male colleague repeats it and suddenly receives a chorus of approval.

The women of rural Hunan Province in south-east China once used an exclusively female script, coded to exclude the male gaze and allowing them to share their most intimate secrets. This is Nüshu, which means 'women's script' and which originally rose to prominence in the nineteenth century as a way of liberating women from the strictures of society at the time, allowing them to express sadness and grief and to openly talk about their personal dreams. They would scratch their thoughts on surfaces using bamboo sticks, or embroider them on cloth and handkerchiefs.

The Nüshu script, which some believe to be ancient, was passed down by generations of women; anyone who couldn't read it learned its codes by sight. Those initiated in the code were known as 'sworn sisters', able to communicate in a society profoundly dominated by men. Today, the Nüshu language is undergoing something of a resurgence. As one leading scholar puts it, 'Now she leaves beautiful calligraphy, wisdom and brave spirit to future generations.'

27 October

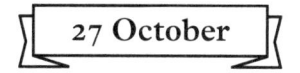

SOPHROSYNE

On this day in 2014 Taylor Swift released *1989*, which she spoke of as her first 'official pop album'. Winner of the Grammy Award for album of the year, it charts the trajectory of love through heartbreak, nostalgia, and on to recovery, leaving its narrator feeling empowered and hopeful. She is, to some degree at least, in possession of 'sophrosyne', a mellifluous word that might have come straight from Swift's own lyrics but which entered English in the nineteenth century to mean 'soundness of mind' and 'self-control'. Pronounced as 'so-frozz-ini', with the emphasis on the middle syllable, it is based on the Greek for 'prudence' and 'moderation'.

The star's extremely committed fans are known as Swifties, even though many a word-lover has long been a Swifty, albeit of a rather different kind. A 'Tom Swifty' is named after the title character in a series of children's adventure books published from 1910. The stories are ripping yarns where no verb lacks an adverb, typically of the purplest variety. In language a 'Tom Swifty' is therefore a kind of wordplay inspired by these stories, involving a ridiculous but pleasingly punning relationship between an adverb and the statement it refers to:

> 'If you want me, I shall be in the attic,' said Tom, loftily.
> 'Don't you love sleeping outdoors?' Tom said intently.
> 'My favourite singer is Taylor,' Tom said swiftly.

28 October

RAZBLIUTO

Take any music album from any era, and feeling 'torchy' is almost par for the course. The word evokes the pain and wistfulness of unrequited love, a theme that spans the decades and takes in such classics as 'Unchained Melody' by the Righteous Brothers, Radiohead's 'Creep', and Adele's 'I Can't Make You Love Me'. That word 'torchy' is an offshoot of the torch song, a metaphor lit in ancient times when wedding torches would be set aflame in a bride's hearth on her wedding night as a tribute to the gods of marriage. In music, the torch is of a kind that still burns inside the singer even when it has been extinguished in the object of their love. The French know this as *la douleur exquise*: the 'exquisite pain' that comes from wanting a person who can never be yours. The Russians are more hands-on: for them, *razbliuto* describes the lingering sentimental feeling felt for a former lover: the relationship may be over, but a part of you will always love the person you lost.

The dictionary tends to offer little solace for those destined to carry a torch for eternity, except for one word, now obsolete, hidden within its artefacts. 'Redamancy' is defined in one seventeenth-century glossary as 'a loving of him, or her that loves us, a loving again, a mutual loving'. It may not be soothing to the ear, but it is nice to know such a word exists for unrequited love that is at last requited.

29 October

WHANGDOODLE

Upon a rugged throne of petrified turtle soup stood the mighty A. Jacks, eating a slice of buttered beeswax ...

'Bring forth the whangdoodle, and place it on the hewgag!' he exclaimed with a terrific voice.

This early florid account in a New Hampshire newspaper of some fictional object called a 'whangdoodle' (quite apart from the 'hewgag') gives us an idea of the fantastical and nonsensical contexts in which it was used. Five years later, in 1857, it was greatly popularized by a humorous mock sermon reported in the *Daily Enquirer* in which it appears in an invented biblical quotation as the name of a mythical creature:

> And they shall gnaw a file and flee unto the mountains of Hepzidam, where the lion roareth and the wang-doodle mourneth for its first-born.

Within just a few years a 'whangdoodle' was variously used as a person or thing whose name one either can't remember, doesn't know, or doesn't wish to mention. In poker, it became a round in which the stakes are raised, especially after a big hand has been shown. All of which goes to show that we can use 'whangdoodle' as a placeholder for pretty much anything, and that it won't be long before a person can be a Whangdoodle too.

30 October

CHATOYANT

On a dark and foggy night in the winter of 1933, Percy Shaw was driving home from his local pub in Boothtown, West Yorkshire, when he reached a particularly serpentine stretch of road. Despite his familiarity with it, the pitch darkness and lack of any visible marks on the road made the journey feel more hazardous than usual. It was then that Shaw spotted two points of light reflected in his car's headlights: the eyes of a cat sitting on a fence near the road.

The intense glow of a cat's eyes are caused by incoming light bouncing back off the *tapetum lucidum*, Latin for 'shining carpet'. This is a layer of cells that reflects light back through the animal's retina. For Shaw, it was the inspiration for revolutionizing road safety, for he realized that a reflective device fitted to road surfaces could guide drivers in similar situations to the one he faced on his journey. He duly called them 'cat's eyes', and they were patented the following year.

There is a word for the precise kind of illumination that Shaw witnessed that night. The French *chatoyer* means 'to shine like a cat's eye', while the beautiful *chatoyant* means 'shimmering brightly'.

31 October

NIGHTMARE

It would be easy to assume that a 'nightmare' involves one of the horsemen of the Apocalypse or any dark rider from hell. In fact, the 'mare' here is unrelated to anything equine, and comes instead from the Old English *mære*, meaning 'incubus'. This was a male demon thought to have sex with sleeping women. In this case, the fiend was also thought to lie so heavily upon the sleeper that they were suffocated. A grisly thought for Halloween.

A far less familiar word suitable for this night is 'wisht', a word with various meanings including 'unlucky', 'uncanny', 'sickly', 'haggard', or 'ashen-faced'. It is the quality that comes with 'wishtness': witchcraft or its embodiment in the form of a ghost. 'Wisht-hounds', or spectral hounds of hell, are straight out of the nightmare cupboard.

NOVEMBER

1 November

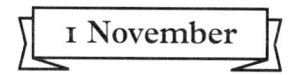

KAAMOS

Waking up on this All Saints' Day, it is impossible to deny that winter is upon us, and that the months ahead are going to be increasingly dark and cold.

In Finland, *kaamos*, literally 'polar nights', is the period of time between November and February when the sun sets for months. It provokes a range of feelings, from the longing for sunshine to a distinct lack of enthusiasm and, at the extreme end, to depression. But it is also good to recognize that this time of torpor is part of the cycle from hibernation to revivification, and dotted in-between are moments of sunshine when the warmth penetrates the frost (*see* APRICATE, 24 April). Hibernophiles – winter-lovers – will welcome this time with open arms. The rest of us can retreat into our hibernacles and wait for the light to return.

2 November

SKULDUGGERY

The Day of the Dead is all about skulls. The colourful sugar skulls that can be seen across many parts of South America on this day are known as *calaveras*. Each carries the name of a much-missed person, so that their spirit can be welcomed and celebrated as if they were still present.

Today is notable for a far darker link with death, as it was on 2 November 1828 that the bodysnatchers William Burke and William Hare were finally captured. At the time, the practice of bodysnatching was so widespread that a device called the 'mortsafe' was developed, a form of iron cage that surrounded a coffin and prevented abduction of the occupant. Those who succeeded in this skulduggery, despite such measures, sold their 'product' to medical schools, and were grimly known as 'resurrectionists'. Burke and Hare notoriously went one horrific step further when their own supplies ran low: in the year between 1827 and 1828 the pair killed at least sixteen people, selling the cadavers to Dr Robert Knox's anatomy school.

There is something inherently menacing about the word 'skulduggery'. Most of us would split it into 'skull' and 'dug' and assume the link is something as macabre as Burke and Hare's evil trade. Yet the original and more common spelling has just one 'l', which suggests the word's origins had no connection to either skulls or digging.

The term is apparently an American invention, first appearing in print around 1867, where it referred to the misappropriation of funds and fraud. Like Burke and Hare's crimes, it hailed from Scotland, where 'sculduddery' meant 'fornication', 'unchastity', and 'lewd behaviour'. The word may be based on the term 'dud', which in the Scottish church was the sackcloth of repentance. Today, folk etymology has ensured that 'skullduggery' is gaining ground in the spelling stakes as a shorthand for dishonest, unscrupulous, and likely underground behaviour – which is perhaps only fitting.

3 November

WILD GOOSE CHASE

Nay, if our wits run the wild goose chase, I am done, for thou hast more of the wild goose in one of thy wits than I am sure I have in my whole five. Was I with you there for the goose?

In *Romeo and Juliet*, Mercutio speaks of losing the battle of wits against Romeo as they walk the streets of Verona, apparently comparing their hunt for the perfect one-liner to hunting wild geese.

While the play, published in 1597, gives us our first record of the expression 'wild goose chase', its connections even then were far more concerned with horses than birds. The term was used for an equestrian sport in which the second and succeeding horses had to accurately follow the course of the leader, forming a similar flight formation to a flock of wild geese observed in the winter skies. While the geese's flight plan is highly effective, to the human eye the horse race that imitates it must have seemed erratic and impulsive, with each rider choosing when to follow. Consequently, by the time Samuel Johnson was writing his dictionary in 1755, a wild goose chase was 'a pursuit of something as unlikely to be caught as the wild goose' – in other words a fruitless quest and a fool's errand.

4 November

BACKENDISH

The Russians call it *rasputitsa*, 'the season of bad roads', but in various spots in the north of England, the end of autumn and the latter part of the year is commonly referred to as the 'backend'. In Lancashire and Yorkshire, a particularly wet and blustery day might be described as 'backendish'.

The range of vocabulary for rain and cold in English is, inevitably, vast. Driving rain in particular invites vibrant expression, including the 'cowquaker': a cloudburst so dramatic and sudden it makes every animal shake. You might assume a different creature inspired the northern 'stoating', but the word is a version of the Scots 'stot', meaning 'to bounce', suggesting a shower whose pelting drops ricochet off the ground.

If it's coming down in stair-rods, it is also 'plothering': an onomatopoeic word belonging to a large family that also includes the dialect 'plouter', meaning to wade through mud. Speaking of stair-rods, the metaphorical equivalents for torrential rain are extensive – the French might tell you it's raining *comme une vache qui pisse*, 'like a pissing cow'. When the weather is particularly wet, the Welsh will say *mae hi'n bwrw hen wragedd â ffyn*, 'it's raining old women and sticks'. In several languages, it's shoemakers who get a mention: Germany's *es regnet Schusterjungs* means 'it's raining cobblers' sons'.

As for our own 'raining cats and dogs', dozens of theories have been put forward to explain the expression, ranging from the use of cats as witches' attendants, to rain so heavy that animals would be washed down from thatched roofs. More likely is that it simply provides a good metaphor – in France it rains frogs while in Slovakia 'tractors are falling'.

5 November

BEAVER MOON

The first full moon of November is known as the beaver moon. Its name is said to be a nod to beavers making their winter homes in November, while some believe that indigenous Native American peoples would set beaver traps around this time to secure their fur for the freezing months to come.

This month, beneath the beaver moon, bonfires and skies will be lit without much thought to the dark histories that inspired this celebration. The word 'bonfire' is fittingly gloomy, for its original form was a 'bone-fire', upon which animal and human bones would be burned. Bonfires aren't, of course, restricted to this day of the year. In the Celtic calendar, they are lit at the beginning of summer at Beltane, a pagan festival whose name means 'the fires of Bel', in which Bel is a probable reference to the Celtic god of the sun, Belenus. At Beltane the fires are celebrated as protective rather than malevolent. But today, it's hard to avoid a shiver as effigies of Guy Fawkes are ritually thrown into the flames and Catherine wheels ignite. Some say this spinning firework takes its name from St Catherine of Alexandria, who was condemned to death on a spiked wheel for her Christian faith. After all this, thank goodness for the innocence of sparklers. And beaver moons.

6 November

SHEMOMEDJAMO

Snaccidents will happen. Few of us would be unfamiliar with the feeling of eating past fullness because we are enjoying the food too much. If only there was a word for this specific food emotion. Thankfully, the Georgians have one: *shemomedjamo*. Its literal translation? 'I accidentally ate the whole thing.' The Finns have another in *älmätä*, used to describe the eating of something very greedily and fast, equivalent to 'snaffle' but with an added touch of disdain. It suits those situations when a child or sweet-toothed adult complains of stomach-ache after devouring an entire packet of biscuits.

7 November

MUSCLE

Just as our intestines were once known as our 'arse-ropes' (*see* 14 January), so our muscles in the sixteenth century were called 'flesh-strings'. It would be hard to argue with this straightforwardness, but it denies 'muscle' its etymology, which is one of the sweetest in the English language. In ancient times, athletes would regularly exercise in the nude to best show off their physical prowess. The word 'gym', short for 'gymnasium', famously began with the Greek for 'exercise naked'. To the Roman imagination, the flexing biceps of a proudly BUFF athlete resembled a tiny rodent scuttling beneath the skin. They consequently chose to call each of them a *musculus*, 'little mouse'.

8 November

VENTRILOQUIST

CORKY: There was never me, only us.
FATS: Schmucko . . . us was you.

On this day in 1978 the film *Magic* was released, ensuring that ventriloquists' dummies would never be seen in the same way again.

In ancient Greece, those believed to be possessed by an evil spirit were thought to speak from the depths of their stomach, where demonic possession took hold. They were consequently labelled with the term *engastrimuthos*, which was translated into Latin as *ventriloquus*, meaning a 'belly speaker'. When 'ventriloquist' was adopted into English in the seventeenth century, the belief in demons inhabiting human bodies, and in pacts between the ventriloquist and the exorcist, persisted. The modern application to someone who can make their voice seem to come from somewhere else, as Anthony Hopkins does in the role of Corky with his dummy Fats, is not recorded until the end of the eighteenth century.

Incidentally, the ancestors of football fans were thought to be equally possessed: *fanaticus* means 'from a temple', i.e. inspired by a god.

9 November

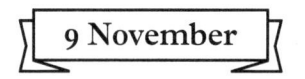

SPONDULICKS

'Bread', 'sugar', 'mazooma', 'wonga', 'dosh', 'greenery' ... whatever you choose to call it, money is one of the biggest themes in any slang dictionary. Much of its vocabulary draws on the idea that life is impossible without it, giving rise to a raft of terms connecting money and food. 'Bread' was chosen because it is the staple of life, while 'dough' riffs on the same theme. 'Sugar', 'jam', and 'cake' all carry the suggestion that money sweetens our lives.

As ever with slang, etymologies are often hard to come by, but that hasn't stopped us guessing. 'Dosh', one of the more recent additions to the money lexicon, may be a blend of 'dollars' and 'cash', but a more likely source is the word 'doss', a place to sleep, which of course needs to be paid for. Before becoming our favourite slang term for a pound sterling, the first meaning of 'quid' was a sovereign. Its probable origin is the Latin *quid*, meaning 'what', with 'one needs' as the unspoken add-on.

And then there is 'spondulicks', known to older generations as a teasing byword for ready cash. A firm favourite of Bertie Wooster in P.G. Wodehouse's Jeeves novels, the earliest records of it date back to the 1850s, and root it firmly in the US. Its source may well be the Greek *spondylo-*, which is found in several English words that refer to the spine. A college textbook from 1867 defines 'spondulics' as 'coins piled for counting'. It seems very possible that a stack of coins was seen by someone with knowledge of Greek and a sense of humour as resembling a spine, with each coin representing another vertebra.

10 November

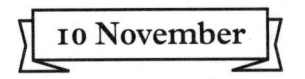

HAD-I-WIST

'How sad would be November if we had no knowledge of the spring!' The photographer and naturalist Edwin Way Teale knew more than most about nature's reflection of the passing year. His four-book series The American Seasons took him some 75,000 miles across North America following the changing seasons. As the days darkle (an old term for the dimming of light) it is tempting to look back with regret rather than forward to the sunshine. For such occasions English offers the melancholic 'had-I-wist', an utterance of remorse for something we did because we didn't know what we now do.

11 November

MURMURATION

'Murmuration' is one of the most familiar collective nouns in current English, for it describes a phenomenon that more and more of us observe with wonder every year, when hundreds – sometimes thousands – of these iridescent birds swarm and swirl above their roosting site in a choreographed whirlwind. Smaller flocks will join bigger ones until the sky is black with wings. The name 'murmuration' refers to the deep, low murmur of the birds as they swirl in unison.

The starling is one of the bird world's most talented linguists. It can mimic other birds, and can even imitate characteristics of human speech. Mozart famously kept one for several years, teaching his pet bird to sing and composing a funeral commemoration on its death. Some of Mozart's own compositions are said to bear the vocal autograph of the starling. Shakespeare mentions the bird only once, in *Henry IV, Part 1*, where Henry Hotspur fantasizes about training a starling to repeat the name 'Mortimer' as a means of goading the king into ransoming his brother-in-law:

> Nay, I'll have a starling shall be taught to speak
> Nothing but 'Mortimer', and give it him
> To keep his anger still in motion.

Shakespeare's words may have had remarkable consequences. The starling's prolific presence in North America is said to be down to a single act of homage to the Bard in 1890, when an eccentric socialite named Eugene Schieffelin released forty pairs of starlings into New York's Central Park, part of his mission to bring every one of the birds mentioned by Shakespeare to North America. The starling has filled a continent's skies with murmurations ever since.

12 November

PEISKOS

Manx speakers 'brabbag', while in England we 'cloffin'. Both words describe the simple pleasure of warming the back of one's legs in front of an open fire.

The hearth has long been the central point of a home. Not for nothing does the word 'focus' come from the Latin for 'fireplace', before becoming the burning point of a lens and, eventually, the centre of any interest or activity. In French *focus* became *foyer*, originally also a hearth, and later the focal meeting point within buildings such as theatres.

Lest you might think you have the full set of words for fireside comfort, Norwegian deepens it with *peiskos*, a word based on *peis*, meaning 'fireplace', and *kos*, 'cosiness'. Norway's winters are long and harsh, and so *peiskos* holds a special place in the cultural imagination, offering a respite from the cold and a way to savour moments of solace.

13 November

TREACLE

'Once upon a time there were three little sisters,' the Dormouse began in a great hurry; 'and their names were Elsie, Lacie, and Tillie; and they lived at the bottom of a well ...'

'What did they live on?' said Alice, who always took a great interest in questions of eating and drinking.

'They lived on treacle,' said the Dormouse.

Lewis Carroll began writing the story that was to become *Alice's Adventures in Wonderland* on this date in 1856. It is a story that has bewitched readers for generations, and it also introduced the possibility of treacle wells.

While modern treacle belongs to syrupy puddings and tarts, its original meaning was worlds away. When the word was borrowed into medieval English from the Old French *triacle*, it described an ointment that counteracted venomous bites. Its ultimate roots lie in the Greek *thēriakē*, an antidote against venom, and *thērion*, 'wild beast'. 'Treacle' later extended its meaning to embrace any remedy or medicine, and by the seventeenth century it took another turn, thanks to the traditional use of a sugary syrup to help medicine go down, Mary Poppins-style.

But it was on the healing sense that Lewis Carroll played when he introduced a treacle well in his story, for he was referring to one particular well situated in Binsey, just outside Oxford. As the author knew, the history of St Margaret's Well extends much further back than the pilgrims who came to seek remedy in its waters, for in Oxfordshire legend its spring was summoned by the city's patron saint, St Frideswide. It is said that its physiological powers were sought by Henry VIII and his queen, Catherine of Aragon, who turned to it for help producing a son and heir. In this instance at least, the well and its 'treacle' did not produce the desired results. Had the cure worked as hoped, the English Reformation might never have happened – in which case Binsey might have become a very different kind of pilgrimage site.

14 November

SNOTTER

A nineteenth-century slang dictionary defines the straight-talking word 'snotter' as 'a pickpocket who commits great depredations upon gentlemen's pocket-handkerchiefs'. No surprises there, given that by this time 'snotter' had been used for a piece of nasal mucus for some three centuries. *The English Dialect Dictionary* lists several more examples of its use: a 'snotter-bob', for example, is 'the membranous appendage to the beak of a turkey-cock', a 'snotter-box' is the nose, a 'snotter-clout' a hankie, and a 'snotter-cap' a 'dull, stupid, boorish fellow'.

Among builders, there is a distinctly different take in their use of 'snotter', for they apply it to some object that should never be there, such as a hair caught below plaster or paint.

15 November

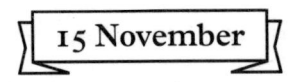

DESIDERATE

'The fault, dear Brutus, is not in our stars,/But in ourselves, that we are underlings.'

In early November 1572, at just eight years old, William Shakespeare lived through a supernova – a powerfully luminous explosion of a star – which flared into view in the Cassiopeia constellation in the northern sky as brightly as Venus. The event was to upend the accepted view of the universe and ultimately sparked a scientific revolution.

The prevailing view of the cosmos had remained largely unchanged since the time of the ancient Greek astronomer Ptolemy. His geocentric view fixed the earth at the centre of the universe, orbited by the sun and the other planets. Now, by measuring the supernova's position relative to the moon, the Danish astronomer Tycho Brahe and others were able to prove that the stars were not fixed at the same distance from the earth. Just four decades later, the Italian physicist Galileo Galilei, born the same year as Shakespeare, used his new telescope design to record four moons circling Jupiter on orbits that were not dependent on the earth and supported instead the heliocentric theory that most celestial objects orbit the sun. It was becoming rapidly clear to Elizabethans that they were far from the centre of the universe.

To 'desiderate' is to yearn for something we once had but that is now lost. At its heart is the Latin *sidus, sider-*, 'constellation', suggesting a sense of looking to the stars for something to return. Its relatives include 'desire' and 'consider', both reflecting the act of wishing upon the stars for satisfaction and wisdom. Today, 'desiderate' allows us to articulate a longing for the return of something we regret ever having let go.

16 November

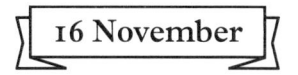

HUMGRUFFIN

Watch out for 'matutolypea', a word based on Latin and Greek and which literally means 'morning grief'. The emotion can be brought on by various things, whether a lack of coffee, food, or friendship, or just the prospect of a particularly bad day.

Any of them might turn us temporarily into a 'humgruffin': 'a terrible or repulsive person'. The term is likely to be a whimsical creation, based on the sound of grumbling and gruffness, with perhaps a touch of a fantastical 'griffin' thrown in for good measure. It first appears in a book of humorous poems published in 1842 – 'One horrid Humgruffin, who seem'd by his talk,/And the airs he assumed, to be Cock of the walk' – but has had surprisingly little oxygen since. For anyone feeling crumpsy and creased when they wake, 'humgruffin' is ready for the taking.

17 November

COMPANAGE

On National Homemade Bread Day, it is worth reflecting on the sweet spot that bread holds in our language. Throughout history it has been used as a placeholder for the most valuable things of life, be they financial or social, or when we 'break bread' with others in fellowship, a core tenet of Christianity. In Scots, one was once either in 'good bread' or 'bad bread', depending on whether one's circumstances were favourable or dire.

In some cases, the importance of bread has become so embedded in our vocabulary that it has lost its specificity. The word 'companion', in its most literal sense, is someone with (*com*) whom we share bread (the Latin *panis*), just as a 'mate' was once one who ate their 'meat' alongside us. For workers, the eating of bread as a meal was once such a given that any accompaniment, such as cheese, was known as 'companage', literally 'with bread'. Its greatest embodiment might just be the various ingredients of a ploughman's lunch.

18 November

HUNCHWEATHER

A nineteenth-century glossary of the dialect of East Anglia offers us a pleasingly pithy term for those days whose chill penetrates the bones and never leaves. This is 'hunchweather': the kind that makes you look down at the ground, shoulders bent, as you trudge beneath it with gritted teeth. Such a stoop would in fact render you 'hurply', a word from old Yorkshire dialect which is described in a Swaledale glossary as sticking up the back like 'a beast sheltering under a hedge in cold weather'.

19 November

YUGEN

Much of Japanese culture rests on ancient ideals and aesthetics. Many are expressed in single, beautiful words that are nigh impossible to translate with precision and clarity. These include *shibui*, a profound but unobtrusive beauty, and *wabi-sabi*, an acceptance of imperfection and an appreciation of the aging process.

Yugen, which is made up of two kanjis meaning 'shadowy' and 'profound', describes a deep and subtle sense of beauty that is almost impossible to pin down. It is found in the indistinct and the impermanent – something fully felt but only partially seen, a whisper rather than a statement. If you were to look at a rose with *yugen*, you would see it in a much deeper context. The rose has a life before and after that moment, while its petals tell the story of dozens of natural processes that have made them what they are: soil nutrition, bees spreading pollen, sun and rain. The life of the rose too is transitory, a knowledge that intensifies its beauty even further.

Yugen can be applied to contexts as sublime as a misty forest and as commonplace as interior design. What most seem agreed on is that, as a fourteenth-century Japanese playwright described it, it is 'an elegant, mysterious beauty that lies beyond words'.

20 November

GRUFELING

There are days when life leaves you 'gloppened', a useful old word that means open-mouthed in astonishment. For those times when you can scarcely believe your eyes, ears, or the news, English thankfully provides a few expressions for suspending reality and its unwelcome surprises for a while.

One of them is 'coorie', the Scots equivalent of the English 'cower', which has the added dimension of nestling down and settling in for the duration. It is just one term within a suitably well-furnished lexicon for snuggling, in which you can also find 'neezling', 'snoozling', 'snuggening', and 'croodling': all multi-taskers for when you need a quiet lie-down to forget about the chaos unfolding around you.

And finally there is 'grufeling', a word defined as 'to lie close wrapped up, and in a comfortable-looking manner'.

21 November

BOGWURPLING

There is nothing like a family saying to instinctively bind its members together. Many of us accept our parents' odd turns of phrase on the assumption that every other family uses them too, only to discover in later life that no, it was just us. This family lexicon is in turn handed down to other generations and taken on like a comfort blanket whenever we need a touch of home.

For their collection of *Kitchen-Table Lingo*, the English Project discovered a multitude of words and sayings that have been kept within families for generations. Among its finds are such delights as 'noofling', every parent's habit of licking a hankie and wiping their child's face with it; 'grooglums', the unspeakable debris left in a sink after washing up; 'barmbedarm', the bloated stomach after a full English; and 'testiculating', waving your arms around while talking bollocks (a word that quickly saw its way into the mainstream). Surely one of the very best, however, is 'bogwurpling', one family's creation for walking across a muddy, squelchy field.

22 November

SMULTRONSTÄLLE

In the depths of winter many of us will look ahead yearningly to summer. Holidays may be booked and photographs returned to as a reminder of halcyon days of warmth. Swedish offers us a multilayered word for such moments, which is more than the sum of its parts. *Smultronställe*, 'the place where the wild strawberries grow', is a cherished location in our lives that may be returned to in the imagination whenever recovery and peace are required. The term is most associated with Ingmar Bergman's 1957 film of the same name, in which a man reflects upon his youth and his life's meaningful moments.

Today, a personal strawberry patch may be as simple as a park bench, or as memory-packed as a family home. The abiding emotion that accompanies it is one of ease and fondness.

23 November

HEELS OVER HEAD

When William Faulkner was asked to list the three greatest novels, he replied: '*Anna Karenina, Anna Karenina,* and *Anna Karenina*'. First published in 1878, Leo Tolstoy's tumultuous tale of love, and the extent to which it can withstand societal expectations, still resonates as deeply with readers today. Its central tale is of Anna, the eponymous married heroine, and her passionate, head-over-heels affair with the cavalry officer Count Alexei Vronsky.

'Head over heels' has expressed the uncontrollable plunge into love for centuries. On closer examination, however, you might wonder how it expresses a plunge at all, given that it merely describes the physical position we spend most of our lives in, rather than one that renders us topsy-turvy.

The explanation lies in the erroneous transmission of the expression over time. Its earliest incarnation, in the late fourteenth century, was 'heels over head', the metaphor of an emotional somersault. But three centuries on, the words 'head' and 'heels' were swapped so that the idiom itself was (fittingly) turned upside down, and others unthinkingly perpetuated the same mistake. The two forms of the expression coexisted for a time before our modern version won the day.

Whichever way the body turns, the capacity of love to turn things upside down is at the heart of *Anna Karenina*. 'He stepped down, trying not to look at her, as if she was the sun. Yet he saw her, like the sun, even without looking.'

24 November

ORT

'Then what art colleyfoglin' for? I'm not havin' your orts an' slarts.' D.H. Lawrence was a master of dialect, capturing with great beauty and precision the vocabulary and accents unique to the mining communities of Derbyshire and Nottinghamshire. In this line from his *Love Poems*, a lively and lovely collection in which the poet uses dialect as a vehicle for gossip, scolding, and affection, he admonishes his listener for scheming ('colleyfoglin'') by giving him leftovers rather than a proper portion. An 'ort', in many regional dialects, is a fragment of food left over from a meal and applies as much to fodder left by cattle as the leavings at the table. The expression 'to make orts of' consequently meant to 'treat with contempt'. 'Slart' is equally expressive of 'scraps' or slim pickings.

More useful still, perhaps, 'ort' can be a verb meaning 'to pick out the best bits of food and leave the rest'. We all know dinner guests (and teenagers) like that.

25 November

CODDIWOMPLE

English speakers love a pootle, as is evidenced by the dozens of words for it up and down the dictionary. We may decide to 'tootle', 'saunter', 'soodle', 'moodle', 'dander', 'streek', or 'streel', for starters. If we're being dragged along without enthusiasm, we are 'trampoosing'. And we can choose to be 'boulevardiers', 'flâneurs', 'round-towners', or 'sidewalk superintendents' (those who love nothing more than strolling around and giving unsolicited advice). But yet to be officiated for the dictionary is the word 'coddiwompling', which is to travel in a purposeful manner towards a destination as yet unknown. In other words, coddiwompling is all about the journey, but rather than involving an idly aimless saunter, this is a walk with determination. You may not know where you're heading, but you will make sure you get there. Though a recent coinage, it has caught on fast and is even the subject of a 2019 TED Talk from Nancy Osborne, a former United Nations security adviser, who persuasively argues that coddiwompling could be the key to a happy and satisfying life.

26 November

ANATHEMA

Most of us know about a valediction, but what about its evil twin, 'malediction'? While the former means 'speaking well' of someone, the latter involves 'speaking ill'. More simply, a malediction is a curse.

On this day in 1922 the tomb of Tutankhamun was discovered by the British archaeologist Howard Carter, thereby unleashing, if legend is believed, the curse of the pharaohs. An article in the *New York Times* less than a month later reported the account of another Egyptologist, James Henry Breasted, who worked with Carter soon after the first opening of the tomb. Breasted told how Carter had sent a messenger on an errand to his house, where the messenger claimed to hear a 'faint, almost human cry' and then discovered a birdcage containing a cobra, the emblem of the Egyptian monarchy, which had devoured Carter's canary. This was interpreted by local residents as the result of a curse invoked when Tutankhamun's tomb had been entered.

A belief in vengeful spirits and malevolent gods has inspired maledictions and spells for millennia. In the late 1970s at the Roman baths at Bath, 130 ancient 'curse tablets', or *defixiones*, were unearthed, bearing inscriptions that plead for the death and destruction of an enemy. *Defixiones* is rooted in the Latin *defigere*, 'to fasten', since it was believed that, through a curse, evil would bind itself to the enemy. One tablet wills the gods to ensure that 'he who carried off Vilbia from me become liquid as the water. May she who so obscenely devoured her become dumb . . . and have all her intestines eaten away.'

In the Middle Ages, book curses were widely employed, designed to deter thieves from stealing valuable manuscripts. At a time when superstition was deeply entrenched in the imagination, such curses threatened to invoke the wrath of God if a book or scroll was unlawfully taken. In a Bible translation from around 1172, the scribe included this warning:

> If anyone take away this book, let him die the death; let him be fried in a pan; let the falling sickness and fever seize him; let him be broken on the wheel, and hanged. Amen.

If God or evil spirits didn't get to the thief first, excommunication was a certain forfeit, also known as 'anathema'. This word from Greek means 'thing dedicated', and later, specifically, a 'thing devoted to evil'.

27 November

FOOFARAW

On this day in 1810, Theodore Edward Hook made a bet that he could make any house the most talked about in London, and proceeded to bring the city to a standstill. At around 5 a.m. a chimney sweep arrived at 54 Berners Street, claiming to have been called to the address. The maid, assuming it to be a mistake, sent him on his way, only to answer the door a few minutes later to another sweep, and another, followed by a medley of cake-makers, apothecaries, doctors, vicars, undertakers with coffins, and a group of piano-makers with bulky instruments. By now Berners Street was in chaos, and as news spread, even more people turned up to watch and wonder at the procession of tradespeople arriving at number 54. The more observant among them may have noticed a man standing on the pavement opposite handing his friend a guinea, for Hook had irrefutably won his bet. It's estimated that he summoned around 4,000 people from a dizzying array of professions to knock on the door opposite. Known thereafter as the 'Berners Street Hoax', it became one of the most notorious foofaraws of its day.

'Foofaraw' itself is an incontestably wonderful word which originated in the American West, where pioneers used it for frivolous trinkets, baubles, and gewgaws. Partly a borrowing from French, where a *fanfaron* is a boastful braggart, and partly from Spanish, in which *fanfarrón* means 'ostentatious' and 'vain', it may have been influenced by French *froufrou*, a word for the rustling of a woman's skirts, suggestive of showy ornamentation and therefore a bit of a fuss.

28 November

DAMFINO

It would be hard to remember a time without the debate as to whether swearing is becoming more prolific among younger generations – mostly held among parents and newspapers rather than the swearers themselves. While swearing in private spaces may well have remained largely stable, the very public kind is undoubtedly more noticeable, and many of those who would have stopped and stared at a dropper of the F-bomb on a street corner a generation ago are unlikely to be surprised at it today. As a result, some among us might be feeling that the arsenal of exclamations is lacking some creativity. Should you wish for some more esoteric exclamations to soothe feelings of pain, frustration, stress, surprise, or even joy, then – as so often in life – we should look no further than a historical dictionary.

Here we will find such beauties as 'Gadsbudlikins!', a medieval swerve around blasphemy and a mangling of 'God's body'; 'by cock's bones!', one of the earliest oaths, in which 'cock' is again a euphemism for 'God'; and the curious collection of 'damn my diaphragm!', 'strike me good-looking', 'douse my top lights!', 'bust my gizzard!', and 'dog bite my onions!'. But surely the crème de la crème of all euphemistic fig leaves is 'damfino', a simple retort from Victorian times to any annoying question which decodes to the shoulder-shrugging 'damned if I know'.

29 November

CUMBERWORLD

Of all the glorious insults contained in the *Oxford English Dictionary* – and there are many – one of the most withering can be found in 'cumberworld', from the fourteenth century. Although most examples of its use are self-referential and fairly maudlin (generally from depressed poets), it is surely far more useful as a sophisticated put-down that, at its most basic level, tells someone they are a total waste of space, only far more elegantly. Its definition? 'A person or thing that uselessly encumbers the world.'

30 November

METANOIA

'The only transformation that interests me is a total transformation – however minute,' wrote Susan Sontag in her diary. The writer was famous for her continuous reworking of herself, making changes as apparently small as escaping her early pen name 'Sue', lest it tether her to the past, and as great as denouncing her communist politics and turning to liberalism instead. Her last words to her son, as recorded in her biography, suggested she still had much to say: 'I want to tell you . . .'

The word 'metanoia' describes a transformational change of heart, or, in spiritual terms, a total conversion. It comes from the Greek for a 'change of mind', but once borrowed into English it took on the dimensions of a total reorientation of one's way of life – a repentance for the past as well as a new understanding of the future. And when a person stands at a crossroads, Sontag gave them wisdom for that too: 'It is easier to endure than to change. But once one has changed, what was endured is hard to recall.'

DECEMBER

1 December

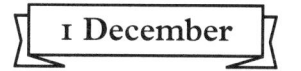

VOORPRET

The etymology of 'Advent' goes back to the Latin *advenire*, 'to come to', for this is a time in the Christian year that builds up to the birthday of Christ and his second coming. In lay terms, this day marks the start of the countdown to holidays and to midwinter, when the sense of anticipation is high. In Japanese, the term *wakuwaku* is the onomatopoeic description of happiness at the prospect of an upcoming event. In Dutch, it is expressed as *voorpret*, 'pre-fun'. Thanks to those living in the eighteenth century, English speakers needn't miss out either: for us there is 'betwitterment', a pleasingly fluttery word that describes thrilling if nervous excitement.

2 December

MALO MALO MALO MALO

We all love a bit of wordplay at Christmastime – even when it comes with the corniest of Christmas cracker puns. If you're looking for something a little more sophisticated, you might like the rhetorical device known as 'antanaclasis', a characteristically elegant Greek borrowing for something that is rather clever, namely the use of the same word in multiple different senses. Perhaps the most famous example is 'Buffalo buffalo Buffalo buffalo buffalo buffalo Buffalo buffalo', an admittedly unlikely sentence that translates roughly as 'Buffalo buffalo [bison from Buffalo NY] [that] Buffalo buffalo buffalo [that the bison from Buffalo NY bully] buffalo Buffalo buffalo [are bullying bison from Buffalo NY].'

There are far older examples. The Romans, for instance, had fun with *malo malo malo malo*, an arguably even more inventive sentence designed to teach pupils the ablative and locative cases, and which translates rather incredibly to 'I would rather be in an apple tree than a naughty boy in trouble' – the Latin *malo* has all these senses depending on context and emphasis.

If at this forgiving time you prefer to stick to the cheesy, there is always another favourite: 'Time flies like an arrow. Fruit flies like a banana.'

3 December

GEBORGENHEIT

In 2004, the Deutscher Sprachrat (German Language Council) and the Goethe Institute selected *Geborgenheit* as the second most beautiful word in the German language after *Habseligkeiten* (the paltry but cherished belongings of someone poor). *Geborgenheit* has no direct equivalent in English, for it is the total sum of a variety of feelings whose common threads are warmth, security, closeness, and comfort. You may find it in the hug of a long-lost friend, the timelessness of your childhood bedroom, or the traditional dish that graces the Christmas table each year.

4 December

FERHOODLED

English lacks a word to succinctly convey the sticky mess of uncooperative Sellotape that can ensue while wrapping presents, as well as the chaos of a disorderly sock drawer, or the tangle of phone leads lurking below every desk or bedside table (what the Germans know as a *Kabelsalat,* 'cable salad'). In Pennsylvanian Dutch, each of these situations might be described as 'ferhoodled': utterly mixed up. Its name is a relative of the German *verhuddeln,* meaning 'to bungle, blemish, or bring everything into disarray'. Even people can be 'ferhoodled' if they are momentarily befuddled.

On the brighter side, some families have created an edible version of such muddle which they also know as a 'ferhoodle': think scrambled eggs, potatoes, ham, peppers, or whatever happens to be in the fridge.

5 December

BUFF

On the evening of 5 December 1876, one of the most catastrophic fires in New York history broke out in the city's Brooklyn Theatre. The production of the play *The Two Orphans* featured a wooden reconstruction of an old boathouse on the bank of the Seine, which was made of painted canvas on a flimsy wooden frame that turned out to be highly flammable. Ignited by a gas lamp, the conflagration that followed resulted in a death toll of nearly 300 people, primarily in the upper galleries of the theatre housing the cheapest seats. When Thomas Nevins, chief engineer of the Brooklyn Fire Department, eventually arrived at the theatre with his men, he was forced to conclude that the building was lost and that his job was now one of recovery.

Nevins's team may have included several 'buffs', volunteer firemen in New York City whose name came from the fact that their uniforms were made of buff leather to keep them warm during the icy winters. The New York *Sun* would go on to describe them as 'men and boys whose love of fires, firefighting, and firemen is a predominant characteristic'.

It seems a significant leap to go from these warmly clad fire-chasers to the experts we know as 'buffs' today, but as time went on the name was extended to cover an aficionado of any subject that ignited their passion. The final link in the chain is the expression 'in the buff', i.e. naked, since the colour of buffalo or 'buff' leather was thought to be similar to that of human flesh.

6 December

SISU

Today is Independence Day in Finland, commemorating the country's freedom from Russian rule and its recognition as a sovereign nation.

Sisu is often described as 'the word that defines Finland'. Said to represent the quintessence of the Finnish spirit, it means both resilience and the ability to fight through hardship no matter what. The word's popularity emerged in the face of the nation's gutsy perseverance during the country's invasion by the Soviet Union. As *Time* magazine reported in 1940:

> The Finns have something they call *sisu*. It is a compound of bravado and bravery, of ferocity and tenacity, of the ability to keep fighting after most people would have quit, and to fight with the will to win.

Indeed, *sisu* has been described as so essential to the Finnish national character that 'to be a real Finn, you must have it'. The rest of us can only look on and admire.

7 December

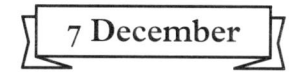

MAMIHLAPINATAPAI

From opportunistic smooches beneath the mistletoe to the 'miskissing' (fourteenth-century speak for the 'improper' kind) at the office party, December can be as much a spur for romance as the early thrills of spring. On such occasions we often turn to French for the language of love, but it is far from the only tongue that can teach us something. The word *mamihlapinatapai* is derived from the Yaghan language of Tierra del Fuego, and was listed in the *Guinness Book of World Records* as the 'most succinct word' in existence. It is as untranslatable as it is unpronounceable, but roughly put, *mamihlapinatapai* involves two parties looking at each other and hoping that the other will initiate something that the other is too nervous to start themselves.

8 December

TOE-COVER

Desperate shopping and excessive spending at this time of year is a given, and it follows that we have created one or two words for it. Take 'abligurition', an ugly word from the eighteenth century for the inadvisable but inevitable 'extravagant spending on food and drink'. The lexicographer Nathan Bailey's *Universal Etymological English Dictionary* of 1724 offers a slightly more heartening definition, namely 'prodigal spending in belly-cheer', in which 'belly-cheer' perfectly encapsulates the buying of food for comfort (or greed) rather than necessity.

Overspending on presents is another matter, and most of us are seduced at some point by 'discounted' items by the tills that may look wonderful but will almost certainly disappoint – what the Victorians knew as 'wonderclouts'. For anyone in need of a gentler adjective for something utterly worthless, it is worth remembering 'quisquilious', a word based on a Latin word for dregs or refuse that manages to sound quite beautiful. The keen shopper starts Christmas shopping with high hopes of finding the perfect gift but often ends up buying socks instead. Luckily, there is an exasperated word for that too – this time from the point of view of the receiver – 'toe-cover' is 1940s slang for a cheap and disappointing present.

9 December

RAMRACKET

As the holidays approach, the levels of excitement rise, and depending on where in Britain you happen to be, a fidgety and restless child can be described as 'lissom' (Berkshire, Wiltshire, or Staffordshire), 'sprack' (Wiltshire), 'spry' (Dorset), 'wick' (all over the north), 'pert' (Sussex), or 'wiggy-arsed' (Wiltshire); they can 'have a clew in their bottom' (Northumberland), or be 'full of ganning on' (Northumberland), or 'on the rouk', 'on the wander', or 'riving' in Yorkshire. Marvellous as all these descriptions are, it would be hard to top the Somerset adjective 'upstrigolous', which somehow manages to combine affection with annoyance towards a child who simply can't sit still.

Meanwhile, as fever builds, let's hear it for 'ramracketting', defined in the *English Dialect Dictionary* as 'Christmas gambols' – or jumping about playfully at Yuletide.

10 December

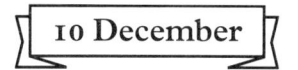

ORANGE

This is the time of year when the shops start filling with the heady scent of citrus. No 'Christingle' service for children is complete without oranges (each fruit representing the world) studded with sweets on sticks and lit with candles whose flames threaten to kindle more than Christmas spirit. Such candles, which symbolize Christ as the light of the world, take their name from the German dialect term *Christkindl*, 'Christ child', since the tradition originated in the Moravian churches of Germany.

Oranges are the focus not only of Christingle, but of many a linguistic discussion that hangs on the question, 'Which came first, the colour or the fruit?' The answer is most definitely the latter, which was first cultivated in South-East Asia. In the Middle Ages, the Seville variety was brought by the Arabs to Sicily, whence it spread to the rest of Europe. Its name changed several times over the course of its long journey. In Arabic it was known as a *naranj*, and in Spanish as a *naranja*; by the time it arrived in French and English in the 1400s, the 'n' had migrated to the article before it. The popularity of the sweet fruit grew quickly, but it was to take another century before orange as a colour emerged to replace the cumbersome *giolureade*, 'yellow red'. On this day in 1688 the accident-prone James II, last of the Stuart kings, fled the country in fear of the superior forces of his Dutch son-in-law William of Orange, only to be caught by some fishermen at Faversham. As a result, Britain's new royal family were Orange.

11 December

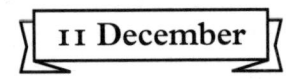

GIGIL

Any word that sounds like 'giggle' promises a child-like sense of fun. And 'gigil', originally from the Philippines, doesn't disappoint. In the official language of Tagalog, this word describes the overwhelming feeling of joy in the face of almost unbearable cuteness. It might be the fresh-faced smile of a young child, or the liquid eyes of a puppy staring back at you. 'Gigil' is the impulse that inspires you to smile, exclaim, or, more often, physically squeeze the object of cuteness in an outburst of affection. In this sense, 'gigil' remains the preserve of elderly relatives.

Not everything is sweetness and light, however. In the same way as it connotes an exaggerated explosion of joy, 'gigil' can also induce extreme irritation in the person at the other end of it. This impulse, just as strong, is nicely encapsulated in the counter-response *nakakagigil ka*, which roughly means 'I could kill you'.

12 December

BINFLUENCER

Forget social media. Our street is the only site any of us really needs to engage with. On every one there is a neighbour who conscientiously puts out their bins, ready for bin day, first. Everyone else notices this and promptly puts out their own. It follows then that this resident is none other than the local 'binfluencer', a recent coinage we never knew we needed.

There is even an influencer bin – Count Binface, the creation of British comedian Jon Harvey, who has run as a high-profile satirical candidate in various elections. Wearing a customized bin as a helmet and a flapping cloak, he made his first appearance on this day in 2018, and ran in the following year against the sitting UK prime minister, Boris Johnson, with the aim of promoting electoral participation through ridicule. His manifesto includes nationalizing both Adele and model railways and inviting the other countries in Europe to join the UK.

There is a common misconception that the job of a refuse collector is entirely menial and unskilled. This myth can be dispelled simply by looking at the forty-seven-page induction document that each new recruit must absorb and follow, not to mention the complicated street systems that many must navigate, often with just a hair's breadth of space to manoeuvre. Such quick thinking and creativity are amply reflected in the tribal lexicon of the bin collectors, who will speak of a 'Tiffany' if a road has been left sparklingly clean, and of 'air mail' when rubbish is thrown by a panicked resident into the claws of the truck from a window. Surely the best description of all, however, belongs to the daily sight in summer of wriggling and writhing maggots among the bursting bin bags. These, in the slang of the 'garbologists', are known as 'disco rice'.

13 December

WAITS

Go to any town or city in the Middle Ages and you would have found a group of 'waits': a band of musicians, particularly wind instrumentalists, whose duties included waking citizens on dark winter days by playing loudly in the streets. They would also entertain prominent visitors at the city gates, including monarchs. A chronicle of 1587 relates how 'The waits of the citie were placed with lowd musicke, who cheerefullie &

melodiouslie welcomed hir maiestie into the citie, this song being soong by the best voices in the same.'

Although the public office of waits was abolished in 1835, the term survived to encompass groups of singers and musicians who sang around their home town or city at night, especially carols at Christmastime.

14 December

BAUBLE-BEARER

Deck the halls. Dress the tree. Christmas is a particularly sparkly time of year, when tinsel glitters beneath the fairy lights. Originally the name for a cloth that was woven with shining metal threads to mimic the appearance of ice, tinsel makes our homes positively 'clinquant', a pickup from French that means 'glittering with silver and gold' or, as Samuel Johnson put it in his *Dictionary*, 'dressed in spangles'.

Aside from the tangy sweets some of us enjoyed as children, what exactly is a 'spangle'? The dictionary will tell you it is a 'little spang', a small glittering ornament that shares a root with a Viking term for a clasp, buckle, or brooch. In the late Middle Ages, the name was applied to a piece of sparkling metal with a hole in its centre and a thread pulled through it. Such ornaments were used for the decoration of textile fabrics and other materials, including, eventually, Christmas baubles.

Spangles may have ended their story there had it not been for the US lawyer Francis Scott Key, who boarded HMS *Tonnant* during the War of 1812 with the intention of negotiating with the British fleet for the release of his fellow countrymen who were being held prisoner. Ironically, he himself was not allowed to leave until the British attacked Baltimore the next morning, forcing him to watch the bombardment from a ship belonging to the enemy. It was here that he wrote the lines that were to become the US national anthem, the first verse of which concludes, 'O, say does that star-spangled banner yet wave,/O'er the land of the free and the home of the brave?'

'Bauble' derives from *beaubelet*, an Old French word for a child's toy or plaything, and dates back to at least the fourteenth century, when it carried today's meaning of a showy ornament. In the years that followed, 'bauble' doubled up to mean the baton carried by court jesters (who were nicknamed 'bauble-bearers' in Tudor England) as well as a foolish person. 'To give someone the bauble', in seventeenth-century English, meant to make fun of them.

15 December

DROWN THE MILLER

Welcome to 'quafftide': the fifteenth-century word that announces it is very much time for a drink. Today is International Tea Day, one on which all 'theists' (how the poet Shelley, an immoderate tea-drinker, used to describe himself) celebrate what is variously known across Britain as 'putting on a brew', 'mashing', 'biding and drawing', 'steeping', 'empting', 'helling', and 'lading'. When people gather around a teapot, one of the assembled might ask 'who's mother?', an expression that also led to the punchier Victorian phrase 'bitching the pot'.

The temperance movement, established in the nineteenth century to fight against the pernicious effects of alcohol, embraced tea as its replacement so heartily that the word 'teetotal' has often been spelled 'tea-total'. In fact, 'teetotal' is an emphatic underlining of the 't' in 'total' as a pledge to abstain entirely from alcohol.

Meanwhile, any hater of weak tea might do well to learn the phrase 'drown the miller', used to indicate that too much water has been added to the pot. In the Royal Navy, it was rations of grog or rum that were the scene of a miller's drowning, thereby ruining what promised to be a very good thing.

16 December

ÆLFSOGOÐA

'Jiminy Christmas! ... I'm a cotton-headed ninny muggins.' *Elf* regularly tops the lists of heart-warming festive movies. But the elves of earlier times were not the red-cheeked, Noddy-hatted helpers of today's Christmas grottoes. Instead, these earliest versions were dwarfish creatures responsible for disease, nightmares, and the stealing of children. Their name is a relative of both the German *Alp*, 'nightmare', and the English 'oaf', thought to be a changeling left behind by the elves when they stole a child from its home. To be 'elf-shot', in the seventeenth century, was to be pierced by the arrow of a tiny archer and afflicted with a disease or other supernatural curse.

The dictionary lets in the occasional chink of light, however, for these elves can be as mischievous and witty as Buddy the Elf when they want to be. Anyone displaying 'elflocks' of a morning, for example, has woken up with excessively tangled hair, thought to be the work of mischievous sprites overnight who have played merry havoc with our barnet. And to have *ælfsogoða*, in a book of Anglo-Saxon magic, was to have a fit of the hiccups as the result of an elfish prank.

Elves could also be wise when they chose. The first name of England's cleverest Saxon king, Alfred, literally means 'elf-counsel'.

17 December

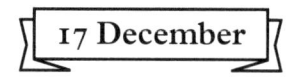

RETROUVAILLES

'Tis the season for renewing friendships via Christmas cards or round robins, and for seeking out those we may see just once a year but who tether us to family and continuity. While not all visits go perfectly to plan, the French have a word for the happiest reunions that take place after a long time apart. A *retrouvailles*, literally speaking, is a 'refinding', or the happy rediscovery of old friends.

In Basque, *aspaldiko* equally decribes the euphoria felt when catching up with someone who has been missing from your life for too long.

18 December

FUROSHIKI

The term 'bath-spread' doesn't sound particularly enticing, unless the spread in question is a glass of red and a few canapés as you sink below the bubbles. This is, however, the literal meaning of the Japanese term *furoshiki*, and its origins, though watery, are rather different. Its earliest outings relate to the careful wrapping of a bather's clothes before entering a *sento*, or public bath, to protect them from and prevent them getting lost. This wrapping was far from the usual roll or bundle, however; rather it involved square pieces of traditional cloth that could also be used for wrapping food or gifts. At Christmas, the art of *furoshiki* comes into its own, when present-givers choose exquisitely patterned cloth as an alternative to conventional wrapping paper. There is just as much symbolism in the knot with which the cloths are tied: the more delicate and elaborate, the greater the respect towards the recipient. It certainly puts to shame the traditional dash to the supermarket on Christmas Eve for the last bit of grotty wrapping paper.

19 December

ON-DING

Forget fifty Inuit words for snow. There are more than 400 terms for the white stuff in Scots – covering its imminence, texture, heaviness, flutters, joys, and sounds.

This word-hoard includes 'feefle', to swirl; 'smirr', a smattering of snow; 'unbrak', the beginning of a thaw; 'flindrikin', a slight snow shower; and 'flother' and 'figgerin', both descriptions of a single flake of snow that might be a harbinger of more. 'Skovin' is a large snowflake, while a 'snaw-ghast' is an apparition seen in the snow. A particularly heavy snowstorm, such as many of us wish for at Christmas, was once known as an 'on-ding', in which a 'ding' represents a forceful blow or sharp smack, as though the ground is suddenly covered in one swift slap of the skies.

20 December

YULE-SHARD

Today is officially 'Dot Your I's Day' (*see* TITTLE, 26 September), a reminder to all of us to pay attention to detail and to be less slipshod in life. Perhaps this particular date was chosen as a warning against becoming a 'Yule-shard': the person who leaves the office for the holidays with a lot of work unfinished.

The French have a particularly good expression to describe any last-minute push towards a work goal, particularly at this festive season. *Charrette* harks back to an old practice in nineteenth-century Paris among students of architecture, who would transport their elaborate building models in a cart (grandiosely referred to as a chariot) across the city at the very last minute, frantically making alterations as they went to meet their final deadline. Anything not on the cart by the end of the night would not be counted towards their final grade; hence the last night of term was known as 'night of the chariot'.

21 December

PERTOLERATE

Today is the winter solstice, the shortest day and the longest night of the year. It is the precise point of midwinter, after which light begins its slow climb back to us and night is no longer dominant. When the sun pauses for a moment, there is a glimpse of renewal as it begins its journey north towards midsummer. These darkest and most dormant days of winter have been celebrated in rituals since ancient times, from the Roman Saturnalia to the pagan Yule and on to the Christian Christmas. In Iran it is known as Yalda, a time when friends and family gather together to eat, drink, and read poetry. Fruit and nuts are eaten, especially pomegranates and watermelon, whose red colour symbolizes the crimson hues of dawn and the glow of life. The end is in sight at last.

December is a month when we may well feel we have 'pertolerated' the year, drawing on a now-obsolete term that meant, according to Cockeram's seventeenth-century *English Dictionarie*, 'to endure to the end'.

22 December

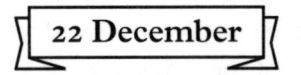

IKTSUARPOK

The festive season tends to produce two types of host. Firstly, there is the kind who never seems to have enough time for the cleaning and cooking required when friends and family descend, resulting in a fit of manic 'scurryfunging' – old US dialect for the tidying frenzy that occurs even as the guests are walking down your path. Conversely, there is the person who has been fully prepared for several weeks, their wrapped presents safely stowed beneath the tree, and their fridge plentifully stocked after a highly efficient and list-driven expedition to the shops. This second category of host is often restless, eager for it all to begin after so much preparation, and listening out expectantly for the car pulling up and the ring of the bell. English has yet to find the right term for this category, but we would do well to borrow from the Inuit language of Inuktitut, in which *iktsuarpok* describes the repeated process, born of a mix of anxiety and excitement, of going outside to check for the approach of a long-awaited guest.

23 December

RESPAIR

Although most of us would associate 'halcyon days' with the serenity of summer, they actually belong to winter and the fortnight around its solstice. The *alkuōn* of Greek myth was a fabled creature identified with the kingfisher, whose name translates as 'sea-conceiving'. Its legend focuses upon the goddess Alcyone, who, upon hearing the news of her husband Ceyx's drowning, is said to have cast herself into the sea in grief.

Moved by her plight, the rest of the gods turned both Alcyone and Ceyx into kingfishers. Every year, Alcyone would build her nest on the surface of the sea, while her father Aeolus, divine keeper of the winds, kept them calm and unruffled.

Halcyon days are surely ones of 'respair', a word recorded just once in the *Oxford English Dictionary* and one of the greatest of all the lost positives, for it means 'fresh hope', and a recovery from despair.

24 December

JOLABOKAFLOD

'\'Twas the night before Christmas.' Christmas Eve is the time for present-giving in many cultures, when children may be told they have been visited by jolly-timbered St Nicholas, by the Christkind (Christ child) or, in Latin America, by El Niño Jesús. The gifts bequeathed by these benefactors may be traditional or modern, but in Iceland they go one better. Here, Christmas is filled with the results of a *jolabokaflod*, 'Yule book flood', when publishers fill the bookshops with new titles ready to be given on Christmas Eve. The real joy comes afterwards, when the family reads into the night tucked under cosy blankets, hands cupped around mugs of steaming hot chocolate. The ritual is said to have begun during the dark days of the Second World War, when paper was one of the few things to escape rationing.

25 December

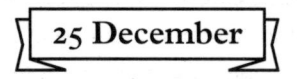

BUMMOCK

In Scotland, Yuletide is also affectionately dubbed the 'Daft Days' thanks to its abundance of entertainment and games. When it comes to the celebrating, the nineteenth-century 'bummock' describes both the huge amount of booze consumed at Christmas and a 'Christmas party thrown by landlords for their tenants'. As for the food served at the bummock, one name for a male turkey was 'bubbly jock', although the dictionary doesn't relate if the bird's mood shifted in the run-up to Christmas.

At its best, Christmas is about togetherness, and at the heart of the beautiful Greek word 'irenic', meaning 'peace-bringing', is an ancient root meaning 'thread'. The idea is of binding people together in reconciliation and harmony, when hatchets are buried and differences forgotten. There can be few better words for Christmas Day.

26 December

BLELLUM

Sadly we can't all be as saintly as Good King Wenceslas, who according to our favourite Christmas carol strode off on this St Stephen's Day across the heavy snow to bring food and firewood to a poor peasant. For most of us, this is a time of semi-friendly family fisticuffs over Scrabble, the remote control, or the dregs of the Quality Street tin.

Luckily, we are well armed to cope with such minor brouhahas, at least linguistically speaking. From 'collieshangie' and 'argy-bargy', to the 'wringle-wrangle' or 'stairhead rammy' (should any arguments extend to neighbours), there is usually a suitable name. And at this point in proceedings watch out for the catalyst for any one of them: the 'blellum', a name that describes the family member or guest who simply won't stop talking. The only record given in the *Oxford English Dictionary* gives us its full flavour, thanks to Rabbie Burns: 'A blethering, blustering, drunken blellum.' Perhaps there was one of those in Wenceslas's Bohemian castle, inspiring his overwhelming desire for a long walk into a blizzard.

27 December

CURMURRING

The Scots enjoy the admirable tradition of 'crawmassing', making the most of the leftovers from the Christmas feast to avoid any waste. In this hazy run of days that goes by various names, including 'Twixtmas', the 'Merryneum', or 'Blursday', when the 'Yule-hole' (the last hole in your belt that needs to be turned to at Christmastime) is creaking, we may need to find some delicate expressions for the bodily consequences of our excess. You might, for example, experience some grumbling in your 'groozlins' (intestines), as well as a 'wambling' of the stomach – far from referencing furry creatures of Wimbledon, to 'wamble' is described in Samuel Johnson's *Dictionary* as 'to roll with nausea and sickness'.

Perhaps the least offensive of the crapulent lexicon is 'curmurring', a word that already sounds a little irritable and which indicates 'a rumbling sound, especially that made in the bowels by flatulence'. Then again, the Scottish novelist Walter Scott clearly took kindly to a hair of the dog: 'A glass of brandy to three glasses of wine,' he wrote, 'prevents the curmurring in the stomach.'

28 December

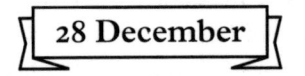

QUERENCIA

The adage that guests, like fish, go off after three days has become proverbial wisdom in so many languages that it must surely be a universal truth. If 'apanthropy' (the desire to be left alone) has fully kicked in by this point of the year, then Spanish can offer the soothing prospect of a *querencia*. Forget its sense in English as the place where a bull stands in a bullring before its cruel baiting takes place (where, according to Ernest Hemingway, the poor animal is 'inestimably more dangerous and impossible to kill'), in its native tongue *querencia* is about emotional rather than brutish strength. *Querencia* is an animal's favourite haunt: the one that conveys safety as well as protection. Its root is the word *querer*, which means 'to want', 'to desire', and 'to love'.

If you prefer to stick to a rather less poetic English word, you might reach for the verb 'latibulate', which came and went in the seventeenth century, and which is defined as 'privily to hide ones selfe in the corner'.

29 December

PEREGRINATE

This can also be the time of year when we begin to feel restless and start to plan ways in which to satiate our wanderlust.

In 1162, Henry II, the great-grandson of William the Conqueror, made the bold move of appointing Thomas à Becket, a layman, as archbishop of Canterbury. He did so in the hope that Becket, a close confidant, would support the Crown's rather than the Church's interests. The subsequent conflicts between the two men focused particularly on Becket's insistence that clergymen suspected of heinous crimes should enjoy the privilege of a church trial, and culminated in the covert (and, Henry insisted, unauthorized) assassination of the archbishop by four knights within the walls of Canterbury Cathedral on 29 December 1170. Following Becket's canonization in 1173, the martyr's shrine became one of the major destinations for pilgrimages throughout Europe and this day became his feast day.

The term 'pilgrim' derives from Latin via the Anglo-Norman *pilegrin* and shares a root with 'peregrine', 'a stranger from foreign parts'. (The peregrine falcon is the 'pilgrim falcon', because the birds were caught fully grown on migration rather than taken from the nest.) Although pilgrimages were often made to distant holy places, more local ones were inevitably more accessible, and Canterbury became a principal centre for many pilgrims, including most famously those in Chaucer's *Canterbury Tales*.

These pilgrims would make their journey to Becket's shrine at a comfortable pace, exchanging gossip and stories as they went. The leisurely pace of their travels was known as a 'Canterbury trot', frequently shortened simply to 'Canterbury', and then still further to the modern 'canter'. What they were most certainly doing was 'peregrinating', a useful verb for this fidgety period meaning 'to journey' as well as 'to live in foreign places'.

30 December

MNEMONIC

On this day in 1460, Richard, Duke of York, was killed in the Battle of Wakefield, a major engagement in the Wars of the Roses and an early victory for the Lancastrians. His rule was brief and he was killed before he could be crowned. But he left an unlikely legacy in language, as the inspiration for one of the most famous mnemonics in the world, in which 'Richard of York Gave Battle in Vain' gives us the colours of the rainbow: red, orange, yellow, green, blue, indigo, and violet.

The Greeks believed that there were two kinds of memory: the 'natural' and the 'artificial'. The first is instinctive, while the second needs to be trained through the practice of a variety of mnemonic techniques. The word 'mnemonic' shares its history with Mnemosyne, the Greek goddess of memory, who took her name in turn from the Greek *mnēmōn*, meaning 'mindful'. One of the Titans, daughter of Uranus and Gaia, Mnemosyne was the mother of the nine Muses, the sister goddesses in Greek mythology who presided over song and poetry as well as the arts and sciences. Her name seems a fitting choice for aids to memory and knowledge.

31 December

L'APPEL DU VIDE

Beer goggles or no, New Year's Eve often represents a willing leap into the unknown, when anything seems possible. As we wait for what the Germans call the *Rausschmeisser* ('kicker-outer') – the last song played at a bar before closing time, signalling the time to leave – we may feel full of optimism for the year ahead. The more cautious among us might experience an emotion the same Germans would express as *Schwellenangst*: the fear of crossing a threshold to embark on something new.

For this unique liminal moment of the year, French offers us something even more profound. If you have ever stood on the precipice of a cliff and contemplated the feeling of jumping off, you have experienced *l'appel du vide*, 'the call of the void'. Thankfully, most of us resist it, but what if a morbid curiosity in the idea of oblivion, and the drawing back from it, is in fact the best way of affirming and confirming the desire to live? The call of the void is actually about human survival. With each new year we are leaping into what might be. So here's to you. Let's make it a good one.

ACKNOWLEDGEMENTS

The more books I write, the more I appreciate the efforts and dedication of those behind the scenes: the advisers, designers, proofreaders, publicists, sale teams, walking companions, and cake purveyors. This is particularly true of *Words for Life*, which has been carried through by all of the above with energy, good humour, and skill.

As always, my editor, Georgina Laycock, has breathed life into this book from its embryonic stage right up until the frantic stages of proofs and press releases. I have yet to discover anything George can't do. To her I dedicate the Swedish word *lagom*: a Goldilocks term which means 'not too much, and not too little, but just right'.

The team working alongside her at John Murray have been as excellent as ever. Never 'depooperit', and certainly never guilty of a *Verschlimmbesserung*. Thank you to Caroline Westmore, the source of endless wisdom (and leniency over deadlines), my clever publicist Anna-Marie Fitzgerald, and Sara Marafini for another great cover. Thanks also to Tim Waller, my eagle-eyed copy-editor.

My agents Rosemary Scoular and Natalia Lucas are the stalwarts of my professional life and I'm thankful to them both for always going the extra *poronkusema* to support me.

I also pay tribute to all editors of the *Oxford English Dictionary* past and present. You are responsible for one of the greatest joys of my life, one that brings me resipiscence on the cloudiest of days. And, for more inspiration, I thank in particular Joshua Blackburn, David Crystal, and the editors at Merriam-Webster.

Finally, thanks are due in gowpens galore to my family and friends. To Chris, my favourite binfluencer, Reb and Charlotte,

ACKNOWLEDGEMENTS

my world-correctors, and my two girls for always bringing me smiles and biscuits. To Rob, for understanding that he and I have become total *Tamalous*, and to my sisters Nicky and Naomi, my copemates always. If apricity can be bestowed by humans as well as the sun, they are the bringers of it. Next time my glass is full, I shall raise a fathom-health to you all.

INDEX

@ symbol, 41
Abba, 147
abligurition, 301
absquatulate, 97
accolade, 38
Adam and Eve, 248–9
Adams, Douglas, 125
Adams, Fanny, 139
Advent, 297
ælfsogoða, 308
aftermath cheese, 209–10
agriculture, 22
AI (artificial intelligence), 114
Ainu, 64
ajar, 164
al-Khwarizmi, Abū Jaʿfar Muhammad ibn Mūsa, 228
alarm, 14
Albany beef, 52–3
albatross around one's neck, 152
alcohol, 32, 83–4, 119, 120, 228, 250, 251, 307–8
Alcyone (goddess), 312
alert, 15
Alfred the Great, 18, 308
algebra, 227–8
Alice's Adventures in Wonderland (Carroll), 280
All is True (Shakespeare & Fletcher), 156
all my eye and Betty Martin, 139
alleyways, 252
Althing, 144
aluminum, 62
amainiris, 63
Ambassadors, The (Holbein), 155
ambrosia, 110
American Dictionary of the English Language, 255
American Seasons, The (Teale), 278
American War of Independence, 255
ammil, 10
anathema, 289–90
anatomical snuffbox, 233–4
Anaya, Ignacio, 260
Anglo-Dutch wars, 211
Anglo-Norman language, 236, 243, 317
Anglo-Saxons, 27, 128, 145, 149, 308
animals, 30, 98: asses, 12; bears, 15, 37; cats, 194, 233, 267–8; dogs, 197; fox, 249–50; lions, 110; monkeys, 29, 250; newts, 32; skunks, 116; weather and, 249–50; *see also* birds; insects
Anna Karenina (Tolstoy), 287–8
another think/thing coming, 85–6
antanaclasis, 297
antipelargy, 261
apanthropy, 316
apapachar, 17
Aphrodite, 148
l'appel du vide, 318–19
apples, 251; apple-catchers, 227
apricate, 96
Arabic word origins, 21, 39, 196, 227–8, 303
Arctic, 15
Are You a Bromide? (Burgess), 117
Aristotle, 143
Arlington, Henry, 128
Arnold, Walter, 22
arse, 81
arse-ropes, 12–13
arsefoot, 96–7
Ashley, Anthony, 128
ASMR, 90
asses, 12
astronomy, 282
Athena, 64
aubade, 73–4
Aunt Pollys, 210
Australia, 70
autological words, 34
awkly, 24
Aztecs, 17, 202

Babington, Charles, 35–6

INDEX

back-slang, 40
backendish, 273–4
backfriend, 61
Baden-Powell, Robert and Olave, 43
bafflegab, 90, 221
Baghdad, Iraq, 228
bagsy, 58
Bailey, Nathan, 55, 65, 301
Baker, Frederick, 139
Bantu language, 7
barbecue, 191–2
Barbier de la Serre, Nicolas-Marie-Charles, 45–6
Barker, Ronnie, 140
basorexia, 37–8
Basque, 309
bated breath, 95–6
bath day, 127–8
battles: Bannockburn, 150; Britain, 226; the Frontiers, 202; Wakefield, 317; Waterloo, 146
bauble-bearer, 306–7
Baum, L. Frank, 119
beards, 18–19
bearn-lufu, 260–1
bears, 15, 37
Beast from 20,000 Fathoms, The (film), 145
beauty, 148
beaver moon, 274–5
beck and call, 95
Becket, Thomas à, 316–17
Beckett, Samuel, 108
bees, 110
beetles, 36
beggar's velvet, 224–5
Belladonna, 151–2
Beltane, 274–5

Beowulf, 47
Bergen, Edgar, 205
Bergman, Ingmar, 287
Berners Street Hoax, 291
Betjeman, John, 184
betrayal, 61
betwitterment, 297
Bible, 12, 110, 118, 129, 227, 290
Bierce, Ambrose, 151
Bihar, India, 84
binfluencer, 304–5
bingo terms, 11–12
birds, 98, 112:
  albatross, 152; bird in the hand, 35–6; birdsong, 36–7, 39, 44; crows, 44; cuckoos, 80–1; falcons, 35, 237, 317; geese, 238–9, 272–3; great auk, 96–7; kingfishers, 312–13; lapwings, 44; migration, 112; murmuration, 278–9; ostriches, 98; owls, 64; pelicans, 261; penguins, 93–4, 96–7; sparrows, 98; starlings, 112, 278–9; swallows, 112
bizarre, 19
Black Death, 247
blackberries, 251
Blackburn, Joshua, 90
blah, 28
Bleak House (Dickens), 11
blellum, 314–15
blowing smoke up someone's arse, 81

blue pencil, 197–8
Bluetooth, 171
blurb, 117–18
bodhi tree, 84
body parts, 233–4:
  anatomical snuff box, 233–4; arse, 12–13, 81; Aunt Pollys (testicles), 210; bollocks, 12–13, 210; eyes, 188; muscles, 275–6; navels, 248–9; prat, 123; twat, 65–6
bodysnatching, 271–2
bogwurpling, 286
bollocks, 12–13, 210
bonfire, 274–5
books, 122–3, 182, 263, 313
Booth, John Wilkes, 98
Boswell, James, 167
'bow-wow' theory, 30
Boy George, 72
Boyle, Robert, 177
brabbag, 279
Brahe, Tycho, 282
Braille, Louis, 45–6
brain rot, 98–9
Brando, Marlon, 87
brass monkeys, 29
Brazil, 109, 111, 113
bread, 283–4; bread rolls, 175
Breasted, James Henry, 289–90
breathing while, 177–8
Brenchley, Winifred, 58–9
Bridewell, 154–5
British etiquette, 42
British National Corpus, 144

INDEX

Brooklyn Theatre, New York, 299
Browning, Robert, 65
bruin, 15
bubbly jock, 314
bubonic plague, 247
buccaneer, 191–2
Buchan, John 210
Buckingham, George, 128
Buddha, 84
buff, 299–300
bugbear, 222
bugs, 221–2
Buli language, 54
bumbershoot, 94
bumf, 221
bummock, 314
Burgess, Gelett, 117–18
Burke and Hare, 271–2
Burney, Frances 'Fanny', Madame d'Arblay, 142
Burns, Robert, 119–20, 315
butterfly, 172

Cabal, 128–9
Caesar, Julius, Roman Emperor, 61
cafuné, 109
Cagney, James, 87
cake, 140–1
cakewalk, 140
calendars, 215–16
call shotgun, 58
camouflage, 81
cannonballs, 29
cant, 167
Canterbury Cathedral, 317
Canterbury Tales (Chaucer), 317
Capote, Truman, 207
Carey, Henry, 165

Carmiggelt, Simon, 55
Carpenter, Ralph, 57–8
carrawitchet, 165
Carroll, Lewis, 280
Carter, Howard, 289–90
Casement, Roger, 189
Cassius Dio, 161
Castle Gay (Buchan), 210
cat's eyes, 267–8
catchfart, 261
caterpillar, 172
Catherine of Aragon, 156, 281
caucus, 190
cellar door, 191
Celts, 107, 274–5
censorship, 199
cerring, 164–5
CGI, 115
Chambers Dictionary, 14
Chaplin, Charlie, 200–1
Charing Cross, London, 164
Charles I, King of England, 204
Charles II, King of England, 105, 128
Charles V, Holy Roman Emperor, 155
chatoyant, 267–8
chatter, 36–7
Chaucer, Geoffrey, 165, 317
chav, 133
Cheshire, 194
children, 302
China, 264
Chinese, 109
chissup, 5
Christmas, 6, 297–8, 302, 303, 306–15

Christingle, 303
Christmas Eve, 313
chuggypig, 257–8
Churchill, Winston, 71
churu-churu, 175
circumbendibus, 246–7
Clarke, Arthur C., 176
Clarke, John Cooper, 66
Classical Dictionary of the Vulgar Tongue, A (Grose), 42
Clement, Pope, 231
Cleopatra Glossaries, 12
Clifford, Thomas, 128
clinchpoop, 13
clink, 155
clinkabell, 16
clobber, 226–7
cloffin, 279
clothing: 74, 168–9, 225, 257
Cobbett, William, 42
cock, 292
cockalorum, 147
cockney rhyming slang, 68–70, 133
coddiwomple, 288–9
codger, 236–7
coffee, 7
Coleridge, Samuel Taylor, 152
Coles, William, 59
Collection of Seventy-Nine Black-Letter Ballads and Broadsides, Printed in the Reign of Queen Elizabeth, A, 153
colours, 179, 199, 303, 318
comfort-eating, 31
commas, 188–9
Commodore, 140
Common Sense (Paine), 9

325

INDEX

companage, 283–4
compliments, 21
computers, 222
Confucius, 4
Congo, Democratic Republic of the, 7
constellation, 282
Cook, James, 229, 245
coorie, 285
copemate, 6
cordate, 84
Coryate, Thomas, 229
Cotton, Robert Bruce, 12
Count Binface, 304–5
Covid pandemic, 99–100
cowquaker, 273
Cranmer, Thomas, 19
crap, 237–8
crapoter, 170
Crapper, Thomas, 237–8
crapplause, 174
crapulence, 3
crawmassing, 315
crazy cat lady, 233
crepitus, 83
cricket, 85–6
Crisp, Quentin, 197
Cromwell, Oliver, 105
cuckold, 80–1
cuckoos, 80–1
cumberworld, 292–3
curmurring, 315
curple, 119
curses, 289–90
cushty, 133
cut the mustard, 88
cut to the chase, 248

D-Day, 137
daalamist, 33
Daft Days, 314
Daily Enquirer, 267
Daily Mail, 181

Daily Telegraph, 221
daisy, 92
damask, 179
damfino, 292
Danish, 37, 148, 172
Darwin, Charles, 35–6, 223
Davies, W.H., 148
Davis, Bette, 82
Davy, Humphry, 62
Day of the Dead, 271
days of the week, 128
De Niro, Robert, 200
dead ringer, 183
death, 232, 271–2
Debrett's, 42
debug, 221–2
Dee, Sandra, 87
deipnosophist, 70–1
Delicate Diet, for daintiemouthde Droonkardes, A (Gascoigne), 168
deliquium, 216
demons, 23, 43, 268
Denham, Henry, 234
depooperit, 250
Derbyshire, 288
desenrascanço, 43
desiderate, 282
devil rides upon a fiddle-stick, 199–200
Devil's Dictionary (Bierce), 151–2
Devon, 10, 149
Dickens, Charles, 4, 11, 27, 168, 180, 198–9
dictionaries, 79, 218–19
Dictionaries of the Scots Language, 21
Dictionary of Modern Slang, Cant, and Vulgar Words

(Hotten), 224
Dictionary of Obscure Sorrows (Koenig), 122
Dictionary of the English Language (Johnson), 61, 193, 229, 306, 315
digitus impudicus, 44–5
dildo, 66
dimples, 166; dimples of Venus, 233
Dire Straits, 72
diseases, 121–2
Disney, Walt, 199
doing a Harry, 68–70
dollars, 9
Donald Ducking, 99–100
doofer, 235
doog, 40
doomscrolling, 98–9
Doorway Effect, 178
doppelgängers, 182–3
dørstokkmila, 8
dosh, 277
doublets, 141–2
doup-scud, 123
Doyle, Arthur Conan, 154
Dr Seuss, 205
Drake, Francis, 18–19
dreams, 113; *see also* nightmares
dreckly, 149
Dreikanter, 93–4
drinks, 7, 42–3, 307–8; *see also* alcohol
dromomania, 73
drown the miller, 307–8
drunkenness, 32, 83–4, 250
duration, 177–8
Dürer, Albrecht, 122
dust bunnies, 224–5

INDEX

Dutch, 55, 75, 95, 136, 172, 181, 211, 297
Dutton, Denis, 196
Dylan, Bob, 72

eating, 275
Eats, Shoots & Leaves (Truss), 188
eau-de-nil, 179
eavesdropping, 194–5
eclair, 14
eclipses, 216–17
eclosion, 121
Edinburgh Festival, 165
Edison, Thomas, 5, 222
Edward I, King of England, 54, 165
Edward II, King of England, 232
Edward VI, King of England, 19, 155, 179
eggcorns, 130, 173
Egypt, 192, 289–90
eight minutes, 60–1
Eleanor of Castile, 165
Elf (film), 308
elves, 308
emails, 17–18
Eminem, 199
English Civil War (1642–51), 204–5
English Dialect Dictionary (Wright), 5, 225, 281, 302
English Dictionarie (Cockeram), 311
Enigma codes, 154
Ephraimites, 118
Ericsson, 171
erumpent, 105
escape, 106
Espy, Willard R., 144
esquivalience, 79

Essay on Satirical Entertainment, 147
estivate, 169–70
euphemisms, 197–9
eutrapely, 143
Evelina, or the History of a Young Lady's Entrance into the World (Burney), 143
ex cappa, 106–7
exclamation marks, 147
exhaustion, 250
explaterate, 97
exsufflate, 81
eye, 188
eyethirls, 127

Falafel, Olaf, 165
falconry, 35, 237
Fanger, P. Ole, 39
fashion, 168–9
fathom-health, 145
fauchle, 21–2
Faulkner, William, 287
Feast of the Ass, 12
feckful, 53
Fergusson, Robert, 120
ferhoodled, 298–9
Fernweh, 73, 164
fiddlesticks, 199–200
Fiddlesticks (cartoon), 199
Fielding, Henry, 124
Fields, W.C., 96
figs, 261
film industry, 87–8; sound effects, 87–8
finger-fumbler, 20
finifugal, 206
Finland, 271
Finnegans Wake (Joyce), 108

Finnish, 41, 85, 100, 275, 300
firemen, 299
first-footers, 3
First World War (1914–18), 81, 189, 202–3
slang, 203
fish, 97, 153
Fisher, John 'Jacky' Arbuthnot, 71
fizmer, 115–16
fizzle, 115
flappers, 60–1
Fleet River, London, 155
Fletcher, John, 156
Fletcher's Book of Rhyming Slang (Barker), 140
flibbertigibbet, 23
Flip the Frog, 199–200
Flitterwochen, 38–9
Florentinus, 111
Florio, John, 168–9
flowers *see* plants and trees
Foley artists, 87–8
folk-leasing, 193
FOMO, 85
food: Albany beef, 52–3; as aphrodisiacs, 201–2; bread, 283–4; bread rolls, 175; butter, 148; cake, 140–1; cheese, 209–10; eclair, 14; *kuchisabishii*, 31–2; meat, 145; mustard, 88–9; nachos, 259–60; noodles, 175; ort, 288; pasta, 256–7; *pelinti*, 54;

327

INDEX

food (*cont.*)
shemomedjamo,
275; turkey, 314;
vänskapskaka,
225–6; Welsh
rarebit, 52–3; *see
also* fruit and
vegetables
foofaraw, 291
fool's ballocks, 58–9
forgettery, 178–9
forgiveness, 7–8
forwallowed, 16
fox, 249–50
France, 215
Fred Ott's Sneeze
(film), 5
freelancer, 106
French Connection, The
(film), 248
French marbles, 121–2
French Revolution
(1789), 170
French word roots,
23–4, 124, 172,
211, 236–7, 274:
alley, 251–2;
l'appel du vide,
318–19; aubade,
73–4; auriculaires,
195; bauble, 307;
bizarre, 19;
bouquiner, 123;
buccaneer, 191–2;
camouflage, 81;
charrette, 311;
crapoter, 170;
eclair, 14;
embrace, 37;
ennui, 141–2; *entre
chien et loup*, 126;
exturdire, 32;
foofaraw, 291;
gazebo, 192–3;
Mayday, 105;
names for rooms,
10–11; passenger,
23–4; pom-
egranate, 161–2;
queue, 41–2;
rebarbative, 19;
rendezvous,
14–15; *la rentrée*,
215; *retrouvailles*,
309; risqué, 124;
san fairy ann,
202–3; shimmy,
136–7; *Tamalous*,
239; treacle,
280–1; turquoise,
179
frēond-spēdig, 183
Friedkin, William, 248
friend of Dorothy, 119
friendship, 183
frienemy, 61
frobly-mobly, 52
Frost, Robert, 259
frowst, 47–8
fruit and vegetables:
apples, 227, 251;
bananas, 91;
blackberries, 251;
figs, 261; oranges,
303; pomegranate,
161–2; potato,
129–30, 202;
strawberries,
286–7; tomato
(love apple),
201–2; vegetables,
146
frumberdling, 18–19
fudgel, 55
furoshiki, 309–10

Gadsbudlikins!, 292
gadwaddick, 209
Galileo Galilei, 282
gallinipper, 201
gamp, 180
Garland, Judy, 119
Gascoigne, George,
168
gattara, 233
gazebo, 192–3
Geborgenheit, 298
geek, 205–6
gelasin, 166
Gemini, constellation
of, 107
Georgia, 31, 275
German/Germany,
138, 172, 253, 245
Germanic word roots,
177, 274:
dollars, 9;
Dreikanter, 93–4;
Eigengrau, 57;
Fernweh, 73, 164;
Fingerspitzengefühl,
80; *Flitterwochen*,
38–9;
Geborgenheit, 298;
insults, 8–9;
jein, 252–3;
Katzenjammer, 3;
kennings, 46–7;
kitsch, 33;
Kummerspeck, 31;
muggeseggele, 101;
Pantoffeln, 168–9;
Rausschmeisser,
318; schmaltz,
33–4;
Schwellenangst,
318; *Sehnsucht*,
164; shive, 225;
soul, 153;
schlimmbesserung,
138; *Zugunruhe*,
112
Gerry, Elbridge, 190
gerrymandering, 190
Ghana, 54
gigil, 304
Gileadites, 118
glazomer, 79–80

glid, 162–3
glimmer-gowk, 64
Globe theatre, London, 156
gloppened, 285
gluggaveður, 10
gobbledygook, 37
goblin mode, 13
les goddams, 124
going Dutch, 211
Golden Girls, The (US TV sitcom), 225–6
gone for a Burton, 226–7
goose, 238–9, 272–3
gossip, 6, 23, 42–3, 220
Götterdämmerung (Wagner), 58
government styles, 68
gowpen, 195
great auk, 96–7
Great Expectations (Dickens), 4–5, 198
Great Moon Hoax, 208
Greece, 192
Greek mythology, 64, 161–2, 217, 318
Greek word roots, 68, 70–1, 118, 276, 318: ambrosia, 110; antanaclasis, 297; aphercotrophism, 223; *arktikos*, 15; *engastrimuthos*, 276; euphemisms, 197–9; eutrapely, 143; irenic, 314; *kalos*, 148; *kōnōps*, 201; metanoia, 293; mnemonic, 317–18; nectar, 110; *ōps*, 188;

ostracon, 205; *pneuma*, 217; *podariko*, 3; *rhabarbarum*, 28; *skholē*, 70; *storgē*, 261; *strix*, 64; sycophant, 261; *thēriakē*, 280; thing, 144; wine, 135–6
green-mete, 146
Green, Jonathon, 65
Green's Dictionary of Slang, 210
Greene, Robert, 38
Gregorian calendar, 215
Grelling–Nelson Paradox, 34
grenade, 161–2
groozlins, 315
groping a gull, 207–8
Grose, Francis, 42
growlery, 10–11
grufeling, 285
gruglede, 175–6
Guardian, 130, 166
Gugliucci, Nicole, 264
Guinness Book of World Records, 301
gypsy, 133

Hackman, Gene, 248
had-I-wist, 278
Haiti, 191
halcyon days, 312–13
Hamlet (Shakespeare), 92
hammer and thongs, 130
hapless, 156
Harald 'Bluetooth' Gormsson, King of Denmark and Norway, 171
harbinger, 23

Harpenden, 125
harvest, 187, 209–10, 225, 243
harvest swain, 243
Harvey, Jon, 304
haste post haste, 181
Haunted Bookshop, The (Morley), 263
have one's cake and eat it, 140
head-gem, 46–7
Heaney, Seamus, 47
Hearst, William Randolph, 151
hearth, 279–80
heartspoon, 234
heels over head, 287–8
Hemingway, Ernest, 316
Henry II, King of England, 316–17
Henry IV (Shakespeare), 200, 279
Henry VIII, King of England, 155, 156, 281
Hepburn, Audrey, 321
Herodotus, 216
Herrick, Robert, 243
Herschel, John, 208
heterograms, 118
heterological, 34
Heywood, John, 35
Highsmith, Patricia, 157
hilarity, 113
hirple, 119–20
Historical Thesaurus of English, 149
Hitchcock, Alfred, 57
Hitchhiker's Guide to the Galaxy, The (Adams), 125
Hoag, Aleck, 139
hoax, 208

329

INDEX

Holbein, Hans 155
holidays, 169–70, 175–6, 215
Holmes, Sherlock, 154
Holt, Harold, 70
Homer, 224
homosexuality, 119
honeymoons, 38–9
Hook, Theodore Edward, 291
Hoover, J. Edgar, 136
Hopkins, Anthony, 276
Hopkins, Gerard Manley, 66–7
hornswoggle, 97
hornywink, 44
horology, 246
hot-spong, 120
Hotten, John Camden, 224, 230
Howard, Ronald, 232
Hudson, Rock, 87
hugging, 17, 37–8
humgruffin, 283
Humphrey, Duke of Gloucester, 173
humusk, 244–5
hunchweather, 284
Hundred Years War, 124, 173
Hungarian, 100
hurply, 284
hustings, 144
Huygens, Christiaan, 246

i before *e* . . ., 218–19
Iceland/Icelandic, 10, 33, 47, 96, 144, 313
icicles, 16
If I Ran the Zoo (Dr Seuss), 205
iktsuarpok, 312
ilunga, 7–8
incunabula, 122–3

insects: bees, 110; beetles, 36; butterfly, 172; caterpillar, 172; mayflies, 121; mosquito, 201; naming of, 172; spiders, 149–50; woodlice, 257–8
Institucion of a Gentleman, The, 13
insults, 8–9, 83–4, 292–3
interdespise, 206–7
interrobang, 234–5
Inuit language, 312
Inuktitut language, 312
iota, 236
Iran, 311
Ireland/Irish, 6, 63, 134, 187, 189, 203
irenic, 314
IRL, 111
Islamic Golden Age, 228
Isle of Man, 3, 279
It ain't over till the fat lady sings, 57–8
Italy/Italian, 6–7, 14–15, 46, 74, 172, 223, 231–2, 233, 256–7
Iwerks, Ub, 199

jachelt, 259
Jack the Lad, 139
Jahai, 244
James II, King of England, 303
Jamestown, North America, 116
Japan/Japanese, 21, 64, 84, 111, 167, 175: *bukimi no tani*, 114; *furoshiki*, 309–10; *koi no yokan*, 48; *komorebi*, 66–7; *kuchisabishii*, 31–2; *shibui*, 284; summer rain, 197; *tsundoku*, 182; *wabi-sabi*, 284; *wakuwaku*, 297; *yugen*, 284–5
jargon, 36–7
Jaws (film), 153
Jazz Singer, The (film), 87
Jefferson, Blind Lemon, 201
jein, 252–3
jettatore, 46
Johnson, Boris, 305
Johnson, Samuel, 37, 61, 112, 167–8, 193, 229, 238–9, 273, 306, 315
jokes, 165, 203–4
jolabokaflod, 313
JOMO, 85
Joyce, James, 11, 17, 108
Judaism, 129

kaamos, 271
kadigans, 144–5
kalsarikänni, 85
Kasparov, Garry, 114
Kay, Peter, 72
keen as mustard, 88–9
Keillor, Garrison, 63
kekeke, 111
Kelly, Ned, 11
Kendal Mercury, 112
kennings, 46–7
Kent, 208
Key, Francis Scott, 306
King Arthur, 107
King Lear (Shakespeare), 23
King's evil, 121–2

kingfishers, 312–13
Kircher, Athanasius, 194–5
kissing, 38
Kitchen-Table Lingo (English Project), 286
kitsch, 33–4
Knock apparition, 203
knock-knock jokes, 203–4
knocker-uppers, 4–5
Koenig, John, 122
komorebi, 66–7
Korean, 111, 140–1, 249–50
kuchisabishii, 31–2

Lady Godiva, 140
lagom, 208–9
Lammas, 187
Lancashire, 273
language: English, 218–19; evolution of, 30; family language, 235, 286; secret languages, 68–70
lanspresado, 64
lapwings, 44
Lara, Brian, 85–6
latibulate, 316
Latimer, Hugh, Bishop of Worcester, 19
Latin word roots: *brumalis*, 33; *cantare*, 167; constellation, 282; *cordate*, 84; *crepare*, 83; *defixiones*, 290; *deliquium*, 216; *ex cappa*, 106–7; *granatum*, 162; *incunabula*, 123; littoral, 134; *malo malo malo malo*, 297–8; *olfactus*, 39; *patrissare*, 184; *pecunia non olet*, 161; *percontari*, 234; perendinate, 63; *punctus*, 176; *quantus*, 89; recrudescence, 86–7; *resipiscere*, 4; rival, 107; *scandalum*, 193; sesquipedalian, 34; shimmy, 136–7; sinister, 24; *spirare*, 217; *trepalium*, 176; ventriloquist, 276; *vox*, 90; wine, 135–6
laughter, 111
Lawrence, D.H., 288
laziness, 253
Learned History on Dumpling, A (Carey), 165
Leechbook, 150
left-handedness, 24
'Leisure' (Davies), 148
'Leith Races' (Fergusson), 120
'Letter to a Young Lady' (Coleridge), 152–3
librocubicularist, 263
lickspittle, 261
like, 142–3
Lincoln, Abraham, 97–8
Lindisfarne Gospels, 24
linguistic fossils, 95–6
lion-colour, 179
lions, 110
littoral, 134
Liverpool, 239
Lloyd, John, 125

LOL, 71, 111
Lombards, 18
London, 27, 291
London Magazine, 117
Louvre Palace, Paris, 195
love apple, 201–2
Love Island (TV series), 142
Love Poems (Lawrence), 288
love, 260–1
Lubberland, 253
luck, 46
luncheon, 53

macaroni, 256–7
Macaroni Club, London, 257
Macbeth (Shakespeare), 204
MacGyver, Angus (TV spy), 43
maculate, 247
Magdalen College, Oxford, 105
Magic (film), 276
mail, 181
Maitland, John, Earl of Lauderdale, 128
malapropisms, 173–4
Malaysia/Malay, 172, 244
malediction, 289
malo malo malo malo, 297–8
mamihlapinatapai, 301
Man of Pleasure's Companion, The, 124
man-dream, 113
mansplaining, 264
maps, fictitious entries, 79
marriage, 82

INDEX

Martin Chuzzlewit (Dickens), 180
Mary, Queen of Scots, 106
Maryland, USA, 91
matrisate, 184
matutolypea, 283
Maverick, Samuel, 37
mawkish, 34
May Day, 105
Mayday, 105
mayflies, 121
Mayhew, Henry, 27
Meaning of Liff, The (Adams & Lloyd), 125
measurements, 100–1, 145, 195
meat, 145
medalling, 62
medical terms, 83
de' Medici, Catherine, 195
medicine, 280
meet your Waterloo, 146–7
Melville, Herman, 171
memory, 317–18
Merchant Shipping Act (1876), 135
Merriam-Webster dictionary, 219
Merry Wives of Windsor, The (Shakespeare), 129
messenger, 23
metanoia, 293
metathesis, 254
Mexico, 260
Michaelmas, 238
Michelangelo, 249
Mickey Mouse, 199
micromort, 232
Middle English, 145, 176

Milne, A.A., 15, 183
milver, 119
minced oaths, 198
misle, 108–9
misophonia, 90–1
mnemonic, 317–18
Mnemosyne (goddess), 318
Moby-Dick (Melville), 171
Modern Times (film), 200–1
mondegreens, 72
money, 9, 133, 140, 161, 277: overspending, 301–2
monkeys, 29, 250
months of the year, 127–8
Monty Python's Flying Circus (TV series), 246–7
moon, 38, 216: beaver moon, 274–5; honeymoon, 38–9; moonlight, 35
Mori, Masahiro, 114
Morley, Christopher, 263
morning, 39
Morning Star, 130
morris dancing, 23
mosquito, 201
'Mosquito Moan' (song), 201
mother-in-law's dream, 48
motivation, 8
Mount Athos, Greece, 249
mountweazel, 79
Mozart, Wolfgang Amadeus, 278
mudlarking, 27
Mulberry harbour, 137

murmuration, 112, 278–9
muscles, 275–6
music, 265, 266, 305–6
mustard, 88–9
mutual loathing, 206–7

na'eeman, 21
nacho, 259–60
Nahuatl language, 17, 202
Napoleon Bonaparte, 146–7
Napoleonic wars, 29
NASA, 176
Nation and Athenaeum newspaper, 33
Native American, 116, 190, 274
nature, 66–7, 96, 167, 196
navels, 248–9
nectar, 110–11
nedoperepil, 32
neek, 205–6
Nelson, Horatio, 32
nerd, 205
Nerval, Gérard de, 141
Nevins, Thomas, 299
New Columbia Encyclopedia, The, 79
New Dictionary of the Terms Ancient and Modern of the Canting Crew, A, 168
New Englands Prospect (Wood), 116
New Oxford American Dictionary, 79
New Year's Eve, 318–19
New York Times, 289
New Zealand, 129
Newgate Prison, 155

332

INDEX

Newland, Richard, 86
newspaper corrections, 130
newts, 32
night-writing, 45–6
nightingale, 23–4
nightmare, 268
1989 (album), 265
Nixon, Richard, 193
nod-craftiness, 100
nohow, 142–3
noise, 90–1
noodles, 175
Norfolk, 209, 227
Norman Conquest, 236
Norse mythology, 92, 128
Norway/Norwegian, 8, 175–6, 279–80
nosy parker, 220
Nottinghamshire, 288
novercant, 258
nucular, 254
nuddling, 194
Nüshu script, 264
nuwoseo tteok meokgi, 140–1

O'Brien, Howard Vincent, 28
Obama, Barack, 210
obscene gestures, 44–5, 61
ochlocracy, 68
off one's own bat/back, 85–6
off the cuff, 200–1
Oiche Nollaig na mBan (Eve of Women's Christmas), 6
Oktoberfest, 245
Old English word roots, 113, 128, 144, 149, 163, 210: *æppel*, 227; *amel*, 10; *atter-coppe*, 150; *cerr*, 164; *crawe*, 44; *dæges éage*, 92; folk-leasing, 193; *frēond-spēdig*, 183; *frumberdling*, 19; *gerd*, 100; *gowk*, 80; *hærfest*, 243; *mære*, 268; *merecandel*, 47; *mete*, 146; *nihtegala*, 24; *ruth*, 164; *shadde*, 193; *thwitan*, 65; tide, 246; *uhtcearu*, 57
Old Norse, 20, 47, 127, 128, 144
Old Ways, 252
olf, 39
Olivier, Laurence, 87
Omai, 229
omfietswijn, 135–6
OMG, 71–2
Omphalopsychic, 248–9
'On Duty with Inspector Field' (Dickens), 198
on-ding, 310
online meetings, 100
Only Fools and Horses (TV sitcom), 133
opacarophile, 196
opera, 57–8
orange, 303
orchidaceous, 33–4
orchids, 59
ort, 288
Osborne, Nancy, 289
ostracize, 205
ostriches, 98
Our Mutual Friend (Dickens), 27
Our Seamen: An Appeal (Plimsoll), 135

overmorrow, 63
overspending, 301–2
owl-light, 125–6
owls, 64
Oxford, 105
Oxford English Dictionary, 11, 28, 54, 65, 96, 120, 143, 191, 254, 258, 259–60, 292–3, 312, 315

pagar a la inglesa, 211
Paine, Thomas, 9
Pantoffeln, 168–9
parents, 184
Parini, Jay, 207
Parker, Matthew, Archbishop of Canterbury, 220
Parthia, kingdom of, 22
parting shot, 22
passeggiata, 222–3
passenger, 23–4
pasta, names of, 256–7
patrisate, 184
pebbles, 93–4
Peck, Gregory, 231
Pecksniffian, 180
pecunia non olet, 161
peiskos, 279–80
pelicans, 261
pelinti, 54
penguins, 93–4, 96–7
Pennsylvanian Dutch, 289
percycution, 174
peregrinate, 316–17
peregrine falcon, 317
perepodvypodvert, 90
Persephone, legend of, 161
Persia, 192, 196
pertolerate, 311
Peter the Great, Tsar of Russia, 127

333

INDEX

petrichor, 244
Philip VI, King of France, 124
Philippines, 304
philocaly, 148
phishing, 207–8
phloem, 91
phonoaesthetics, 191
pickpockets, 281
piece of cake, 141
pig Latin, 40
pilgrim, 317
Pippa Passes (Browning), 65
pirr, 141
Planck, Max, 89
plants and trees, 58–9, 84, 92, 148, 223–4, 259; *see also* fruit and vegetables
Plato, 152
Plimsoll, Samuel, 135
Plimsoll line, 134–5
plimsolls, 134–5
Plinian eruption, 262–3
Pliny the Elder, 262–3
plothering, 274
plum rain, 197
pluvial, 94
pochemuchka, 196–7
poetry, 47; 'Marguerite' poetry, 92
Polish, 250
politics/politicians, 91–2, 170, 190, 230
Polynesian languages, 15, 245
polytropic, 223–4
pomegranates, 161–2
Pony Express Courier, 58
'pooh-pooh' theory, 30
poputchik, 157
poronkusema, 100–1
Porridge (TV sitcom), 140

Portugal/Portuguese, 19, 43, 109, 113
post haste, 181
potatoes, 129–30
pottering about, 30–1
Pratchett, Terry, 91
pratfall, 123
Presley, Elvis, 136–7
prisons, 154–5
procaffeinator, 7
profanity, 65, 198, 261, 292
pronunciation, 108–9, 254
Proto-Indo-European, 15
proverbs, 209
Ptolemy, 282
publishers, 117–18
von Pückler-Muskau, Prince Hermann Ludwig Heinrich, 73
puff, 117
punctuation, 176–7, 188–9, 234–5
puns, 165–6
pushing the envelope, 226
Putin, Vladimir, 45

QI (TV series), 219
qualtagh, 3
quantum leap, 89
quarantine, 247
Queen Anna's New World of Words (Florio), 169
querencia, 316
queue, 41–2
quid, 277
quidnunc, 220
quisquilious, 302
quockerwodger, 230
qwertyuiop, 17–18

rainbow, 318
raining cats and dogs, 274
rama-rama, 172
ramracket, 302
ranço, 113–14
razbliuto, 266
rebarbative, 19
recrudescence, 86–7
Red-Headed League, The (Doyle), 154
redamancy, 266
reference books, fictitious entries, 79
regional dialects, 115–16
religion, 248–9; blasphemy, 198
rendezvous, 14–15
la rentrée, 215
resipiscence, 4
respair, 312–13
retrouvailles, 309
reunions, 309
reverdie, 74
Reynard the Fox, 15
rhubarb, 28
rhymes, 119–20
rhyming slang, 68–70
Richard, Duke of York, 317–18
Ridley, Nicholas, 19
rigmarole, 54–5
Rime of the Ancient Mariner (Coleridge), 152
risqué, 124
rival, 107
Rivals, The (Sheridan), 173
Rivals of May, 107
Roaring Twenties, 60–1
Robert I (the Bruce), King of Scotland, 150

INDEX

robotics, 114–15
rocket surgery, 173–4
rocks, 93–4
rogitating, 196
Roman baths, Bath, 290
Romans, 32, 44–5, 100, 127, 217, 276, 297–8
Romany, 133
Rome, Italy, 231–2
Romeo and Juliet (Shakespeare), 272–3
rooms, names for, 10–11
Roosevelt, Franklin D., 190
Rowling, J.K., 110
Royal Navy, 32, 307–8
Russia/Russian, 32, 45, 80, 90, 127, 157, 196–7, 218, 266, 273, 300

St Augustine, 231
St Catherine of Alexandria, 275
St Francis, 7
St Frideswide, 281
St Margaret's Well, Binsey, 280–1
St Martin, 139
St Paul's Cathedral, 173, 195
Salem witch trials, 233
Samson, 110–11
san fairy ann, 202–3
San Francisco Examiner, 151
Sankt Joachimsthal, Bohemia, 9
scams, 207–8
scandal, 193
Schieffelin, Eugene, 279

schlimazel, 46
Scotland/Scots, 33, 48, 52, 123, 134, 250, 272, 285, 310, 314, 315
Scott, Walter, 315
Scout movement, 43, 67
screamer, 234–5
scrofula, 122
scrumping, 251
scurryfunging, 312
sea-lawyer, 153
seabiscuit, 190
'Seafarer, The', 47
seasons, 244–5, 278: autumn, 243, 244–5; spring, 53, 113, 120–1, 149, 243; summer, 105, 148, 169, 197, 215, 244, 286–7; winter, 33, 53, 96, 105, 112, 169, 243, 271, 311, 312–13
Second World War (1939–45), 69, 119, 137, 154, 199, 226–7, 313
secret languages, 68–70
secretary, 106
seijaku, 167
Seinfeld (US TV sitcom), 163
sent to Coventry, 204–5
Serbia, 210
serenity, 167
sesquipedalian, 34
Shakespeare, William, 15, 23, 62, 92, 122, 129, 156, 165, 200, 204, 272–3, 278–9, 282
sharks, 153
Shaw, Percy, 267–8

shed, 193
Shelley, Percy Bysshe, 307
shemomedjamo, 275
Sheridan, Richard Brinsley, 173
Shetlands, 141, 194
shibboleth, 118–19
shimmy, 136–7
ships, 134–5
shivelight, 67
shivviness, 225
shoes, 168–9
shopping, 301–2
shotclog, 63–4
shturmovshchina, 218
sidler, 163
sign of the meow, 41
Silesia, Poland, 230
silly goose, 238–9
Simpsons, The (TV cartoon series), 221, 254
sinister, 24
sinners, 4
Sister Sledge, 72
sisu, 300
skilljoy, 174
skulduggery, 271–2
skunks, 116
slang, 40, 133, 168, 190, 210, 224–5, 281; back-slang, 40; cockney rhyming slang, 40, 68–70, 140; criminal underworld, 68–9, 224; First World War, 203; money, 277
sleaze, 230
Slovenian, 94–5
slut, 224
Smart Alec, 139
smells, 39, 244

335

INDEX

smeuse, 115
Smith, Henry, 154–5
Smith, Milton A., 221
Smithfield bargain, 82
smultronställe, 286–7
Snake Island, 45
snecklifter, 63–4
sneezing, 5, 83
snollygoster, 91–2
snotter, 281
snow, 310
Snow White and the Seven Dwarfs (film), 30
sobremesa, 162
social media, 99, 177
sockdolager, 97–8
sólarfrí, 96
songs, 72–3, 73–4
sonography, 45
Sontag, Susan, 293
sophrosyne, 265
soubhiye, 39
soulmate, 152–3
sound effects, 87–8
South Africa, 250
Spain/Spanish, 19, 111, 129, 162, 172, 211, 225, 253, 291, 303, 316
spangles, 306
sparrows, 98
speech, forms of, 167
spelling, 218–19, 255
spiders, 149–50
Spielberg, Steven, 153
spitting image, 182–3
spizzerinctum, 67
spondulicks, 277
sporange, 119
sprezzatura, 74
spud, 31, 129–30
spuddling, 30–1
Starbucks, 171
starlings, 112, 278–9
Starship, 72

stepmother's breath, 258
Stewart, Jon, 184
stoating, 273
stoplessness, 176–7
storks, 261
storms, 59–60
Strangers on a Train (film), 157
strigiform, 64
strokes, 121–2
stroking, 109
strong verbs, 162–3
struthious, 98
Sullenberger, Chesley, 210
Sullivan, John, 133
Sun newspaper (New York), 208, 299
sunlight, 66–7
sunsets, 196
supercilian, 187–8
supernova, 282
superstition, 112, 121–2, 290
suspire, 217
swallows, 112
swear words *see* profanity
Swedish, 35, 39, 48, 95, 128, 208–9, 216, 226, 286–7
sweet Fanny Adams, 139
Swift, Taylor, 265
sycophant, 61, 261
Symposium (Plato), 152
syphilis, 122

Tacitus, 44–5, 262
Tagalog language, 304
Taino language, 191
takes the biscuit, 140
taking the Mickey, 139
Tamalous, 239

tandsmør, 148
tattoo, 245
taxes, 161
Taxi Driver (film), 200
tea, 42–3, 307–8
Teale, Edwin Way, 278
teetotal, 307
Teletubbyzurückwinker, 8–9
testicles, 210
text-speak, 72
Thackeray, William Makepeace, 62
Thailand, 111
Thames river, 27, 165
thermopot, 7
thing, 144
thirls, 127
Thoreau, Henry, 99
'Three Times a Lady' (song), 140
three-pipe problem, 154
thunderplump, 94
tidsoptimist, 215–16
Tierra del Fuego, 301
time, 177–8, 218, 246
timekeeping, 215–16
time and tide wait for no man, 246
Time magazine, 300
tinsel, 306
titivil, 42–3
tittle, 236
Titus, Roman Emperor, 161
to a T, 236
to and fro, 95
to dine with Duke Humphrey, 173
toe-cover, 301–2
toilets, 237–8
Tolkien, J.R.R., 143, 191
Tolstoy, Leo, 287

Tom Jones (Fielding), 124
Tom Swifty, 265
Tomlinson, Ray, 17–18
tongue-pad, 167–8
tongue-twisters, 20
tonstrix, 56
torchy, 266
tosspot, 83–4
transformation, 293
travel, 175–6, 288–9
treacle, 280–1
Treason Act (1351), 189
Truss, Lynne, 188
Tshiluba language, 7
tsundoku, 182
tung, 255
Turing, Alan, 154
Turkish, 35
turquoise, 179
Tutankhamun, Egyptian Pharoah, 289–90
Twain, Mark, 138
twat, 65–6
twilight, 125–6
twitten, 251–2
twittle-twattle, 229
Two Orphans, The (play), 299

ugsome, 19–20
uhtcearu, 57
uitwaaien, 75
Ukraine, 45
Ulysses (Joyce), 11
Umberto I, King of Italy, 182–3
umbles, 208
umbraphile, 216–17
umbrellas, 94
uncanny valley, 114–15
United States, 9, 91–2, 97–8, 136, 200, 201, 248–9, 291: national anthem, 306–7; Native American, 116, 190, 274; Post Office, 181; presidential elections, 190; seasons, 243, 278; US English, 62, 163, 255; Watergate scandal, 193
Universal Etymological English Dictionary (Bailey), 55, 65, 301
upstrigolous, 302
Urban Dictionary, 17
Ursa Major, 15

vagrants, 167–8
Valentine's Day, 38
Valiant comic, 11
Vance, J.D., 233
Vanity Fair magazine, 135
vänskapskaka, 225–6
vedriti, 94–5
vegetables, 146
vellichor, 122
ventriloquist, 276
Verschlimmbesserung, 138
Vespasian, Roman Emperor, 161
Vesuvius, Italy, 262
vicious cycle/circle, 85–6
Victorians, 27, 92, 94, 139
Vidal, Gore, 207
Vijayanand, Renu, 67
Vikings, 20, 24, 37, 127, 128, 129, 171, 306
Vitalis, Orderic, 18
Vitula, Roman goddess, 199–200
voice, 90
volcanic eruptions, 262–3
voorpret, 297

wabbit, 52
Waghorn, Henry Thomas, 86
Wagner, Richard, 58
waits, 305–6
walls have ears, 194–5
wambling, 315
wanderlust, 73
War of 1812, 306
Washington Post, 174, 181
Watergate scandal, 193
Watts, Alan, 178
weather, 10, 249–50, 258, 271, 284: animals and, 249–50; cold, 29; heat, 197; ice, 10; mist, 33; rain, 94–5, 197, 244, 250, 273–4; rainbow, 318; snow, 310; storms, 59–60, 94–5; sunshine, 96, 120–1, 249; wind, 75, 115–16, 141, 217
Webster, Noah, 255
Weeds of Farm Land (Brenchley), 59
Wellesley, Arthur, 1st Duke of Wellington, 146
Welsh, 17, 51, 52–3, 96, 115, 187, 274
Welsh rarebit, 52–3
whangdoodle, 266–7
whiles, 177–8

INDEX

whispering galleries, 195
whistle-stop, 190
White, Betty, 225–6
widdendream, 113
wild goose chase, 272–3
Wilde, Oscar 62
William I, 'the Bastard', 237
William of Orange, 303
Williams, John, 153
Williams, Tennessee, 61, 222–3
williwaw, 116
Wilson, William, 119
wimpling, 116
windows, 127
wine, 135–6
Winnie-the-Pooh (Milne), 15, 183
winter solstice, 311, 312
wisht, 268
wistful, 164
witchcraft, 233, 268
Wizard of Oz, The (film), 119
Wodehouse, P.G., 277
women, 6, 48, 56, 264
wonga, 133
Wood, William, 116
woodlice, 257–8
World Gonad Cooking Competition, 210
World Meteorological Organization, 60
Wright, Joseph, 5

Yaghan language, 301
yakamoz, 35
Yalda, 311
Yankie Doodle Dandy, 257
yeoubi, 249–50
Yiddish, 46
yo-he-ho, 30
yob, 40
Yorkshire, 273, 284
Younger Futhark (runic alphabet), 171
yugen, 284–5
Yule-shard, 310–11

Zugunruhe, 112